# THE *Emotions* FROM A *Badge*:

TALES FROM A
*Deputy Sheriff*

STEPHEN CRIBB

Copyright © 2016 Stephen Cribb
All rights reserved
First Edition

PAGE PUBLISHING, INC.
New York, NY

First originally published by Page Publishing, Inc. 2016

ISBN 978-1-68289-342-5 (pbk)
ISBN 978-1-68289-343-2 (digital)

Printed in the United States of America

# Contents

Preface ..................................................................5

Illegal Dumping ....................................................7
SWAT .....................................................................9
Inflatable Irene ....................................................15
Frozen Marijuana ................................................19
Accident or Murder .............................................24
First Autopsy .......................................................48
Children Suicides ................................................50
I'll Get It .............................................................53
Father Kidnaps to Kill ........................................56
Death Penalty .....................................................61
Overkill ...............................................................63
Learning to Swim ................................................76
Vanished ..............................................................79
Swear They Are Dead ..........................................90
Firebomber ..........................................................92

An Expert Witness ................................................................. 133

Family Dispute......................................................................... 135

Oops! ....................................................................................... 152

Olympian Killer ...................................................................... 154

Drop the Gun! ........................................................................ 164

Murder for a Car ..................................................................... 168

Hunted .................................................................................... 177

Turn the Power On ................................................................. 191

Victim Refused to Prosecute................................................... 195

How Long Has He Been Dead?.............................................. 204

Director of Personnel .............................................................. 207

One Boring Day with a Detective .......................................... 213

Shooting in the Park................................................................ 216

Closing a Business ................................................................... 227

Endangered Quarterback......................................................... 234

The Never Again Will I Ride in Your Car ............................. 244

Disrespect One's Oath ............................................................. 248

Cuff and Stuff .......................................................................... 254

Not Invincible ......................................................................... 262

Last Day................................................................................... 283

Epilogue................................................................................... 285

About the Author.................................................................... 288

# Preface

As a child, my dream in life was to be a cop. In all my backyard games, my choice was always the Sheriff not the cattle rustler or train robber. With my life moving forward, it seems that I never really grew up because at the age of nineteen, I became the first teenager commissioned as a Deputy Sheriff in my home county. With not even being twenty-one years of age, I was below the legal age limit to purchase a handgun, so my father had to buy me a revolver allowing me to carry that required sidearm at work. For the next thirty-five years, I lived the greatest career in law enforcement. Yes, my childhood dream came true.

Now let me explain to one and all. When a new deputy is commissioned with the Sheriff's Office, they are issued a radio number to identify them when talking over the radio. The definition of the number identifies the job duties and assignment type of a deputy, and mine continually changed over my many years at the office. My first radio number as a rookie was 619 that could help a person knowledgeable about the agency determine that the Sheriff's Office employed a total of less than one hundred deputies in uniform assignments. At the time of my retirement, I was the master sergeant of the district detectives with 2810 being my call number. By this time, there were nearly one hundred uniform deputies working on the road at any given time of the day. From 619 to 2810, my career moved through a multitude of radio numbers and assignments that provided me more information than I, or anyone, should have ever been able to obtain.

My time as a Deputy Sheriff included all of the various desirable assignments. Some of those positions included patrol deputy, SWAT team member, Selective Enforcement, Intelligence and Homicide with each of these transfers seeming like I was quitting and starting a completely new job. Working in these amazing assignments seemed to place me there at the most interesting times for that type of work in the history of the office. These cases were mass murders, serial murders, courthouse corruption, and misconduct by other law enforcement officers. Some investigations went beyond the local news to both national and international coverage. Television shows, talk shows, and others profiled my cases; and even books have been written about some of these crimes.

Because of my special knowledge, I have always been encouraged to write my own book about my career. Some, both in and out of law enforcement, were concerned about what I might discuss in my book. Some claimed the investigations provided me with way too much of the information that others truly do not ever need to know. Those opinions made me believe that I would need to limit my writings to some selective investigations. At this time, some of those other bits of knowledge need to remain in a safe and secure file location. I'll have to go to my backyard and dig up that coffee can of facts on a much later date.

Some of my jabbering will cover a few of my many homicide investigations, and out of respect for others, I will try not use the real names of the people involved in most of these cases. More often, I will wander over to some other very interesting story or incident. At times, I know you will be angry; other times, you may want to cry, some moments may fill you with pride with the magnificent outcomes, frequently, I hope you will give a little laugh. So let you and me get us a cup of coffee, or other special beverage of your desire, and sit out on the back porch so I can tell you some of my many stories. So at this moment, just sit back and enjoy!

# Illegal Dumping

As I will often tell you in these stories when I began my career with the Sheriff's Office, I was the first teenager to be commissioned as a Deputy Sheriff. This time period from the past was completely different from the concepts of the modern world today. With my youth at the time of my hiring, the decision was to assign me to the Radio Room with several other civilians and deputies. Most of the deputies were very old gentlemen or newly hired females. These young ladies dressed in a uniform that included a skirt rather than pants, and while still packing a revolver in a gun belt were not allowed to work road patrol, neither was this teenager. At that time, the communications method was a total voice system without any assistance from a computer. The incoming calls were written on a paper form, sent through a hole in the wall on a small conveyer belt, and read to the dispatched deputy over the radio. The form was time-stamped for each action, and the radio communication was entered on the radio log using a typewriter, not even an electric typewriter. For those who do not know about a typewriter, you will have to ask your grandparents for an explanation.

The Sheriff who hired me was a very conservative, church going, high-quality person. With his very clean personality, we had to be very careful what we said over his radio. In the worldwide radio communications systems, there is a phonetic alphabet, so when you need to clarify which letter that you speak, there is a specific word to define the letter. For example, to clarify the letter W, one would say the word "Whiskey." Of course, our Sheriff did not allow *that* word to be used over ***his*** radio; the word we had to use was "William." As I said, he was a bit conservative.

One evening, as I sat in the dispatcher's chair, I heard that conveyer belt spin a complaint form through the wall and onto my desk. As it was arriving several other Radio Room personnel rushed into the small area with each and all staring at me. I picked up the newly created dispatch form and immediately discovered the reason of their interest. The form indicated that a man had walked into a country bar way on the south end of the county, dropped his pants, and defecated on the middle of the floor. Yep, that was the real poop or scoop or crap or whatever you want to call this dilemma. No one spoke as we all knew I could not say ***that*** word over ***his*** radio. How could I accomplish this task without angering the Sheriff? I had to do the job. I picked up the form and keyed the microphone.

"Hillsborough to Zone 50, copy a call."

"Zone 50, go ahead Hillsborough."

"Zone 50, be en route to the Country Corner Bar; they have had an illegal dumping inside the building, and Zone 51, you are dispatched as a backup unit."

I had accomplished the difficult task of dispatching the call without saying anything bad on ***his*** radio. Of course the deputy who went to the call was not that clean mouthed when he called me on the telephone. I asked him how could I have done it any better and satisfied the Sheriff. His argument came to an abrupt stop, and he completely agreed about that concern bringing an end to the phone call. Then a short time later came the crack of the radio,

"Zone 50 to Hillsborough, mark this call complete, the problem has been wiped up."

"10-4 Zone 50."

It was all over, the form time-stamped, and the radio was cleared with the call sign, "KIB660."

Be careful now, don't spill your drink while you laugh about that little tale.

# SWAT

Let me know if you need a refill on your drink before we move on to this next story.

My second Sheriff was also a very good and extremely high-quality person, employer, and of course Sheriff. This man was very concerned about the image of the Sheriff's Office because in the long run, that would be his image as viewed by the public. Because of this, he was convinced that his Sheriff's Office did not need, should not have, and would never have a SWAT team. Now, this is the Special Weapons and Tactics team that could handle the most dangerous situations with the most efficient methods for the most desirable outcome. As we all know, the final outcome may be the most unpleasant result of the "green light" command given to the sniper and the suspect eliminated by a single shot creating the three Cs; one criminal, one cartridge, one corpse. With this, the Sheriff was very strong with his opinion that he could resolve all issues without SWAT and would not create such a loathsome group of trained killers.

With the increase of problems in our community, the command staff decided that all of the patrol supervisors should have tear gas issued to them so that it could be used at the immediate time of the problem. At that time in our history, the Deputy Sheriffs were armed with a revolver, and there was no desire or need to move to the semiautomatic military pistol. With the revolver, a new device was created that could be temporarily attached to the barrel, armed with a tear gas canister, and loaded with a special bullet to launch the tear gas can. There was no need for a specially trained team as all of the supervisors had this device.

On one evening, one of our local farmers was celebrating some recent incident in his life and imbibed a large amount of alcoholic beverages to achieve the festivity of joy. Unfortunately, the good man drank a bit too much which caused him to expand the celebration by shooting outside of his house at the street lights, the cars, and at a couple of people. He was just having a good old time that night. The Sheriff's Office quickly responded to the scene where the farmer had barricaded himself inside of his home. This situation created a need for the deputies to surround the house and for a supervisor to respond to the scene. On this evening, two sergeants went to the location as both knew they could resolve the problem; no one would ever need a SWAT team for a person with a high-powered hunting rifle shooting from a barricaded location. These two sergeants both knew they had the tear gas, and that they could easily fumigate that troublesome bug from his home.

Working together, the sergeants unloaded a revolver where they mounted the gas launcher and loaded the launching bullets into the weapon. With great skill, they began to blast the tear gas canisters into the occupied home, the first, the second, and the third, the canisters were bursting in air. With each shot, they heard the smashed glass and saw the gas fumes expand throughout that large house. By then, the sergeant providing the canisters was reading the tear gas can label and asked the sergeant that had been deploying the gas a very simple question, what does this mean when it is labeled "Caution: this is a pyrotechnic device"? The other sergeant could not answer that question, but the house itself was willing and able to explain that term to the good supervisors as the flames began to rise out of the windows. Yes, pyrotechnic means that it can cause a fire, in this case a very large fire. The intoxicated farmer fled from the burning farmhouse, a very large and beautiful home with a listing price of well over a million dollars, a very nice and expensive estate. As the deputies arrested the farmer who, when not drinking, was a well-respected local leader in the farming community, all watched as the mansion engulfed in flames and smoke burned to the ground all the way to the foundation.

It was not long before the now sober farmer, a political supporter of the Sheriff, started legal action to recoup the financial loss of his mansion that the good sergeants had burned all the way to the ground. On reviewing this case, the Sheriff's lawyer provided the best legal advice to resolve this serious situation of being to immediately write that man a big check. The final opinion was the sergeants, without the proper training, had used a device that should not have been used to resolve this situation; now doesn't that just burn you up? The lawyer also advised that to prevent having to continually issue checks with two commas in the numeric dollar value, the Sheriff should have a certain trained group to handle these types of serious situations. I would not have wanted to be in that meeting when they discussed with the Sheriff the requirement to create the SWAT team. The good Sheriff made the final decision; I am so very sure against his desires, to create a new team that he still insisted would not be designated as a SWAT team they would need to create a different label.

The lieutenant in charge of the Selective Enforcement Unit (SEU) was instructed to create the team, select the members, and immediately obtain training for this new group. Lieutenant Ronald was also given a direct order to determine a label for this group as the term of SWAT could not, absolutely would not in any way or fashion be used to define the team. At that time, I was selected to be one of the founding members of the Sheriff's Office team, but not the SWAT team.

With the members selected, we formed the team and began a search for our equipment and training. Fortunately, the FBI was currently offering a class in this type of training at the main military base camp of the state National Guard. We gathered up our equipment and headed north to become experts in the use of Special Weapons and Tactics and to create a name for the team. During the training, we learned the structure for this type of team, trained in rifle and pistol, and methods for hostage rescues and barricaded suspects. We also learned that our methods and equipment of revolvers and rifles housed in the property room would require new rules at our office.

While staying in mobile homes located on the military base, we had meetings to organize our new team and to determine a name for our group. Lieutenant Ronald decided on positions for the team with Deputy Raymond being the sniper, Deputy Robert and Deputy Gordon would be the entry team, Sergeant James would be the team leader, and I would be the omni man. That meant that I was the person assigned to all of the special equipment, the 37-mm tear gas gun, the Taser electronic gun, beanbag launching gun, and other toys that no one else would have; all the neat toys were all mine, mine, mine. Also, when they saw my shooting abilities, the lieutenant assigned me as the backup sniper, so that added a scoped rifle to my new box of toys. If the office psychiatrist knew I had all of those toys, or should I say special equipment, that would have taken him on an emergency run to the closest cardiac care unit.

With the team organized, we began the debate on how to title our new group. There were several concepts and ideas battered around with none of these seeming to be the best answer. Then Lieutenant Ronald with a glow of insight announced that he had the perfect answer, the Fast Action Response Team. I immediately informed the good lieutenant that I would not like to be the gas man on the FART team. The others agreed that the acronym would not provide a professional appearance on the Sheriff's Office uniform. We all "passed" on that idea and selected the title of Emergency Response Team (ERT).

With training completed, we returned home and began the new battles for the operation of the team. We had to get special permission to carry semiautomatic handguns to have our military assault rifles (AR-15) and sniper rifles stored in the trunk of our cars, and for me to have my special equipment kept in my car. With that being approved, Major David prayed that my car was never struck in the rear end in a traffic accident, we then moved to the idea of a uniform. The change was to take an all dark green uniform and have the colorful patches changed to black creating another tough decision for the reluctant Sheriff. The final decision was for all this to be approved, and that only the ERT personnel could carry the assault rifle and the Colt .45 semiautomatic pistol on duty. The ERT was complete and ready to resolve any and all actions of their assignments. Of course, everyone was afraid to use the ERT team as everybody knew it was not the favorite group of the Sheriff.

Finally, late one evening, the callout was initiated for the ERT team to respond to a barricaded suspect, our first call in the history of the team. Upon arriving at the scene, we determined that a young man in the house had a mental breakdown possibly due to a reaction to his mental controlling drugs. The gentleman was armed with a knife and threatening to kill himself and anyone who came in the house. The plan was for the entry team to assist me with getting inside the home, confront the subject, and Taser him to the ground. Let us remember that this was many years ago, and the Taser was a brand-new device that had never been used by our office, maybe even never used in the entire state at that time.

The old Taser looked like a traffic enforcement speed radar device that was a large instrument with a handle coming from the bottom and the flat front accepting two cartridges. Each of the cartridges was the size of a 9-volt battery, and each contained two metal barbs with the appearance of teeny-tiny fishing harpoons, which were about the size of a quarter of the length of a toothpick. When the trigger was pulled, the two barbs for one of the cartridges were launched hooking into the person and remained connected to the device by thin lines that would provide an electric shock of fifty thousand nonlethal volts to the person. The electricity continued to flow while the trigger was held down, but once the trigger was disengaged, the electric charge came to an immediate stop. By pulling the trigger again, the power would again regenerate to flow into the person. The second cartridge was also available if the first did not get both barbs to connect to the person.

With plots and plans completed, it was now time for action, time for me to Taser the subject or clear the way for a shotgun blast to the subject by the entry team. We went to the rear of the home and used special methods of entry—well, we picked the lock based on our previous knowledge in law enforcement that we will not discuss here or ever. Once in the home, the rooms were totally dark as the suspect stood near the front door. We approached the knife-wielding subject and got very close before he saw us sneaking up. The man screamed at our team as he raised the knife over his head and charged toward me in his attack. When the man was within distance of the Taser wires, a very close distance, I fired the weapon and held down the trigger. With the electricity flowing through his body, the man looked as if someone had hit him the back of the legs with a baseball bat. His feet went up in the air, and his shaking body fell to the terrazzo floor. In the darkness, one could see blue sparks jumping in the openings between his fingers. By now, the entire team had entered the house, and Sergeant James told me to stop the charge as it looked as if it was killing the man. When I let go of the power, the man immediately stood up as if nothing had happened and looked directly into my face, he was not very happy. As he again started his attack, I smiled at him and again pulled the trigger on that Taser. He went up into the air, onto the ground, and again flopping around like a fish on the deck of a boat while the team prepared to surround the man. The sergeant told everyone that when I stopped the charge, they would all grab the subject and take him into custody. The next comment from the sergeant was a direct order for me not to electrify the subject while they were holding him. The charge was stopped; the man was grabbed, cuffed up, and taken out of the residence for his trip to a mental evaluation facility. The ERT team's first action was a complete and total success; we did not even burn the house down.

 As we finished up at the scene, I realized that this had occurred just after midnight, so I turned to the team and thanked them for my present. With their questioned look, they were informed that with this time being the beginning of a new day, this had all happened on my birthday. With the success of the team action and a birthday gift of the first to use a Taser, I departed the scene singing the words to tune "You Light Up My Life." It was times like these when one realizes that some supervisors do not have a sense of humor, I never got a chance to finish the song.

# Inflatable Irene

Now let me assure you that this is a true story even though you may not believe me. Get ready for another interesting day at work.

During most of my time on the SWAT team, or to be correct for the Sheriff himself ERT, my daily assignment was in the Selective Enforcement Unit (SEU). With my many assignments with this squad, we have got to add another tale about one of my partners in that group. Now this was a group of eight deputies that were assigned to fix a problem, absolutely fix the problem. There was this one time that we went to a bar to explain how they had to behave themselves because the neighbors were complaining about the establishment. While trying to communicate with the patrons, they were laughing at us and ignoring us as the band turned up the volume of their amplifiers. This caused us to simply leave the building, arm ourselves with shotguns, and return into the business. The corporal was telling them to be quite as one of me reached over and turned off the power to the amplifiers. The story of the shotgun round fired into the ceiling is a total exaggeration of the facts, that's right, a total fabrication. So without the band playing and the patrons not laughing anymore, we were able to explain the problem and request the assistance of the customers. Even the band agreed to lower the volume, so we did not have to arrest them and impound each and every piece of their equipment and keep those items of evidence for months, maybe years until the trial. The assistant manager even agreed to work on resolving this terrible problem, a simple misunderstanding. The manager could not help because he argued with us at the very beginning of the conversation and during his arrest fell to the ground as he struggled to escape. Once that rude man was released from the hospital, it was strait to jail for his criminal actions. At least that's how I remember the story.

One of the members of this special group had been one of my partners when I first started at the office. Both of us young deputies were assigned to the radio room to take complaints and dispatch cars. At that time, Deputy Kevin had emptied his extra bullet pouches of ammunition and filled them with chewing gum and candy. His transfer to the street changed his method of maintaining his equipment.

Good old Deputy Kevin was a very dedicated and determined Deputy Sheriff. By the time he was in SEU, he was aggressively concerned about his safety and the results of his work product. One of his constant problems dealt with his fears about being discovered when we were conducting surveillances or following suspects. He would keep several hats and jackets that he could swap into allowing him to change his appearance while conducting these undercover operations. This did not work as well as he believed because his actions were inside a car with heavily tinted windows and working during the night hours. With this concern eating away at him, he was able to develop the best method of changing the appearance and look of his vehicle. His solution was to purchase a full life-size inflatable doll of a human being. Go ahead as we all laughed as much as you are when he brought that device to work one night. The statements from Deputy Ronald that evening are certainly not publishable, but he did name her Inflatable Irene.

As we worked over the next few weeks, we would see Deputy Kevin driving down the road alone and later in the evening he had someone, or maybe something, in the passenger seat. With all of the inflating and deflating, the entire squad was beyond control with our opinion on this method. Eventually, our plot and plan was created and placed into action.

Deputy Kevin had placed his little lady in the car seat with the seat belt locked in place and allowing him to activate his power air pump to inflate her into the sitting position at any moment. So at that moment, Deputy Kevin would be able to have his date sitting next to him; probably his best chance for a date. Well, the rest of the squad got together and not really broke into his car; we kind of took some action to enter the car, oh, alright, we picked the lock. Once inside, we placed a thumbtack through the seat belt on the passenger's side; of course, the tip was pointed at Inflatable Irene. Later that evening, as we were all checking an area for some criminals, the time arrived when Deputy Kevin activated that power pump and started to inflate his darling Irene. Well, when that plastic lady hit that thumbtack and exploded, the entire squad thought that poor Kevin was going to be killed in a traffic crash. That car swerved all over the roadway before it came to a screeching dead stop. This occurred as all of the rest of us were laughing so hard we were also having trouble driving down the road. It seemed that Irene left Deputy Kevin, left him in the wind.

As Deputy Kevin communicated with us concerning this incident or better defined screamed at the top of his lungs, he appeared to be upset. Telling him that at least she went out with a bang was in no way taken as a condolence.

Needless to say, Deputy Kevin did not replace his dear lost Irene. His main focus was to move forward and to continue with all of his proper actions for the completion of the investigations and for officer safety. The methods of his work were always to be overly cautious to achieve the best outcome for him. On one day, this was going to be a bit difficult for this good man.

In the SEU squad, we were issued unmarked cars to assist with our special investigations. Being unmarked, these cars did not have a cage to place the criminal in the backseat and protect the driver from attack. Those of us with these cars would place the suspect in the front passenger seat and secure them with handcuffs and the seat belt. One afternoon, Deputy Kevin was driving a prisoner to jail in the aforementioned status. As they went down the interstate highway, the arrested subject had slipped out of the handcuffs and unbuckled the seat belt. As they drove down the highway, the criminal grabbed for the pistol in Deputy Kevin's holster. Continuing with the interstate traffic, they fought over the gun while the good deputy brought the car to a stop and jumped from the vehicle. His exit was at the same time the suspect obtained control of the weapon.

As Deputy Kevin ran around the car, the suspect, exiting on the passenger side, was also circling the vehicle as he was shooting at the deputy. After a trip or two around the car, Deputy Kevin was able to obtain his shotgun from the car. Now, the suspect was shooting the revolver, and the deputy was blasting away with the shotgun. Then it finally happened, both of them ran out of bullets. The criminal dropped the pistol and took off running while the deputy dropped his shotgun and thanked the good lord for his survival. With all of the shooting, neither one of them hit the other person. Based on the shooting investigation, they did not hit anything at all; there was no damage from any of the bullets at any location. Fortunately, there was no damage to our partner; he was safe and alive.

The SEU squad got together at the scene and started a search for the dirt bag that shot at one of us, our brother in arms. It did not take long before he was located and taken back into custody. During that arrest, he again tried to resist his apprehension and forced the entire group, each and all of us, to use sufficient physical force to ensure the apprehension of a felony suspect. When a prisoner is in the hospital for that many days they have to be remote booked and a detention deputy from the jail guards them in their hospital room. At least, that's the way I remember it.

That SEU assignment was one of my most enjoyable times at the Sheriff's Office and more so a great honor to work those outstanding partners.

So now that we have told too many funny stories, let us move on to some other interesting stories where I will try to talk about some of the more serious tales of my career. Not all of them are full of hot air like Irene.

# Frozen Marijuana

Let's get another cup of hot coffee before we start this story; you will need something hot while you hear this one, it's a bit cold. Now remember that during most of my time on the Emergency Response Team (ERT), my main duty assignment was in the Selective Enforcement Unit (SEU). The job of SEU was to help other areas when they needed extra manpower but more so to "fix a problem." Many assignments would come to our little unit, most of them on the old pink phone message, and we immediately fixed that problem. That small group of eight people were always "fixing" a problem, and the bosses were happy it was done and determined to never know how it was done, just fixed. These different assignments in SEU were always a new experience and created some unbelievable tales of work. Reading between the lines, you can be assured that these stories will be very selective when discussing actions involving that group. So let us move on and start this next interesting little tale.

One afternoon, we were gathered together by Sergeant James to meet up with a group of smuggling detectives at their office. This was unusual as that group was always involved in secret squirrel types of investigations. During that meeting, as with any in their office, we started with being reminded that we were sworn to secrecy on the information in that meeting. From a current investigation, the SEU group was needed to help on the resolution of their smuggling case. At that time, they had a confidential informant who was assisting them with a major smuggling operation. Based on the investigation, two shrimp boats were currently floating just outside of the local bay and were waiting to deliver their loads later that evening. The contraband was to be loaded into semitrailers and transported to a barn on a farm out in the very rural area of our county. At the barn, a specially trained squad of heavily armed smugglers who would guard the big haul until it could be moved on for sale. With that being said, this may be at least a two-night operation requiring a deputy to have an eye on the property in case they tried to move the drugs and to prepare for the attack when we moved in for the arrest. With the dangerous security force on the property, the request was for our group to be that eye. The plots and plans were created, and after our reminder to the vow of silence, we were sent off to accomplish the task.

The plan was for our squad to change our clothing into a full set of camouflage garb. We needed the equipment to sleep overnight, more than one night, while we hid in the wooded area between the railroad tracks and the road on the north side of the armed fortress. Because we were to remain secret, we could not have any fire or lights that would expose our secret observation post; this even required headphones for the radios. Without the ability to heat the food, we each carried several canteens of water and of course some freeze dried military rations; believe me these food packets will never be shown on The Food Channel. The concern of the armed guards at the barn forced the need for the ERT members in our group to be armed with our military assault rifles. With this order issued, we each went out to gather all of the needed equipment for this dangerous mission.

Dressed in our camouflage with backpacks, daily needs and survival equipment, and of course multiple weapons, we gathered to take the next step in the plan. Before we go any farther, let me add another bit of information to this interesting investigation. This current assignment was occurring in the month of January, the coldest January in my knowledge of local weather history. Now in our big sunshine state, cold means the temperature has plummeted into the sixties or even worse all the way into the fifties. During this assignment, the temperatures would drop into the teens, which would definitely require drinking large amounts of orange juice.

With our group bundled and equipped for the artic assignment, we were dropped off on the railroad tracks several miles from the

## THE EMOTIONS FROM A BADGE

location of the storage barn. With the night being cold, we hiked down the tracks while the temperature was dropping to eventually reach our secret outpost. When we arrived in the woods, the holes and ditches allowed us a good location to hide in those briars and brambles and bushes of the cold orange grove. From our hidden spot, we had an excellent view of the barn and the entrance to the property. The entire move into the location was accomplished and a complete secret to the entire neighborhood. We were stealth fighters.

Later that evening, we followed the radio traffic that indicated the first shrimp boat was unloaded, and several truckloads of the whacky weed were traveling toward our site. As we sat there watching, the three trucks drove onto the property and emptied twenty tons of marijuana into the barn. After the trucks were emptied, they quickly rushed back to the docks. This time, their wait would be longer as the second boat was stuck in the water as the engines would not start.

As the sun was rising, we established shifts for each of us to sleep and to also watch the stash on the property. The day was a bit nicer with the bright sun shining and bringing those cold temperatures way up into the twenties. If the cold was not bad enough, we had to take the freezing water and add that to the long-range patrol rations in order to eat the cold glob of food. By that time, we were all in agreement that during the raid, we might have to accidently shoot the person who decided to put us out in this cold and miserable weather. It was just talk, do not worry it was just talk.

The next night, we again waited for the delivery of that second load of marijuana to be delivered to the big barn. All through the night, we heard that the shrimp boat was still having problems starting the engine. We sat there; the temperature dropped, and we shook and shivered waiting on the next load. That night, the boat did not make it to the pier, yet there came another sunrise.

That following day, we were running out of our gourmet meals while we told unbelievable stories from our past where we were warm and comfortable. With the sun going down and the temperatures falling into the third night, we again brought up the idea of that accidental shooting; remember it was just talk, do not worry it was just talk. The cold night went through with the news that the boat was still stranded in the bay waters. We all agreed on swimming out there and just pulling that darn boat to shore. That idea was nixed when we realized the water would be even colder than our current environment. It was another night in the frozen tundra.

Before sunrise of the fourth day, the command decision was to have the Coast Guard seize the disabled boat and for us to raid the barn. Before the sun was rising, we moved into a closer location to launch the attack. It was hard to continue being stealth in this area; this may have been as we had lived in the woods without a bath for several days, and if you could not see us, it would be so easy to smell us. While we waited in the yard of the neighbor's house, he was the first to see us sneaking about. When confronting us as to our business, the homeowner immediately saw me and realized we were the Sheriff's Office. We had a short conversation about how he knew me from him working at the railroad with my father; my partners reminded me that I always knew someone everywhere and anywhere that we went. The gentleman was informed, to a point, of our action and asked to stay inside. We even had to turn down his offer to bring us out some coffee; that was hard to turn down hot, yep warm hot and steaming coffee.

As the sun rose, the Coast Guard Cutter assaulted the shrimp boat, we got the signal to attack the guarded compound. We moved in with all of the proper tactics including our guns drawn to capture the multiple criminals and disarm them of their automatic assault rifles. On entering the location, we took down all of the occupants without a shot and without an injury. The entire crew guarding the house consisted of just two unarmed people. The man was in his eighties and his darling wife just a tad younger; there was not a gang of armed guards at the fortress.

After reading the search warrant, we entered the barn to see an amazing sight. There were bales of marijuana stacked up all along one side of the barn and up to the ceiling. The bales had the same appearance of a bale of hay with a very different color and smell. None of us had ever seen that much marijuana at any one time. Even the smuggling detectives were stunned as we stood there looking at that much wacky backy.

The case detective came over to our group and offered his gracious and profound thanks for all that we had done to assist with this case. After that nice man walked away, we reminded ourselves that all of the talk about an accidental shooting was just talk. The most desirable next step for us was to locate heat; the inside of the car was so very nice and warm. The problem from that was our driver had a bit of a problem with the smell; as we held onto our rifles, he was told to shut up and keep driving.

After resolving all of the difficulties, and a very long and hot bath, we each got a long night of good sleep. The final outcome of this raid was one of the largest drug seizures ever completed by our office and the conviction of several notorious smugglers. The detective, who was a very good man, had done an excellent job of resolving such a difficult and high-quality investigation. When that good man finally retired from the Sheriff's Office, he held the rank of major; he achieved the rank and retirement because there was not an accidental shooting on that frigid day. Remember that was all talk that's right just talk, very cold glacial talk.

# *Accident or Murder*

I know that you have been waiting to hear a little more serious story than tales of the wild shenanigans of my early career. So let us jump forward in time and talk about one of the more serious investigations, the death of a child.

The county of my jurisdiction contains well over one thousand square miles of land which during my early years on the job had a low number of residents that formed a community of many wide open rural acres. The population to land ratio has continued to grow each year changing our community to a more urban than rural local. Even our school system in those early years had nearly one hundred thousand students less than their current enrollment today. At that time of so many years ago, the southern half of our county contained only one high school and one middle school which were next to each other on one large piece of shared land. During that old time of many yesterdays ago on one Wednesday afternoon in March, both of these schools would face a tragedy.

The two crowded schools were both on a double-session schedule, which creates a separate and independent morning and afternoon session, allowing many of the students to be home from school early in the afternoon. On that particular day, one fourteen-year-old boy who had attended the morning session was home from school ready and willing to enjoy the afternoon. The young man, Howie, jumped on his moped and started to ride around his rural neighborhood. The blonde hair blue-eyed child did not have an appearance of aggression or any look of a threat. He was enrolled in the high school ROTC program with aspirations of one day becoming a United States Marine. From his home, he stopped at residences of several different friends with each person having other obligations preventing him from staying very long at any of the houses. At the last stop, he told Mary, the young girl at that home, that he was going to go to a local spot in the woods where they would usually meet up with one another and hang out with others from the neighborhood. He asked Mary to call Ginger, who was another friend, and tell that girl where she could meet with him. As he drove away on the moped, Mary telephoned Ginger telling her that Howie wanted her to meet with him at that well-known location. Mary did not tell Ginger that Howie was carrying a pistol.

Ginger, an eleven-year-old girl anxiously jumped on her bicycle and peddled off to the well-known rendezvous point. She was a cute little girl who always beamed a bright and broad smile from her face that was surrounded by her curly blonde hair. Her story was so similar to that of some little lady we all know, she was so much that little girl next door. From ballerina, to softball player, and a cheerleader for the youth football teams, she continued to grow through her wonderful life.

By the time she met up with Howie, a second young man had already joined up with the first lad. This second boy Randy, who lived across the street from the spot in the woods, was fifteen years old and sadly had a very small and slight challenge with some of his learning abilities. He was much taller and built bigger than either of the other two in that trio of friends but was a very quiet and timid follower. So with all three friends together at that little opening in the woods, they were all enjoying the day and having some afternoon fun. Then *bang!*

A neighbor, hearing a gunshot, went outside to see what was happening as one of the boys came out of the woods yelling for help. The man Mr. Andy who was Randy's father rushed into the woods to find Ginger shot in the head, and there on the ground next to her bleeding head was the pistol. The wound was a very traumatic injury to the area of the right eye causing her blood to be gushing from the bullet hole. Mr. Andy applied pressure with the bandana that had already been used by Howie with his treatment. When the father started first aid, Howie stepped away and picked up the gun from the ground as Mr. Andy told Howie to leave the gun on the ground and not to touch the weapon any more. As the gun was placed back on the ground, the man loudly yelled for other neighbors to call for an ambulance and the Sheriff to respond to the scene. Several other neighbors came to help, and Howie was sent to notify the girl's parents. It did not take long before the emergency personnel and Ginger's family arrived at the horrible scene. The pretty little girl's head was wrapped up in the bandages that were filling with blood, as she was placed in the ambulance and rushed to the trauma center hospital for immediate surgery. As the ambulance raced from the scene with lights and sirens announcing their path, the neighbors stood there in a sad and concerned state of shock. It was now time to start the investigation.

On the afternoon of this trauma, the sun was beginning to set when I arrived at the crime scene. Two deputies were already conducting their portion of the investigation for this current incident. The primary deputy had secured the scene and was conducting interviews and properly fulfilling the requirements of his job. I knew that deputy would be complete and perfect on all of his obligations to the highest possible level because I was his field training officer when he was first hired with the Sheriff's Office. The other deputy had the obligation of securing the area of the crime scene. At this point, everything was in good order to help resolve this incident or maybe solve a crime.

The other detective and our lieutenant arrived a short time later. After meeting together and obtaining a quick briefing of the events, the lieutenant decided that the other detective would be the case officer, and I would assist him with the investigation. This is the normal action to place one investigator as the lead detective allowing him to be in charge and responsible for the outcome of the process. In all reality, this places a heavy burden on that lead detective.

This other detective, Steve, had grown up with me during our long time together at the Sheriff's Office. Or should I say, we got older together as neither of us ever really grew up. Through our first days of employment working in the radio room, our assignment together in the Selective Enforcement Unit and now as detectives in homicide, we together had resolved many and various difficult jobs. We worked very well together as we knew the methods and personalities that each would use to complete any of our assignments.

With Steve working his part of the case, I met up with the crime scene technician to begin processing the crime scene in the woods. Compared to many other an investigation, there was very little evidence to process at this scene that would help our investigation better define the incident. The .32 caliber semiautomatic pistol lying on the ground was an older model weapon that was in poor condition. The rusted gun was on the ground near a large puddle of blood that had spilled from the victim's head. The pistol was jammed open as a result of what is called a stovepipe. Normally, when a semiautomatic pistol is fired, the top portion of the weapon slides back and ejects the empty shell casing before returning to the loaded position and is ready to fire a second round. A stovepipe jam is when the portion of the gun is sliding back to eject the shell casing, and the shell is not thrown from the gun and where it sticks in the ejection portal preventing the gun from returning to a ready-to-shoot position. This causes the shell casing to stick out of the top of the ejection port and look like a stovepipe chimney sticking out of the top of the pistol. This completely jams the weapon and prevents the gun from having the ability to take a second shot. A second piece of evidence was a blood-soaked bandana stuck in a bush to the side of where the victim had been laying. The bullet fired from the gun that struck the victim and went through her head was never found. The few items of evidence were impounded; photographs of the scene and measurements were taken to create a crime scene diagram completing the overall processing of the incident scene. When finished, I met up with lead Detective Steve to assist with the rest of our duties.

Steve had conducted some interviews at the crime scene before taking Howie and Randy to our crime scene office. Both subjects agreed to have a neutron activation test conducted on their hands. This is a chemical test used to determine if the person had recently fired a firearm by wiping a chemical substance on the hands to recover the gunpowder residue. Steve's next stop was our office in the Criminal Investigations Division where we were now all together.

Howie sat in a small interview room with the two detectives as he told us his story of what had occurred that afternoon. His story started with how he left school for his home where he got into some military camouflage clothing and jumped on his moped to wander the neighborhood. On the moped, he had a side bag where he kept the pistol that was used in the shooting. He kept the gun and a broken pool cue with him to protect himself from being attacked even though he did not know of anybody that may be after him. Both of these weapons were just for his personal protection. Howie had obtained the pistol when it was left at his family home by an uncle who had lived with his mother and him for several months. Recently, his mother sent the uncle away because he was an alcoholic and disrupting the home with all of his drinking. After the uncle moved out of the house, he was looking through some of the items left behind by the uncle. In those items, he found the pistol.

His first stop of the afternoon was when he met up with a fellow ROTC student at that boy's house. They took that boys .22 caliber rifle and Howie's pistol and went to the woods to take some target shooting. After they each had shot both of the weapons, the other boy had to go home for a scheduled trip to the barber shop. This caused him to jump back on the moped and move to another location.

Howie's next stop was at the home of another girl named Mary who lived in the neighborhood. At that house, he determined that she was on some type of restriction, and he could not go inside or stay at that home. He only stayed at that home for a few minutes before moving on to the next stop.

This next residence was the home of Randy who was the witness to the shooting. They got together and decided to go across the street into a wooded area where they so often like to play. Howie stated that they were just standing around and goofing off when they saw the victim riding by on her bicycle, so Randy called out to her. The witness invited Ginger to join up with the two of them in the wooded area.

## THE EMOTIONS FROM A BADGE

Ginger and he were standing there and talking while Randy started to walk further into the woods. Randy was headed in the direction of a fortlike area that they had created further back into that location. Ginger was asking him about the "stick" that he had attached to his moped. Howie explained that it was the large end of a broken pool cue that he carried for his own self-defense. Ginger then asked Howie if that was the only object that he had with him for protection. He told her that he also had the pistol, took the weapon from his side pouch, and showed her the gun by unwrapping from within the bandana. Cute little Ginger asked if she could hold the gun. Howie was sure that would not be a problem of any kind.

Howie stated that he started to walk toward Ginger with the gun in his hand with his arm extended to enable him to hand her the weapon. As he approached Ginger, he tripped over a limb or some other object causing him to stumble. He was afraid that he was going to drop the weapon, so to prevent the gun from falling, he tightened his grip on the weapon. At that time, he was looking at the gun more that at Ginger when the gun discharged causing him to look up at the victim. She was standing there looking at him with a stunned look on her face when the blood started to flow from her face, and she collapsed onto the ground. When he went to her aid, Randy was returning to their location. He could not tell where the blood was coming from, but he used the bandana that had been wrapped around the pistol to try and stop the bleeding. He told Randy to go across the street get his father. As Randy was heading out to get his father, Mr. Andy was already headed their way arriving a short time later, and then his dad took over the first aid. The father yelled out to the neighbors to call for the ambulance and the Sheriff's Office to come to the scene.

Prior to the arrival of the emergency personnel, Mr. Andy told Howie to get on his moped and notify Ginger's father that she had been shot. He then jumped on bike and rushed to the victim's home. When Howie first told Ginger's father what had occurred, he did not seem to believe the story was true. Her father's mind changed with the emergency personnel's arrival in the neighborhood. At that time, Ginger's father got in his car and rushed toward the scene.

With all of the other emergency personnel and neighbors at the scene, he was not able to go back into the area with Ginger. He did see the ambulance take Ginger on a stretcher from the scene. Howie told us this was the truth, and it was all he knew about the incident. Steve and I both noted something very strange about the attitude of this fourteen year old, which had just shot the cute little neighborhood blonde-haired girl in her face; there was not a tear in his eyes.

After the hour long interview of Howie, we started the interview with Randy. He stated that he was in the wooded area with Howie just having an afternoon conversation. As they were talking, Ginger rode up on her bicycle, so he went out of the woods to invite her to join them. He had noticed that Howie had an unknown object wrapped in a bandana in his pocket that day but did not know what was in that bundle. He stayed a short time with the others, and later, he left those other two and started to walk down the trail to their fort. When he was about thirty yards down the trail, he heard the shot. He turned and ran back to the scene. As he was approaching, he could see Howie standing about two feet from Ginger as she was falling to the ground. He did not know that Howie had a gun, and he did not see the actually shooting. He only saw Ginger fall to the ground.

Randy stated that Howie and Ginger were neighborhood friends. In some ways, he believed that Howie liked Ginger and would like to start dating the victim. The two of them never got very close to each other, and they never dated one another. He also said that after the shooting, Howie wanted him to tell everyone that Ginger had shot herself with the pistol. This was because Howie was scared that he may get in big trouble even though it was an accident. He told Howie that he would not get himself in trouble by lying for him. Randy insisted that was all he knew about the incident because he was down the trail and not with the other two when Ginger was shot.

With the investigation continuing and it was approaching midnight, Steve and I released the boys to their parents so they could get themselves home and get some needed sleep. Steve and I also headed out to get some sleep of our own, but on my way home, I stopped by the hospital for an update on the victim's condition. The hospital personnel told me that on her arrival at the hospital, Ginger had been immediately prepared for an emergency surgery. This preparation included the removal of her clothes, and the surgery also required that her head be shaved for the medical procedure. This caused her personal items to be left in the emergency room resulting in a Crime Scene technician being dispatched to the hospital to impound these items for evidence, the clothing and also the locks of her pretty and curly blonde hair, saturated with blood, which had been shaved from her head.

Throughout the next day, Steve and I interviewed all of the people whose names had come up the day before in the investigation. Howie's ROTC friend told us that he had not seen the shooter the day of the incident. He had to stay late for school and was not home when Howie claimed to be with him shooting the guns in the woods. He also told us that he had not ever shot the shooter's pistol and did not shoot any gun with Howie that day.

The next interview was with the girl that Howie told us that he had spoken to her at her house prior to meeting Randy and Ginger in the woods. Mary told us that the shooter did come by her house, but that her parents do not allow her to have a guest when they are not home. She and Howie talked for a few moments while standing together at the front door. During this time, Howie showed her a pistol that he had wrapped up in a bandana. Howie was a bit reckless as he showed the pistol to her, and being uncomfortable, she adjusted her position because of her fear of the gun. He advised her that he had taken gun safety classes where he learned to be safe with any firearm. Because she was nervous about the gun and also her parent's rules, she told Howie that he would have to leave. As he departed on the moped, Howie asked her to call the victim and tell her to meet him down in the woods. After Howie left, she called Ginger to tell her about the meeting. Mary did not tell Ginger that Howie had a gun.

The next part of this story is very difficult to explain. Steve and I determined that Howie had not obtained the pistol from his uncle as he told us in his interview. The gun used in the shooting had belonged to another family that lived in the south end of the county. Over three months before the shooting two other boys, totally unrelated to this incident, decided to run away from home in order to escape the trouble they were having at school. One of the two boys lived with his mother while his father was currently in state prison on a murder conviction. As they prepared to leave, they clandestinely took three guns from his home on the evening before running away and took these weapons with them to school. Once they got to school that morning, they did not know what to do with the weapons so they had another boy, the son of a Deputy Sheriff, keep the guns hidden in his locker. During the school day they left school, totally forgetting about the pistols, and started their run from supervision and were eventually reported missing. The deputy's son who now had the guns was carrying them in his backpack while riding the school bus home. As the "Yellowhound" or school bus bounced down the highway, he started showing the guns to the other passengers and created a situation where some of the kids got a hold of the weapons and swapped them around among those passengers on the bus. Finally, Howie ended up with a gun and did not return the pistol that eventually ended up being used in this shooting. When the two runaway boys returned home, or to be more correct, were returned to their homes, they tried to get the wayward guns back from the ones who had taken them from the bus. They eventually realized they had been moved around to the point to where they could not recover the guns. They were also not very anxious to bring that topic of the missing guns to the dinner table with their mom.

With all of the new information, it was obvious that the story from the night before was not totally truthful creating a need for another conversation. We met up with Howie and had him take us back to the original crime scene. As Howie showed us a reenactment of the incident, we confronted him with the various problems with his story. Howie told us that he was very upset and scared about what would happen to him as a result of the shooting the night before. Finally, Howie told us how the gun had been obtained from that situation I spoke of earlier on the school bus. On their return from their expedition, the two runaways argued and threaten Howie to try to get their gun back from him. After all of the bickering and discussing in the end, Howie decided to just keep the gun.

Howie told us that he had made up the story about shooting guns with his friends because of the gunpowder residue test conducted by the Sheriff's Office. He believed this would allow him to show that he had shot a firearm earlier that day and make the test be inconclusive for the discharge of the murder weapon. This little story was because he was so scared about this accident.

The account continued about asking the witness to change his story which was also true. Howie was concerned about the trouble the shooting could cause him, so he tried to make up the story that reduced the seriousness of his mistakes in the incident. He said he was sorry for trying to change the story, but that he was so scared when he asked the witness to tell that story. He insisted that the important part that in the end, everything he told us about the shooting was the complete truth. He swore that he was walking toward Ginger when he tripped while trying to hand the gun to the girl. He was handing the pistol to Ginger at her request when he started to fall, and the gun accidently went off as he tried to stop the weapon from falling to the ground. He did not want to hurt Ginger in any way, it was an accident. Still, Howie did not cry.

All of the evidence from the crime was shipped off to the crime lab for a forensic examination. The test used to indicate if the boys had fired a gun resulted in an inconclusive test for both of the young men. The firearms technicians determined that the gun used in the shooting was a positive match of the weapon used to discharge the stovepipe shell casing. The projectile was never located to compare that bullet to the gun. The lab results confirmed the other items were all connected to the incident. The results of the laboratory examination did not provide any information that would alter any findings of the ongoing investigation.

After her four days of intensive care treatment, Ginger, the cute little blonde-haired girl, died in the hospital causing this accidental shooting to be upgraded to a death investigation. With all of the interviews, the autopsy results and the lab results combined together, Steve and I conducted a presentation to the State Attorney's Office for their final decision. It took four more days before the attorneys decided that this tragedy was an accident. Based on the prosecutors ruling, we notified all of those involved including Ginger's family and Howie that this was a closed case. A short time later, the little girl was laid to rest and even with Ginger in her grave, Howie still did not cry.

We all moved on with Steve being promoted out of his detective assignment to corporal supervising patrol deputies. I was still working as a detective on one after another and another death investigations and other crimes against people. Nearly two years after the original shooting, I was called from my desk to join a meeting in the major's office. A summon to that office was not one of the greatest desires for any detective during their career, yet with my approach and assignments to many a "special" investigation it was simply another visit for me.

The major explained that the mother of Ginger had once again, as she did so often, called for him to reopen the investigation into the murder of her baby. If the new information that she was providing was correct, there may be a need to look at the case again. The major told me, or as the major always insisted he asked, that I contact the good lady to determine what should be done with this new information. All of us in that office of death investigations knew that it is hard for a parent to truly bury their child.

On contacting the mother, she told me that a girl who had called her daughter on the day of her death telling Ginger that Howie wanted to see her had additional and new information about the shooting death. Realizing that the girl was Mary who had been interviewed in the original investigation, I advised Mom that I would talk to the girl to determine if she had enough information to reopen the case. Ginger's mother was ecstatic believing that we would surely conduct a new investigation into the murder of her little girl.

Later that afternoon, I contacted Mary at her home near the original crime scene. Even with two years passing since the death, everyone involved in the death investigation were still teenagers. Mary advised me that Randy, the witness to the incident, told her that he had not been truthful during the original investigation because out of fear and panic he felt that he could not tell the truth at that time. Randy has been having problems concerning his lack of truthfulness and believes that he should now tell what really happened on that day. He is still very concerned and scared, and he simply does not know what he should do about this tragedy.

Since the shooting, Mary has never talked to Howie about the incident. There are stories floating around the school and neighborhood that Howie often tells people that bother him, "I've already shot one person, and if you don't leave alone, I can do it again." Mary stated that the only one with any true information about this whole situation would be Randy.

After thanking Mary for her help, I went down the road a short distance to the home of the witness, the house across the street from the shooting scene. When I met with Randy, we had to call his mother for permission to conduct an interview with the minor child. The mother was very concerned about her son because he continues to have emotional problems ever since this incident. She felt that one of his parents needed to be with him while I talked with him, so a meeting was scheduled for the following day.

That next morning, I met with Randy and his father at their home. He started by telling me that he could no longer be silent, he could not keep the secret, this was eating at him, and he had to tell the truth. During the time before the shooting, Howie had often used the pistol to scare people by pointing the gun at others and threaten to shoot them. Sometimes, knowing the gun was not loaded, Howie would pull the trigger to scare people while at other times, the gun would be loaded, and the safety was engaged to prevent the gun from actually firing a bullet when Howie would make threats to the others.

On the day of the shooting, Howie knew the gun was loaded and ready to fire. Just before they entered the woods, he saw the shooter chamber a bullet in the gun. They then met up with Ginger as she was riding her bike near their location, and all three of them went into the woods. While they were gathered in the woods, Howie kept trying to talk Ginger into "making out" with him. Ginger did not seem to be interested in fulfilling Howie's request, and a short time later, Howie told him to walk away. He turned away and started to leave down the path to the fort as he heard Howie tell Ginger that if she did not go "all the way," he would shoot her with the pistol. Randy was about ten feet away when he stopped and turned back to look at them. As they stood there, Howie pointed the gun at Ginger and mumbled something about the two of them having sex, or Howie would shoot Ginger then Howie pulled the trigger and shot Ginger in the head. Howie exclaimed, "I shot her!" Neither of them knew what to do next, should they run, maybe claim that Ginger shot herself, they could not decide on their next step. Howie seemed scared of what may happen to him with the outcome of this incident. They got together and decided on the trip and fall story to explain this incident as an accidental shooting. It was then time to get help. His earlier story about going for help and that other people came to help the victim are the same as his original story.

Randy said that he was very scared the night of the shooting and was afraid to tell the truth because he believed that Howie would be in trouble as well as himself. Randy apologized for his fear forcing him to keep the secret for so long even though he knew the whole time that he should tell the truth.

This new statement which sounded much more realistic changed the entire concept of the original investigation. While wrestling with the next step, I decided to seek the advice of the State Attorney's Office. Mark was the assistant state attorney whom I contacted as he was a lead prosecutor of their murder cases who was also a very knowledgeable and good attorney. Mark is also a simply good person who is concerned about the people within our community. His high qualities were acknowledged years later with his election to the position of state attorney. Our discussion decided on the need for a polygraph of the witness to prove which of the two stories would be the truthful one. With all of the tales, it is obvious that one is not true, and it was our responsibility of proving which one was the truth. We had to fulfill our duty to find the truth.

On speaking to Randy and his family, they were reluctant for him to take the polygraph examination. The parents were concerned that Randy still had emotional problems from being a witness to the shooting. I assured them that a polygraph was not dangerous to his physical health, and that getting the deep secret off his shoulders would benefit not only him but everyone in the investigation. Randy's parents told me that they would have to think about allowing him to take the polygraph test. In the long run, their main concern was for the safety and well-being of their own child. I reminded them that without determining the real story, that their son could be considered a liar by the people in their community, and that the test would be able prove which story is the truth. They had to understand that the polygraph would prove the second story to be the truth allowing Randy to be forgiven by coming forward and correcting the first lie, or by doing nothing, he would have to live with this guilt for the rest of his life. I was prepared to wait for their decision.

My next step was to meet with Ginger's mother. At this point in the investigation, I would not tell her about all of the details of the current investigation. I especially would not tell her about the interviews as there was a need to keep certain facts secret until the end of this investigation. The secrecy of the investigation was paramount in order to prevent others from adjusting their real knowledge of this case to match the information of the current information. I promised her that I would proceed with the investigation, and that in the end, she would be provided all of the new details regardless of the final outcome. I then begged her for a very special and for her a difficult favor to be patient.

It was nearly two months before Randy and his family contacted me to agree to have him take the polygraph examination. They felt that the best thing for Randy would be for him to free his conscious about this horrible incident. The polygraph was scheduled and conducted by one of our examiners, an employee of the Sheriff's Office. Prior to becoming a polygraph examiner, he had been one of our detectives with his past experiences aiding him to become an expert in the field. With him, working the machine that was attached to Randy, I had no doubt that we would now have the complete truth. This examination verified that Randy was a direct witness to the shooting and that he heard the statements made by Howie to Ginger at the time of the incident. He was now finally telling the truth, the whole truth.

The prosecutor was provided the results of the polygraph combined with the information from the current investigation. Mark advised me to come to his office to obtain a subpoena for a deposition of the witness. With the witness served his subpoena, the victim's mother was provided another update still not being told any of the details but ensured the investigation was ongoing.

On the date of the deposition, the mother of Randy called and spoke to Mark, the prosecutor and myself. She told us that her own mother, the grandmother of Randy, had passed away that week; and the funeral was scheduled for the date of the deposition. With our condolences and concern, we set the deposition for a later date.

The following week, we conducted the deposition establishing sworn testimony of the witness. The interview with Randy enforced the new statements concerning the shooting and provided a few more points that needed to be resolved before proceeding with the investigation. Mark asked for me to obtain the answers to these questions before we went any further with the case. The main points were to clarify some information with Mary who had started the new interest in the investigation. The second was to interview a recent girlfriend of Howie who dated the shooter after the incident who was no longer seeing the shooter to determine if he ever told her about this story. So I strapped on the old six shooter, saddled up the horse, and headed out to continue the investigation.

The first lady Mary was contacted at her home to clarify some information that we had obtained from the deposition. There were stories that Ginger may have had earlier sexual encounters with Howie and Randy, and that the shooter and the witness threatening to cut the tires of the victim about a week prior to the shooting. Mary stated that she had heard the stories about Howie and Randy pulling knives and threatening to cut Ginger's tires if she did not kiss both of them. That story includes a second part claiming that Ginger pulled a knife to defend herself from the two boys. Mary has no direct knowledge of the incident stating that is was a story on the street, and she also had no information about any sexual contacts with any of the three involved in the incident. Mary also believed that Howie's ex-girlfriend may have more information and provided information on the new girl.

On the following day, I contacted the ex-girlfriend Lisa at the local high school. Lisa's story was that she had known Howie prior to the shooting, but they did not start dating until after the incident, and that they were no longer seeing each other. She knew who the victim was but had no personal contact with the girl. The story on the street is that the investigation had been reopened, and that this had started people talking again around the school. She never spoke with Howie about the incident, only hearing the gossip that Howie tripped as he was handing Ginger the gun, and it went off by accident. Lisa did not have any information or knowledge that would indicate this was anything but an accident.

She added that since the shooting, Howie has had a change in his overall personality. He used to hang out with the country kids but moved to the drug group until recently when he has started back toward the country people but is still straddling the fence between the two groups. She stated that she knows Randy from school, but they are not friends and does not have any contact with him. Lisa told me that she had never spoken to Howie about this crime or heard him talk to anyone about the situation. Since Howie and she broke up, she has had very little contact with the shooter. Lisa has no idea why anyone would say that the shooter told her the whole story because they have never talked about the shooting. She added that there were many rumors going on about this incident recently heating up with the story that it was being investigated again. Lisa stated she had no knowledge of anything concerning this case.

For five months, I had been working on this case that I assisted with two years before this new information. Now the time had come to testify before the grand jury with all of my investigation concerning this sad story. Mark had decided that the best solution would be for the grand jury, rather than a group of prosecutors, to decide how to handle this situation. The story was presented to the panel from the original statements, the crime scene, and now the new information. With all of the information, the final decision of the grand jury was to return an indictment of second degree murder on

Howie. Based on the indictment, I went early the next morning and obtained a warrant for the arrest of Howie. It was now time for me to locate the shooter, or now we should say the killer.

My first stop on that morning was at the high school attended by Howie the killer where I contacted the dean. He was a man that I knew from many contacts with the school system over our many years of work. He was a very good administrator and a great person with his work methods and interactions with the students moving his career forward later retiring as the principal of a school that he helped build from ground up. The students of his last school at the time of finishing his career felt a great loss with his departure for his well-deserved retirement. Another irony is that this man's daughter eventfully married one of my many good friends. Recently, we met again when I attended his grandson's high school graduation celebration at my friend's home. Sometimes, I believe that I live in the biggest small town in America. With the help of the good dean, we discovered that the killer was not in school that day. It was unusual for him to be absent creating the understanding that the rumor mill had been in full motion broadcasting that the case was once again under investigation.

On leaving the school, I took a short trip to where I was able to locate Howie the killer and his mother at their residence. The mother had recently been the victim of a traffic accident that left her with serious injuries to her head creating a need for medical and psychiatric treatments. On advising both of them that Howie was under arrest for murder, it was obvious that she could not be left alone. My partner riding with me that day assisted Howie with contacting a family friend to come to their home so that his mother would not be left alone. An hour later, his mother had that friend with her as we transported Howie to the Sheriff's Office. The fourteen-year-old killer who was now sixteen years old was under arrest for killing the eleven-year-old victim who was not able to add years to her age.

When we arrived at the office, we began the procedures for an interview with the killer. As I started to read the consent to interview form, which advises a suspect of their constitutional rights, Howie requested that he read the document. Howie and I agreed to his request including the condition that he read the form out loud. The presentation during his reading of the form was another indication that he fully understood the information. It was now time for a different interview from those in the past as this time, he would have to tell the truth; since we finally had the real story, Howie would now be required after all of the tales to finally tell the truth.

Howie stated that he would tell the truth as he had always told the truth about the incident. As we sat there, I looked straight into his eyes and made him promise that he would now tell us the entire story, the whole truth. He told us about how he got the gun from the incident on the school bus, including that his uncle wanted to buy the pistol but never did, even though the uncle bought a box of ammunition, and that he eventually took the gun and bullets from his uncle. On the day of the shooting, he had the gun but not the box of ammunition, he only had the bullets that were loaded in the weapon. He stopped by two friends' houses then met Randy and Ginger in the woods. Randy was walking away from them as he was handing Ginger the gun. When he walked toward Ginger, he tripped; and as he stumbled, he grabbed the gun so it would not fall to the ground, and the weapon was fired by accident.

During the interviews at the time of the shooting, he was scared of what might happen to him. He changed the story several times claiming it was a suicide or her accidently shooting herself. After he had made up those stories, he realized that he had been "dumb," and he finally told Detective Steve the truth about this incident. Howie insisted that it was the truth about the accident.

Back then, Detective Steve asked if there was a sexual overtone to the shooting. Howie told the detective then, as he states now, that there were none and that all of the rumors were "bull." He insisted that everyone continues to tell lies about this whole incident. Howie insisted that there were no sexual overtones to the meeting the day of the shooting.

We then asked Howie had he ever threatened anyone else with the gun. He told us that previous to the shooting at a location where a bunch of kids were gathering one night, a friend with him made an obscene jester toward a group of people at that gathering. When the other boys started to come after his group, the friend displayed the weapon, and the others fled from the scene. Howie stated that he did not display the gun because he knew it would be the wrong action and did not to cause any trouble.

To the next question Howie said that since the shooting, that people have spread rumors about him. People claim the incident was because of his ROTC background, and that he is a "crazed jungle fighter" who is after anyone's blood. They also claim that he threatens to shoot other people with one story claiming that he says, "I have shot someone before, and I'll do it again." These stories are all rumors that he insists are lies because he did not intend to shoot Ginger, and that it was an accident.

Howie told us that he has tried to speak to the victim's mother about the shooting. The two of them have tried to set up a meeting on several occasions, but they have never been able to get together. Over the years, he has continually stopped by the victim's grave where he will leave flowers or some trinket by the tombstone. His mother has tried to get him to see a psychiatrist, but he has refused this help as he does not believe in that type of medicine. It has been hard for him to cope with this terrible accident.

At this time in the interview, I reminded Howie that he promised to tell the truth. He replied to me that he was being truthful. I again looked into Howie's eyes and asked about the week before in the woods when he threatened the victim with a knife. Howie seemed surprised that I knew about that occasion. I reminded Howie that I knew about that and even more about this entire story, and I told him to tell the real story, the whole story, to tell the truth.

With a stunned look, Howie stated that he would tell us the whole story, the true story. Howie stated that the week before the shooting, Ginger, Randy, and he had been in the woods at the same spot playing around. He had recently discovered that the victim had a crush on him. Randy and he were joking with Ginger telling her she was a "chicken" and would not do anything sexual with him. As they joked back and forth, she told them that it was late in the day, and she had to leave and go home. The witness and he both pulled out knives and told Ginger they would cut the tires on her bicycle if she tried to leave. They were both joking with her, and Ginger simply got on the bike and rode away. Howie stated that he did not need to display the knife to have been able to have sex with Ginger. Prior to the knife being displayed, he had kissed Ginger and admitted that he wanted to have sex with her as Ginger claimed to already having a sexual relationship with a twenty-three-year-old man of whom she never provided him that man's name. All of the actions that day were all for fun with each of the three of them being involved, but nobody was serious about hurting anyone.

Howie insisted that he never had a sexual encounter with the victim. Ginger had told him that she was not that kind of girl and did not know him well enough for them to become involved sexually. There was no need or reason for him to force Ginger into any sexual activity, and he added that even though he is not a "big stud," he can obtain sex from women on a regular basis.

He insisted that he has never told anyone about the shooting. Howie agreed with the statement that he started dating a girl from high school after the incident. The two of them had talked about the situation in general terms, but never in great detail. My next question was about the day of the shooting once again, I reminded him that I knew more and asked him about the truth which I knew and he knew, and that he needed to provide the truth.

With a bit of a shaken look, he then told us that Randy and he told Ginger that he was in the process of moving to Texas. The two of them were trying to convince the victim that this was their last chance to get together sexually. They wanted to convince Ginger he was leaving so that she would feel sorry for him. Howie hoped that this little ruse would help in getting her to agree to have sex with him. Ginger finally figured out they were kidding her about his move to Texas but still agreed to have sex with him. She told him she would not do this act in the woods, so he suggested the home of the witness that was across the street. Ginger would not agree to go to that location either creating a situation that seemed to prevent any possibility that could arrange the sexual moment. Howie was reminded that the truth can only be achieved by telling the entire story, the whole truth. I looked deep into his surprised and astonished eyes.

Howie added that on other occasions, he has pointed the pistol at other people and at himself. These actions were always in a joking manner and never as a threat to anyone. When he was at Mary's house just before the shooting, he did not point the gun at her. He did have it in his hand but never pointed the weapon at Mary; he wrapped the pistol into the bandana and left her home. We then asked him to continue as we knew there was more to the story.

He squirmed in his chair and looked down at the table showing that it was becoming harder for him to look me in the eyes, as he began his next statement, Howie indicated that he believes Randy made up the story of him purposely shooting the victim for Randy's own benefit. Howie denied Randy's statement claiming he had told Ginger to "give it up or else." He added that the witness is "a fool and a wimp and would imagine anything to cover his ass." Howie was becoming more and more nervous over what I might know about the whole story, the truth. I reminded him once again that he had promised to tell me the truth, so fulfill that promise.

Howie added that he did not remember cocking and loading the pistol that day. He did show Randy how to cock the pistol, and that may have caused the gun to be loaded on the day of the shooting. He insisted that he did not remember putting a bullet in the chamber prior to the shooting. Howie was sure that it was not loaded on that fatal day in conflict with what Randy said when Randy finally told the truth.

He then insisted that he did not point the gun at the victim prior to the tripping that caused the shooting. Howie had heard stories that Ginger had been shot in the back of the head then later, the story changed that she was shot in the eye. He stated that he did not know for sure where the girl had been shot. He froze without being able to answer when I asked him if he had not seen the blood spewing from the bullet wound.

Howie became agitated while responding to my next question insisting that he did not tell Ginger to drop her pants, or he would kill her. He stated that there was absolutely not any statement even similar to that comment made by him to the victim. He was just showing off the gun and being a fool as he handed her the weapon.

Recently, Howie had heard the rumors about the investigation being reopened, and then he heard about the others testifying before the grand jury. Howie said that one of his friends told him they were "looking to fry your ass." Even hearing this, he was sure that it would not happen because the entire incident was an accident.

I reminded him that earlier, he said that he felt like a "fool" at the time of the shooting. He was also reminded that he had also promised to tell me the truth about this situation. I then told him that since I knew this was not the truth, was he not still being a fool? Howie sat in the chair simply staring at the ground when I told him to look at me and not his feet. He looked up toward me, and I said that I had asked him a question and deserved the respect of an answer. We told him we did not need to hear the story of lies he was telling because we knew the real story, and that it was now time for him to finally, after all these years and after all of the lies, tell the truth.

As we looked into each other's eyes locked into a stare, he again started to talk. The three of them were in the woods as he was playing around with the gun and while they were all talking to each other. He told Randy to leave the area and walk back toward the area of their fort. As they stood there chatting with each other, he continued to ask Ginger to have sex with him with him saying they could go back into the woods for this act. Ginger agreed to have sex with him but would not do anything in the woods. He then asked Ginger to go to the home of Randy, but she stated that the father of the witness was at home, and she would not go to that home. As he leaned against his moped, he pointed the gun at her and told her she may not have a choice in the matter she may have to engage in sex with him. She told him to put the gun away before someone got hurt with his reply that nobody would get hurt as he knew what he was doing with a pistol. As he pointed the firearm at her, the gun went off. It was an accident they had been joking around; he did not mean to kill her. As Randy was running back to them, Ginger looked at him and fell to the ground.

After that, Howie told me that this was the first time he had ever told anyone the true story. All the time he has kept this to himself with many people making fun of him about what happened on that day. He would not let that drivel get to him; he simply kept completely quiet about this whole moment. With finally telling the true story, Howie stated that he felt like "twenty tons is off my shoulders."

I looked straight into his eyes again locking our look at each other and then told him that with a gun pointed at Ginger's head, and you insisting that she have sex with you and then after turning you down, by strange and rare chance, the gun accidently went off putting a bullet through the little blonde-haired girl's head, causing blood to spurt back at you from the bullet hole, this horrible situation was all an accident? Finally with the almost whole story, the close-to-real truth out, it was too hard for him to continue, so he just stared at me and said nothing more. The great weight he claimed was off his shoulders was very different from the weight of Ginger's cold dead body when she was weighed at her autopsy. Howie still had not told the entire story and still did not cry.

While the paperwork was completed, I telephoned Ginger's mother to update her on the arrest of the killer. She was elated that the truth had finally come out about the murder of her little Ginger.

Even though Howie was a juvenile, he had been indicted by the grand jury requiring him to be treated as an adult and placed in the county jail. We notified the jail personnel who prepared for the unusual booking of a sixteen-year-old adult with arraignments made to keep him separate from the main population of the county jail. The case was finally solved, and the killer was finally in jail.

A short time later, we went to trial with the killer being represented by a private attorney. The attorney has a good reputation with his quality of work in the courtroom. The judge that we stood before had a nickname of being a hanging judge. The killer decided to plead guilty to a lesser charge allowing the judge to sentence Howie to state prison for killing Ginger the little curly blonde-haired girl. Howie was sentenced as a youthful offender and spent his time of seven years in a youthful offender state prison located in our county while Ginger's entire life was only four years longer than Howie's entire prison sentence. Howie was in state prison; Ginger was in a burial plot.

## THE EMOTIONS FROM A BADGE

With twenty-eight years passing since Howie's crime of murder, the forty-two-year-old killer is out of prison and supposedly living with his family in south Florida near the Gulf Coast. I do not know any of the details concerning the status of Howie's current life. Ginger's mother has yet to overcome her tragedy having never been satisfied with the punishment handed down by the court. She is angry with the judge and the prosecutor and with the overall resolution of this horrible tragedy. We must all understand that there is nothing that could be done that would ever overcome the tragedy of a parent losing a child; and this little girl Ginger, with her curly blonde hair, never having reached her twelfth birthday there can be little help. Her mother, and many others, still mourns the loss of Ginger while Howie, the killer, has still never cried.

It took several years to finally provide to everyone the final answer that this story was not an accident, it was a murder. Sometimes, finding the truth can be helpful to people who are devastated by the loss of a loved one. Most of the time, the solace is short-lived as the outcome does not give them the one and only thing that could fix everything, especially the return of their loved one. Sadly, we cannot change history and bring that innocent person back to life.

# First Autopsy

Hang on now for another interesting little twist in the world of investigations.

As my homicide investigation trainer was driving me to witness my first autopsy, he tried to warn me of the smell and the disgust of the mangled bodies that can create emotional trauma on seeing a human being torn apart to conduct the autopsy. He told me to be strong that after about six autopsies, it will be easier to deal with this portion of the job by thinking of it as a clinical requirement rather than a ghastly sight.

When I arrived at the Medical Examiner's Office that day, we found they were conducting six autopsies all at one time. I told my partner with meeting the requirement of the six, I guess this will immediately get me adjusted to the grotesque trauma. In reality, it was the best learning experience allowing me to compare the multiple bodies and conditions with one another. On that day, the age, sex, physical build, and cause of death seemed to cover a wide gambit from body to body.

The most interesting comparison on that day was between two men on tables that were aligned next to each other. One was of a man in his late seventies who was so extremely overweight that between the interior body parts and his skin were layers of fat. This fat tissue attached to the skin was almost two inches thick and also floating around in the body cavity were multiple lose and large lumps of fat. That gentleman had died from a heart attack while sitting in his lounge chair at his residence watching television. Next to him was a twenty-two-year-old man who died while out running that morning during his daily jogging routine. This young man had a body that looked like a perfect Adonis sculpture having absolutely positively no body fat. That morning, he also died of a heart attack while he was out on his morning run.

This information provided me with the important documented scientific evidence that will forever justify my decision to never again run or exercise. Why exercise oneself to death in the early years of life when we can live a very long and very robust life and stuff our fat faces while we eat ourselves away to our final day of glory. After the completion of the procedure, I stopped by a special store on the way back to the office, made a wonderful purchase, and ate those dozen donuts before lunch, and on many and many more days since, with this all being done so that I can live a very long life. Bon Appétit!

# Children Suicides

I warned you at the start that some of these stories will be rough, so you may need to mix a double to deal with this one.

One year during my time as a homicide detective, we had a rash of children committing suicide. During the twelve months, thirteen young people took their own lives. There did not seem to be a rhyme or reason that could connect any one to another as these kids did not know each other or even go to the same school. We the investigators could never understand how these unnecessary acts could happen and continue to happen. The worst part was watching the number grow, one after another, with no idea of how to stop the tragic flood. Of the thirteen children's deaths, I investigated seven. With these cases fully investigated and resolved, they each and all left the one unanswered question, why?

One young man, just having turned seventeen, was a junior at the local high school. The family lived in a large and clean home in a nice neighborhood with the family income being more than enough to provide for the family needs and even more creating what appeared to be a nice life. The boy was the average teenager with an overall good appearance having the look of a person who could be a handsome model for clothing advertisements in the local newspaper. In school, he was an achieving student with very good grades in some of the more advanced classes. Many of his friends enjoyed his warm personality and good humor. There was no information of drugs or alcohol being a problem with his life. This young man was just the average Joe in high school, but within him, he did have a secret that caused him some internal hardships. His home had a different look inside than it did outside.

His mother had some minor difficulties with her own personality. Sometimes interacting with her was very difficult as she had some very odd moments. A little over a month before the boy's death, the mom had asked the son go with her to get some new flowers for the home. The confusion began when she did not go to the store to buy the plants but stopped in a local business park and started digging the plants out of the median. With her son objecting to the act she demanded, to a point of controlling the boy, for him to also take the plants out of the ground. In the middle of that shopping spree, the Sheriff's Office arrived, at the request of the property owner; and both were arrested for the minor theft. This was a minor problem of a petit crime that never became public knowledge.

For some unknown reason, the young man could not deal with his life. He did not discuss his struggles with anyone, his parents, his girlfriend, his friends; no one had any idea about the level of his depression. Everyone felt that he had recently been a little sad and distant still nobody asked him why, and he told nobody. Whatever was swirling in his mind, whatever was eating at him, whatever was the concern was his own personal very well-kept secret.

On his last day alive, he got home from school and ate dinner with his family. He told his parents that he had some homework to complete, so he would be in his room with his studies the rest of the evening. There was no other conversation as he went toward his bedroom. Sometime later, while in his bed, he laid on his back, fully clothed, placed a high power rifle along his chest and between his legs with the barrel pointing to the bottom of his chin. On hearing the gunshot, his parents rushed to his room. As they looked at the horrible scene, it was obvious that it was too late to provide any help.

On my viewing the scene, it was easy to see that this was a self-inflicted wound. No struggle, no other injuries, the rifle still on his chest and the type of injury caused by the wound. In the bottom of his chin was a small hole typical of an entry wound. The hole was not ripped open indicating no direct contact of the barrel to the skin at the time of discharge. There was a powder burn around the wound that would indicate a discharge with the barrel fairly close to the chin. Then there was the exit wound. The power and pressure of the large caliber bullet ripped the head in half. This tore his face into two mangled portions making it difficult to identify the boy by comparison to a photograph. The top of the skull had exploded from the head with pieces of the skull bone, blood, and brain matter splattered over the headboard. The neat, clean, and well-kept room of this good, young man was a very morbid sight. He was pronounced dead at the scene.

Nothing in his life justified the taking of his own life. The hardest question of this investigation will never be resolved, why did he do this?

Throughout our lives, we all have our moments of ups and downs. When we are in those times of depression, we do not always make the proper decisions. The best decision is to reach out and ask for help from the many people who would be honored to give you a hand or a shoulder. On that other side when you have a loved one, a friend, a child, just anyone who is having a sad moment, you should make sure that you ask what you can do to help. Even though you have those perfect people that you love, and they can do no wrong, you can be completely blind to their screaming for help. We all know that none of our family or friends would ever take their own life. With great sadness I will tell you, no I will scream at you that you are absolutely wrong. We do not know why, but they could do just that. It would be best to ask the why question while they are alive rather than wonder why after the death. Open your eyes and use your heart so you can see the need to provide the best medicine, which might be just a simple hug.

# I'll Get It

Let me try a story this time that will be a tad easier than the last. But hang on, you know how crazy these tales can become. Maybe you should get another drink for this one.

My wife's cousin, who has also been a very good friend of mine and helped introduce me to my great lady, decided that he wanted to become a Deputy Sheriff, so he just went out and got hired by the Sheriff's Office. One day while in the Law Enforcement Academy, he called to tell me the craziest story he had yet heard about a detective doing his job. He told me I would not believe that anyone would do such a disgusting act. No one could be this cold.

Apparently, the instructor for the class that day had once been a sergeant in the Homicide Unit. Some time ago, the supervisor was on the scene of an apparent suicide of a young man. While consoling the man's family, his two detectives were in the house investigating the incident. At this scene, the victim was in a very small room, lying on the floor with his feet pointed at the door of the extremely tiny room requiring the detective to straddle the victim and shuffle his own feet up to see the gentleman's head. Sadly, the man had killed himself with a single gunshot to the head. That room was so very minuscule that only one detective could be in the room with the body while the other stood outside looking in.

The supervisor, who had been in the front yard with the victim's family, told them that he was going to go inside to see if he could get any additional information that would help them with their tragic moment. When he got inside, he stood behind the other detective outside the room. The entire area was very small, so they were forming a line one behind the other with each trying to look into the small room. Unbeknownst to any of the investigators, the entire family had followed the supervisor inside and had joined in the now long line creating the look of a dance around the room line at a wedding reception. While all was quiet, everyone looking into the room, and each person not seeing the several people behind them, the telephone rang. The detective in the room with the dead young man looked down at the deceased, held his hand out as you would to stop someone, and said "Don't get up, I'll get it."

The family screamed out in shock and horror as they all turned and ran from the house crying. The supervisor sneered at both detectives saying something about the good lord, along with several other four letter words, and followed the family outside to begin damage control. The detective standing outside of the room placed his head in his hands and bemoaned that he would be fired over this terrible offense. The detective in the room did not react and simply answered the phone.

With the call answered, the caller responded to the hello asking to speak to the deceased gentleman. Politely, the detective advised that the man could not come to the phone at that moment, and they would have to get together at a later time. It was a relatively short telephone conversation.

The sergeant gathered with the family in the front yard and resolved all of the issues of their concern. The family was satisfied, and that the problem needed to go no further than the sergeant having a discussion with the callous detective to correct the error. The sergeant advised the detective that his actions were horrible, and adding that it was of course not at all a surprise for the detective to act in that loathsome fashion. The sergeant told the class that he was unsuccessful in trying to improve the personality of the detective who was completely cruel and coldhearted and not capable of ever being reformed. The supervisor and the other detective did eventually retire many years later with each holding the rank of major.

My friend and cousin-in-law when he finished laughing after telling the terrible story about such a morbid detective asked if I could ever believe such a horrible story could be true. I told him that those things can occur while dealing with the stress of any investigation. Then I let him know that I was positive the story was absolutely, totally, and completely true because I was that detective. Excuse me, is that the phone ringing?

# Father Kidnaps to Kill

Hang on now, it's time for a story full of energy, crazy, an upsetting energy.

It was a beautiful Sunday afternoon in such a wonderful time of the year as I was off duty driving my unmarked car to the home of my future wife. She lived with her parents who are both from Sicilian families, that is correct not Italian, Sicilian. Every Sunday, her mother cooked a family meal, actually she artistically prepared that meal. This great lady grew up in a portion of our community with a very strong Spanish history, and during her life, she worked in cafeterias of the county school board. With all of this, she was exposed to the Sicilian, Spanish, and Southern styles of cooking in our diverse little community providing her with knowledge that made her the best of the best in the kitchen. The amazing part of this was a special spice that only she could use, it was her little finger. If she touched the dish, it would just make the food taste so much better; actually it was more than better, it was perfect. With great fortune, my wonderful wife inherited that special finger. Still this particular Sunday was even more special, it was Valentine's Day. With lollipops and other chocolates and candies packaged together for my lovely lady, I was going to her home to eat a good meal or, as this down home Cracker boy has learned in Italian, Manga! Or in English eat!

While driving from my home in the city to my future wife's home in the county, the Sheriff's Office radio yelled out with the special alert tone. The dispatcher announced that a man who was driving a small gray pickup truck had just kidnapped his four children during a domestic dispute with his wife. When the man left their home, he forced the kids to go with him as he waved a large butcher knife telling the mother that he was going to kill all of their children. As the details were being announced, I recognized the location of the crime from which the kidnapper had driven away with the kids was a few blocks from my current location. This of course meant duty first, sadly manga later.

I pulled off the expressway and went a block or two to the first traffic light where on one of the corners was a gas station. There in that station was the truck, the man, and the children with dad getting back into the vehicle having just filled the tank with gas. As he pulled out of the station, I did a complete 180-degree turn in the intersection and fell behind the car while announcing over the radio that I was following the suspect's vehicle. The Sheriff's Office radio lit up with transmissions from many of my fellow deputies indicating that the cavalry was on the way. Bugler sound the Charge!

The first marked car quickly caught up with us and turned on his emergency lights and siren to initiate the traffic stop. At that moment, the chase was on! My lights and siren were added to the pursuit as were many others that joined in along the way. The dispatcher fulfilled her required duties and asked the on-duty patrol sergeant if the pursuit should continue or be immediately stopped for safety reasons. The sergeant replied that the life and safety of the children was the primary need with their freedom being the final goal; he ordered to continue the chase. The sergeant then over the radio directed a statement at me in his gruff and stern voice telling me, "Cribb, get that man!"

The rule of the Sheriff's Office at that time was that in a pursuit when an unmarked car is overtaken, the driver will yield to the marked car and fall behind in the chase. As more and more cars continually joined in the chase, I continued to fall back behind another and another and many more marked patrol cars. The kidnapper continued driving along the road before reaching the interstate, and on that highway, he along with us put the hammer down and off we went. As we traveled down the road, I had fallen behind at least ten marked cars including the state highway patrol and many Sheriff's

Office vehicles. In a short time, we reached the next county, then the next county, and then another county. As we went down the interstate, we were traveling in the direction of an internationally well-known, high-quality entertainment park. Many buses full of people that were traveling to the park were also being passed by all of the law enforcement vehicles in the chase. People were leaning out of the bus windows to take pictures of the large parade of law enforcement vehicles fully illuminated and sirens blaring as they chased the suspect with his victims. As I drove by, I was the last one in the line of the parade, excuse me pursuit, I smiled and waved at the many curious bus riders leaving them with a questioned look and a smile on each and every face, a few even returned the wave.

After reaching nearly one hundred miles from the starting point of the chase, the suspect attempted to turn around in the median causing the truck to become stuck in the sand. As we all approached the suspect on foot, he pushed a small child partially out the window while holding a knife to the child's throat as he threatened to kill him. With my past experience and training as a founding member of the Sheriff's Office Special Weapons and Tactics Team (SWAT), I knew my distance and ability were good for a perfect single fatal shot directly into the hostage taker's head. I also knew that the child he was holding was struggling, and there were other children behind him in the continued path of the bullet. My hesitation was also based on knowing my shot would crack open the man's head and splatter his brains and blood all over his children as they watched their father die. Even a successful termination of the suspect could be a physical and surely an emotional danger to the innocent children. Dead in my sights with the gun pointed at his right eye, I held my fire.

The truck struggled in the dirt and then leaped forward as he revived the chase back toward home. About half of the way back in one of the many counties that we had traveled through, those deputies decided that they would stop the car, bring it to a full and complete stop. Two of the deputies pulled up one on each side of the vehicle and squeezed together as they crushed the small truck between them. At that moment, the truck also blew its engine and began to coast to a stop in the middle of the interstate highway. Without an ability to

## THE EMOTIONS FROM A BADGE

continue to flee, the suspect changed his approach from the previous stop and did not return to his previous action of threatening to kill any of the children. The many law enforcement officers involved in the long pursuit assisted the suspect with his exit from the vehicle. So many officers were trying to help the gentleman from the vehicle that the suspect accidently fell to the ground injuring his face and several or maybe many other body parts. The children were safely removed from the truck and protected by one of the uniformed officers without any of them being hurt.

Command decisions were quickly made to meet the entire requirements of the law. The suspect was to be treated at a local hospital, booked in the local jail, and released to a deputy from my office to return him to our county jail. As I was the only unmarked car, I was responsible for loading the four children in my noncaged vehicle, so they could be safely returned to their awaiting mother. So off we went to return that full backseat of youngsters to their mommy.

As I drove the long distance back home, the children started giggling and laughing as they sat there in the backseat of my car. When I had a chance to look in the back, I was able to see that they were all sitting there, having a good time while laughing and joking and eating *all* of the lollipops and chocolates and candies that had been in my backseat to deliver to my lady. They seemed to have more chocolate all over their faces than had ever been contained in the entire bag from where they had acquired the delicious candy. They were more than happy about that candy.

On arrival back at the home, their mother was thrilled to have all of her little children back home, safe and sound. She was very irate with her no good, filthy, worthless, scoundrel of a husband. I thought these words would be better than the real ones that were used on that particular date. Leaving her with the children and an explanation of the events given to the mother, I was again on my way to an Italian feast. Unfortunately, I could not use my lights and siren for this action.

On arriving at my original destination, the many people in the family had already eaten requiring a need to reheat my plate of food. My lady was not very happy that I brought her nothing for

Valentine's Day and created this unbelievable story about a 150-mile chase of a kidnapper to cover my error. She still showed me that she is a wonderful person and provided me a very large Valentine's Day gift; and as always, and many, many other times, forgave me for my forever foolish ways. I am such a lucky man, and the food was outstanding. Manga Bella!

Later on, I was subpoenaed to court to provide testimony against this felon and criminal for his horrible crime. At the courthouse, I met up in the hallway with the children, their mother, and within the group was their lawless father. Their mom told the judge that she and all of the children loved the father as he was such a magnificent man. The entire situation was just a bad moment, and that his love and devotion for them would never allow him to hurt any of the children or her. He was so wonderful, and she begged for the case to be dropped and this pious man to be freed from this unjust tragedy. It was hard to believe this was the same woman who spoke of him in a very different tone and dialect, the day I returned her the kidnapped children from the man with the knife who wanted to kill them. The case was resolved without any difficulties for the family on that miraculous day of redemption.

I often wonder if the father knows how close he came that day, while stuck in the median, holding his little child with a knife to the boy's throat, of me using my SWAT training and my long practiced ability to put a single .45 caliber hollow-point bullet through his right eye, causing pieces of his brain to splatter all over his children that were sitting next to him. Overall, I guess it worked out the best for all of us that day.

# Death Penalty

Please forgive me, but I must have a moment to rant about some of my most horrible cases.

During my career, I worked on two different serial murder investigations. One went through the county killing ladies that he would meet on the roadways. Before he was finished with his spree, he had killed ten women. We never were able to get a number on the many, very many rapes that he committed throughout the entire state by responding to items for sale in the classified newspaper advertisements. The second one only killed three young ladies in our town. He kidnapped them from retail parking lots, just like the stores and shopping malls where you and your loved ones conduct business. His youngest murder victim was a high school student who worked after school in a shopping plaza. None, not a one, of these the thirteen young ladies deserved to die.

Both of these venomous animals are currently living on death row. Each one has lived on death row longer than any one of their victims ever lived on this earth.

As both of these cases are continually and forever appealed and brought back for a new trial, I do not believe that a discussion on these cases should be included with my stories. I would not want to do anything that could jeopardize the court proceedings or change their death sentences in either of these investigations. These cases are already appealed and overturned for a new trial based on the most trivial reasons.

The death penalty is a topic that can easily start a conversation. Most of the talks end up with the two sides of for and against each being very strong in their convictions. We all live in a world that would love for there to be no need for capital punishment. Sadly, people like this live in our world. Both of these killers are willing to escape, both have plotted failed attempts to escape, both desire to be free, both are ready and able to kill again and again. Since there is no cure, like a rabid animal, like these two beasts, the sick and malicious animal must be put to death so many others can live.

# *Overkill*

**O**kay, refresh that drink and let us get to another interesting story.

While working the night shift in homicide, I was often asked to help others on their ongoing investigations. This one evening, another one of those assignments was provided as I entered the office door to begin my shift. The duty on that afternoon was to help two of my partners who were currently working a murder on the northwest side of the county. The request was for me to take the video camera to the scene so we could film the entire crime scene. The very large and heavy old camera was loaded into my car, and it was off to the crime scene to assist with the investigation. This quick action would turn into a very long all-night task.

On arriving at the scene, I met up with a large number of people including my supervisors and my two fellow homicide detectives. Detective John and Detective Paul were the case detectives and were moving through the crime scene conducting their normal actions for a perfect inquiry. It was obvious that with these two working on the case meant the outcome would be a resolution with the killer in jail. With the help of Detective Paul, my assignment was to create a video tape of the entire crime scene. Moving through the residence with the camera, I photographed the victim, the blood, and all of the other forensic evidence at the scene. The crime scene was a very horrible sight.

The victim, who we will call Don, was a seventy-five-year-old man of Italian descent who was a very small built gentleman. Due to some recent health concerns, he required the assistance of a walking cane and was being assisted by his family while living with his son. This poor victim was lying on his stomach in an open room of the house. In various locations on the body, it was easy to see the damage where the man's walking cane was used to beat the elderly gentleman. The cane created injuries to the point that the victim's teeth were broken out of his mouth with the pieces scattered around the room. The evidence showed that the cane eventually broke apart causing pieces of wood to be protruding from some of the wounds. The suspect then took a kitchen knife and stabbed the poor old fellow forty-five times, with only two of the forty-five wounds being fatal— yes, forty-five stab wounds. One of these deadly lacerations was to the back of the left side of the neck cutting an artery and the other to the right front side that went into the heart. The final insult was that on the victim's back were shoeprints, blood-stained footprints where the killer stomped on the victim as he lay there dying on the floor. It must have been hard to defeat the elderly man who stood just over five feet tall and weighed less than 150 pounds.

The room where the victim lay smashed on the floor had a large amount of blood splattered on the wall and the floor. Some of the blood was smeared along the wall indicating the victim had slid down the wall during the attack. Other spots of the blood indicated a back splash of the blood being thrown off of the bloody cane as it was swung back and forth striking the victim. Other blood spatter was on the wall and pooled on the floor as it spewed from the victim's body from the stab wounds, the forty-five knife wounds. The blood was all over the entire room, having the appearance like someone had taken several red spray paint cans and vandalized the walls and floor.

Throughout the room and the house were bloody footprints that matched the sole design that was stomped on the victims clothing. These shoeprints were an extremely unique design that is specific to a certain brand of athletic shoe, the one and only with the circle, squares, and triangles. I was familiar with this brand because during my years in high school, these were the really neat shoes for all of those super cool people to wear; even with that being said, I also wore those shoes. During the time of the homicide, that shoe brand was not as popular as it had been in the past but still were available in the stores. That specific unique sole designed shoe is still sold in today's market.

The last bit of insult was in the kitchen were the broken part of the cane, and the blood-stained knife were set on the counter placed across one another to form an X. The broken wood cane had pieces of human flesh protruding from the jagged broken end. The knife was covered with blood that had dripped onto the counter. These were the weapons used to X out the life of the frail little elderly victim.

Looking through the house, it was easy to see the leftover electric wires and the open spaces that lacked dust indicating that several items had been stolen from the home. This was a burglary, a theft, and a murder that we can never understand the stupidity of the person who would commit any of these crimes, much less such a horrible act.

The investigation had been initiated when the transportation service driver who came to the home three days a week to drive our victim Don to the Senior Community Service Center had not been able to contact him on the previous visit or on that day. With their concerns, the service contacted the Sheriff's Office to check on his well-being. On entering the house, the deputy discovered this horrible scene of Don on the floor after being slaughtered by a thief. Detective John and Detective Paul had determined that Antonio, Don's son, has to leave his father alone at the house while he travels for business purposes. It had been several days since he had seen his father but tries to talk with Don as much as he can during his trips. It was a very difficult investigation as the crime scene held a volume of evidence, but the evidence provided no direction on where to go with this case, at that moment.

Major Ronald, the FART team lieutenant, and Captain Robert, the frozen marijuana case investigator, were the supervisors of the district that covered the residence of this nasty crime. Both of these commanding officers had entered the crime scene, a location beyond the crime scene tape where they should not have been, to view the evidence. Based on their observations and experience, they provided their expert opinions of being certain that the large amount of blood, the displaying of the blood, the weapons crossed on the kitchen counter, all of the evidence indicated that this murder was committed by a cult. They immediately convinced others in the room of their flawless solution, and the word went out to identify everyone associated with a cult near this scene. Detective Paul looked at me, and as we rolled our eyes, we verified their decision with my comment of whatever.

About this time, a deputy came up to the house informing us that a man was out front who had been doing some of the maintenance work to the home and was requesting access to some of his tools that were in the house. Lieutenant Richard advised me to take care of the person by advising he could not enter an active crime scene, and that the other detectives were very busy working the investigation. So it was off to the front yard, following the deputy, who introduced me to the man that I was told to shoo off from this scene.

The introduction and the short discussion provided me with the knowledge that Junior Fernandez was a small-sized, nice-looking, polite, young man with a strong build and was a twenty-two years old construction worker who had been doing some damage repair to the home as a result of a fire that had occurred several months ago. With his work, he had several tools at the house that he needed for some of his other jobs. As always, this nosy little detective used my eyes to search Junior's entire body. It was obvious that he was not carrying a gun or a knife; as my eyes went down the body search, all seemed good until the search went to his feet, everything stopped. The shoes this young man was wearing were the same brand that had the very unique sole of the shoeprints stomped on the victim's back. As my eyes focused on the shoe, it was easy to see the red spots on the canvas top and the red markings on the sides of the rubber soles. All that red looked so much like dried blood, the same blood splattered around the house and the victim. At that point, Junior was advised of my deep concern for his problems and requested to wait for me to have the investigators resolve his concerns. It was time to get back to the house and gather up the troops.

Once I was back inside the house, the others were advised that the killer was standing in the front yard. They looked at me then turned away to continue the discussion of which cult committed the crime. Once again, my interruption brought Lieutenant Richard to ask for me to define the reasons of my suspicions. Describing the brand of the shoe from the bloody shoeprints, the matching shoes worn by the subject and the spots of blood, it was obvious that he was involved in the crime. In return, there was an explanation of me not being a certified expert on athletic shoes and Junior not being in a cult; so it was certain, and absolutely positive, that my opinion was not valid. At that point, Detective Paul spoke up and said the best action would be to take a look at this person to better evaluate my opinion. Detective Paul knew that I would always find the obscure little clues hidden away that nobody else could even imagine were possible and use them to solve the unsolvable case. They all agreed with Detective Paul that this would be a reasonable step, and we set our plans in action while the others continued to research the cults.

Neither Detective John nor Detective Paul could identify the shoe sole design left at the scene from any of their past experiences. This caused them the need to see the design of the soles of the shoes on Junior's feet. Both of the good investigators went out to the front and met up with Junior to discuss the concerns for his tools. Detective John was a compassionate gentleman who offered Junior the opportunity to show him the specific tools. To accomplish this task, Detective John asked Junior to walk with him to the back of the house so they would not disturb the crime scene. The short walk took them through an area of flat and level dirt that created a shoeprint from the sole of Junior's shoes. As I stood there watching them travel through the dirt, Junior and Detective John were in front with the stocky Detective Paul behind them bent down in a duckwalk eyeing those shoeprints, now that should have been included on the video. As Detective Paul stood up from his duck squat, he turned toward me displaying the thumbs up sign with a very large smile on his face. At this point, the evidence had finally told us the direction to go with the investigation. After a few moments inside the house, the two sleuths invited the young man to go to the District Office to complete an interview that would assist with the investigation. Junior was in the hands of the truth finders.

With the three of them headed to the office, the rest of our group continued to process the crime scene. Good Major Ronald and Captain Robert forgot to tell me good-bye when they quickly left the location so they could advise the others to stop the search for the local cults, whatever. The evidence processing, the medical examiner and the many tasks required of a crime scene continued as we waited to hear from our partners conducting the interview, the search for the truth.

With the interview in progress, Junior told the investigators that he was working for a company that had done some repairs to Antonio's home. Several months before, there had been a fire at the house that required those repairs. The company had finished the work, but Antonio wanted some additional work done at the home. As Junior had been looking for extra work, he approached Antonio about the job opportunity. They both agreed to the actions, and he had been conducting the part-time repair work at the home. During this same time, Junior and his wife had been to the home for dinner, and they discussed with Antonio about buying the extra car that was in the driveway. With this communication, Junior and his wife were in the process of buying that vehicle from their new friends. Junior told them he knew nothing about the murder and had simply stopped by to get his tools from the residence. This was the typical first part of a criminal's statement when the guilty party explains their innocence, where they don't tell the truth.

Detective John told Junior that the story was very interesting, but that he wanted the truth. Junior, while insisting it was the truth, was asked to put his feet up on the table. The soles of his shoes were covered in blood and lying on the table was a photograph of the shoeprints stomped onto the victim's body matching his shoes. Totally stunned, Junior stared at Detective John and was again asked to tell the truth. Junior knew he had been caught, no one can hide the truth from Detective John and Detective Paul; they would solve this case right here and now.

As Junior sat with the detectives, he told them that he had been home with his wife on the evening of the murder. They were visiting with some friends in the apartment complex when his seventeen-year-old brother Earl Fernandez came over to their place. He got together with Earl and told the others they had to go out to another friend's house to get a stereo installed in his brother's truck. When they were away from the others, he told Earl that they were going to go over to a house where he was doing some repairs so they could break in and steal some things. He told Earl that an old man would be at the home, but that would not be a problem with stealing the items. At first, Earl did not want to go but eventually agreed to assist with the crime. When they got to the scene, Earl stayed in his truck and parked across the street. Junior stated that he went in the house to steal the television, stereo, and some other items. When he got inside, he was stacking the items to steal when the old man came out of his room and confronted him. The argument turned into a fight, and he hit the old man with the cane and stabbed him a couple of times with the knife during the short altercation, a couple of stabs seem to be less than forty-five. When the fight was over, Don was dead on the ground. At that point, he got the items together and went to the front door to get Earl to back the truck up to the house. Once the truck was in place, he loaded up the vehicle with the stolen items, and Earl drove them from the scene. Junior insisted that Earl never entered the house and was not involved in the fight. They both drove away leaving the little old man lying facedown on the floor in a pool of blood and dead from a couple of stab wounds, forty-five stab wounds.

After leaving the murder scene, he and Earl stopped in a dark area of the roadway swapped some of their clothes, so he would not go home with blood on his clothing that could be discovered by his wife. After the swapping of the bloody clothing, Earl dropped him off at this house and took the stolen items to the home where Earl lives with his father. He believes that Earl hid the items at that house. Detective Paul inquired to Junior about how Earl swapped bloody clothing but did not know there had been a murder in the house. Junior insisted that his brother, who knew they were going to steal the property by breaking into the house that had a person inside, was not involved in the killing of Don and had no knowledge of the murder. Junior stood strong in his blood-covered shoes to protect his little brother.

At the crime scene, other detectives conducted neighborhood survey's and interviews with friends determining nothing that would help with the investigation. The medical examiner took custody of the body and the crime scene was sealed up to maintain the scene for the possibility of future processing. The biggest problem at this point was locating the victim's son Antonio, who was out of town on business, so that we could deliver to him the most unwanted news about his father. By this time, the good news reached the supervisors that Junior had confessed to the crime, and that his brother was also involved in the incident. Lieutenant Richard assigned Detective Lee to team with me and continue the investigation. Our assignments were to interview Junior's wife and to seek and find his brother Earl. There was no information concerning the suspect's involvement with a cult, whatever.

The next stop of the evening was to contact Susan, Junior's wife, at their home. Ironically, Susan had seen the news report of the murder and telephoned the crime scene to see if she could provide any information. Detective Lee had spoken to her on the phone and made arraignments to meet with her at her apartment. When Detective Lee and I came face to face with Susan, she was not aware that Junior was under arrest for the murder. Susan was very concerned and wanted to help us contact Antonio advising she had no idea about who may have committed the murder. After a short interview, Susan was informed that Junior and Earl were the killers. As the tears fell, she told us that she needed her parents to come to her home; we quickly honored that request. Detective John and Detective Paul had obtained a consent to search of his house, signed by Junior, and we obtained from Susan a duplicate signed document. On searching the residence, we located some of the clothing that had been worn by Junior the night of the murder, clothes with spots of our victims' blood. With our actions complete, we packed up and headed north to the next county to search for the second criminal.

Since we were in another county, Detective Lee and I had to meet up with some deputies from that county so they would have jurisdiction and the legal right to assist with our case; they were more than eager to help with a murder investigation. After checking several locations, our mini task force located Earl at his place of business, a grocery store where he was a front service clerk, a bagger. The seventeen-year-old high school athlete was like his brother, a small and strong built, nice-looking kid. As we left the store, Earl put on his high school letter jacket with the wrestling team icon on the front, the same jacket that he was wearing the night of the murder. Just across the street from the store was the substation for the local Sheriff's Office, so we moved everyone to that building.

Sitting in the room with Earl and Detective Lee, we informed the young man that the murder had been discovered, his brother Junior now under arrest had confessed and implemented him in the crime. As the news was being delivered, the squirming young man became more sullen and more fearful of the next step. On being advised of his rights, Earl insisted that he wanted to talk with us, and that he did not want his father involved in this fiasco. The father was a very good man who is a public servant, a firefighter in the local big city, who is now being shamed by his two sons of whom he is so proud. The story that Earl told was very similar to the one that Junior had provided to the other detectives. On the night of the murder, he met up with his brother Junior at his house. Junior talked him into going to the house to break in and steal some things even though the old man would be in the house. At first, he did not want to go but later agreed to help his brother with the crime. While his brother broke into the house, he waited across the street in his truck. After a short wait, Junior came out the front door, and he backed his truck up to the door. Junior loaded the items into the truck and then left the house. Earl insisted that he did not even go into the house; he did not see the old man, and he did not have anything to do with killing the victim. In response to our question, he told us that he knew he was going to an occupied house to commit a burglary and steal property from the homeowner. By his own statement, Earl, based on the laws of our State, was just as guilty of killing Don as was Junior. Now two young men were under arrest for this vicious crime; the two young men who had just destroyed their own lives.

After the interview, Earl took us to his home to recover some of the stolen property that he had hidden at that location. Some of the items were in his garage, but most of the items were hidden in the woods behind the house. A crime scene investigator from our office came to the scene and recovered all of these stolen items. The young man's letter jacket that he wore to the murder was also impounded during this search. Some other items found in the house included some of the clothes that Earl and Junior swapped after they committed the murder. One of these was a pair of blue jeans that had been worn by Junior during the beating, stabbing, and stomping of Don; a pair of jeans with blood spatters all over the lower legs. Earl had traded pants with Junior because of the blood all over his pants, yet Earl did not know that Don had been killed during the burglary, theft, and murder. Earl never provided an answer to that concern.

The last item of evidence was Earl's pickup truck that had been used in the crime. The truck was parked in the parking lot of the grocery store where we located the young criminal. The little truck sat there on a brand-new set of fancy wheels that were purchased with the cash stolen from the home. The truck was impounded and later processed where the windbreaker jacket worn by Junior during the murder was also recovered from the vehicle. That jacket was covered with blood spots splattered over the front. Before returning the vehicle, the fancy wheels, purchased with the stolen money, were removed and placed into evidence as fruits of the crime.

Before sunrise, we had a teleconference with the Assistant State Attorney Charles to apprise him of our investigation. Based on the information obtained by the investigation, we were advised to place both subjects in the county jail for first-degree murder, burglary, and grand theft. The paperwork was completed, and both of the killers were booked into the jail.

Early the next morning, a concern that was raised and resolved the previous night was again brought to the table. Earl was only seventeen and a juvenile which would require him to be contained in juvenile detention rather than the county jail. We were informed that night that both should go to jail, and we were informed that morning to come and get the juvenile for a transfer to the juvenile detention.

The new paperwork was created, and the transfer was performed at the very beginning of the day.

The following week, the juvenile councilor left a phone message for me to call her concerning Earl's detention. When I called her that afternoon, it was easy for us to resolve the issues of the poor little juvenile being held in their facility. The councilor was informed of the grand jury indicting Junior and Earl on charges of first-degree murder on that morning. That indictment meant that Earl would now be moved to the county jail and would face his crimes in the adult court. In a short time, the young juvenile killer became an adult and was transferred to the real jail.

As with any case the evidence was shipped to the lab for testing, depositions were conducted by the attorneys, and the trial date was set to resolve this brutal violation of the law. Before the trial date arrived, Junior had his attorney work out a deal with the prosecutor. Junior wanted to plead guilty to the crimes for which he would receive a life sentence only if Earl could plead and receive a lesser sentence. The deal was not accepted.

It was just eight months after the crime when the defendants went trial with each facing the charges of burglary of a dwelling, armed robbery, and of course first-degree murder. That charge of first degree was increased based on the murder occurring during the other felony crimes; the level of the type of murder increases when one kills someone during a robbery. The prosecution was a very quick and simple task with all of the evidence and statements conducted during an outstanding investigation; Detectives Paul and John were good investigators. With little information to counter the excellent investigation, the defense quickly placed the fate of the two young men into the hands of the jury. Once again, it did not take long for that group of peers to return with a verdict. The jury found Junior guilty on all three charges. The judge would sentence Junior to four years each for the robbery with a deadly weapon and burglary of an occupied dwelling; and on the first-degree murder, the sentence was life, the rest of his life in prison. Young Earl did better than his brother that was just five years his elder. The jury found Earl guilty of the robbery and the burglary charge and not guilty on the murder charge. As it was not proven that the little boy entered the house, the jury would not hold him responsible for the murder of the elderly gentleman. By law, he could be held responsible as they were committing the robbery, yet the jury would not punish the young man for the actions of his older brother. The judge was also very kind to Earl with a nolle prossed action on the robbery; in plain English, he just closed the charge with no sentencing. The final charge of burglary was shown as guilty requiring Earl to deal with a two-year sentence of community control. This meant that he had to be under the control of the Department of Corrections, pay fees, work, and of course, behave himself during the two-year period. Another point of the control required Earl to be home at all times he was not working. Those very tough restriction would not be anything like that young man being sent to prison; the convicted felon was a fortunate lad.

At this time, Junior has been in state prison for over twenty-five years; it would be obvious that Junior has served the four years on the robbery and burglary crimes. Now, as Junior moves toward the age of fifty, he knows that he will be in prison for the rest of his life; his freedom stopped at the young age of just twenty-two. The more terrible fact is that Don's life ended at the age of seventy-five; beaten, stabbed, and stomped to death by the young man who also ended his own freedom.

After his short time in community control, young Earl was released and prepared to continue with his own life. Soon after his release, he contacted me to have his letter jacket and his truck wheels returned to him. The jacket was an easy item to return, but Earl could not understand that the wheels would not be returned to him as he was not the legal owner. He insisted that he was the one who bought the tires, bought them with the money stolen in the burglary and robbery where his brother killed the man. Earl was very angry that he could not recover his wheels that the Sheriff's Office had stolen from him. That anger elevated when I showed him the best way to resolve the issue by walking him out the front door of the office and closing that door in his face as he stood outside. Earl could not understand that the wheels were purchased with money that was stolen, stolen just like the life that was stolen from Don.

When everything was over and done with this case, the two detectives received certificates for their outstanding work product on solving the investigation. We all knew from the start that the cream of the crop investigators would do a superior job and solve this heinous crime. It just makes me so jealous that I could not do anything like that; heck, I was not even able to help them this case. Oh, well, at least it was another case closed.

Now with any murder investigation, one has to have the greatest sympathy for the tragedy suffered by the family of the victim. When you look at everyone involved, the question screams out as to why would anyone do such a terrible act? Then you look at the killers who were both very young, one only twenty-two and the other a teenager of just seventeen years. Why did they choose to do such a stupid, idiotic, tragic action that would destroy their own life as much as that of the victim? The rest of us should look at these three people and moan a cry of sorrow for the two that no longer have a life; one dead and one locked away in prison until he too dies.

# Learning to Swim

**B**efore we start on this story, you might want to get a box of tissue. Hang on to your heart, this one's tough.

As the night detective in homicide, my duties required that I be dispatched to all of the death investigations. One evening, while heading to have my dinner, the dispatcher called my radio number. With my response to the call, the dispatcher provided a dispatch that sent me to the drowning death of a child. My dinner would have to wait.

The location of the death was out in the rural area of the county adding some time to my trip. When I arrived at the scene, I met up with the patrol deputy that was initiating this investigation who provided me with a quick briefing and pointed across the yard to the neighbor's pool. That poor deputy was not very anxious to return the scene of the death. The first step of this investigation was to interview the parents and another man who were inside the boy's home. They each and all explained that the eight-year-old boy had a life dream to learn to swim. The little boy was ecstatic that he was reaching his goal to be a swimmer but still had a long way to go even with his training going so very well. The other man with the family told me that the boy's family did not have a pool, so he was teaching the child in his own pool which was a separate pool from the one where the child lost his life. When he heard that the boy was missing, he joined together with the family to help locate the child. They found the young man in the other neighbor's dirty pool which had not been used for a long time. Once they found him, they immediately tried to revive the child, and then paramedics worked on the lad; they did everything possible, still it was too late. As I spoke to the grieving parents, I could only wonder what one can say to console parents who have lost a child. In all of my years of law enforcement, I never found those words. The tears in the room that night could have filled yet another swimming pool.

I left the family and went over to the pool to observe the incident scene and continue my investigation. Lying on the pool deck was a small body that was not moving covered with a medical sheet. The pool had water only to the middle level with a green mold covering the walls of the pool below the waterline. On the side near the screen door entrance, the mold was disturbed all along the side of the deep end of the pool by the scraping of the mold from the tiny fingers of the child. At the start of the scrapes, one could see they were strong, multiple, and long and as they moved toward the ladder on the far side with the scrapings becoming fewer and fewer, weaker and weaker. As I stood there, looking at those scrapes, it was easy to see the length of the scrape; and the distance between them indicated that his fight for life was fading as he moved around the pool. Near the end of where the strokes seemed to be the weakest, it was just a few feet, not very far at all, and just barely a short distance from the pool ladder where the strokes stopped. That short distance was simply too far.

When I checked on the victim, he had the typical appearance of a drowning victim with a damp and cold body. The color of the skin and blue tint around the lips and other areas of the body had the look of a very cold person, a drowning victim. The only injury to the body was the fingertips that were bloody with broken nails applicable to his scraping of the pool wall. The cute little boy looked so much like a fallen angel.

The finger scrapings on the wall of the pool were the little boy's obvious attempt and struggle, his battle to save his own life. The struggle was defined with the strength and the fading of those scrapings on the wall as he fought his best efforts to get to that ladder and free himself from the pool. Just a few more strokes, such a short distance, he was so close to the ladder that the tragedy seemed even worse. Just a minute longer, a few moments, a few more strokes may have saved his life. Then I looked at the other direction from where he fell into the pool which if he had struggled the other direction, he was a few feet from the other ladder. The closer ladder was less than a quarter of the total distance that he scraped, struggled, and fought to reach that far ladder. The shorter distance would have allowed him to reach that location in just seconds and climb out on that ladder to safety. Sadly, that cute little angel in a state of panic had gone the other direction with that wrong way costing that small boy his life.

We completed the investigation with the medical examiner ruling this to be an accidental drowning, the body of the small child transported to the morgue, closed down the incident scene, and I went back to my other duties for the rest of the night. Eventually, I had time to have that meal; I did not eat much that evening.

# Vanished

One of the stranger assignments that a homicide detective receives are the reports of missing adults as there is so little if any evidence to evaluate in these reports. We seem to believe that a teenager will often run away because that act is required to achieve a high school diploma. The missing kid so often returns home where they are hugged and kissed knowing they are safe with the next step of grounding the defiant delinquent. Often, an adult will also disappear for any of many reasons of which none of their family or friends can grasp. These difficult cases are the ones where you feel that something is wrong, you believe the person is in danger; you know that the person needs help. In these cases, you have to investigate all the leads and ideas to try and find the missing person so that everyone can stop their worries and their fears. The unknown whereabouts of the victim causes so many of the people that are close to the missing person to be on edge with their concerns for the safety of the missing person. The investigation may take years, it may never be resolved, or the final answer may not be that desired result of their prayers. So sit back and let me tell you about one of my most unusual cases of a missing adult who simply vanished into thin air one night. You need a refill on that drink?

Before my promotion to a detective, the Sheriff's Office started an investigation into the report of a lady missing from her home. One morning in the early part of November, Tim Bright asked for a deputy to come to his home so he could report his wife missing. It is not unusual for an adult, who has the full legal right to do so, to simply drop out of site for a few days to enjoy a short time of freedom. With this knowledge, law enforcement does not always accept a missing person report until they are gone for a few days. Providing the gentleman with this information, the deputy encouraged Mr. Bright and went on with his other duties.

Now let me tell you about the life of Tim and Diane Bright so you can better understand this family. Tim was a fifty-three-year-old man who was married and had several children while working as a football coach at one of our local high schools. As life was progressing, he left the school system, and he also left his wife and children. When he was once again a single man, he met up with Diane, a forty-five year old who had also been married and had children in her family prior to her divorce. These two were eventually married and had been together for several years before she disappeared from the face of the earth. To all of our surprise, the children from each of the two previous families were not happy with or about the other new parent.

It took three days before Tim called back to the Sheriff's Office to file the missing person report. This time, the deputy took the report, and the investigation was in progress. Detective Buford was the case investigator who was able to determine a large volume of information that simply created concerns within this experienced investigator—yes, his badge was itching. The story from Mr. Bright was that he and his wife were in the living room of their mobile home watching television. They each had a drink or two before he got up and went to bed while Diane stayed in the living room. When he woke up the next morning, he was not able to locate his wife. During the evening, she had said nothing about leaving; they had not had a fight or even an argument, and there was no reason for her to leave. When asked how she had left, he told the detective that one of their cars was missing from the front yard. The car is one that they never used and only move it occasionally to mow the yard. Tim pointed to a large area on unkempt, tall and brown grass where the car had been parked. Detective Buford noticed that a pocketbook was sitting on the kitchen table and inquired if that was Diane's purse. The response indicated that Diane had left her purse containing her wallet, driver's license, credit cards, cash, and keys on the kitchen table. Now Detective Buford thought to himself why a woman without telling anyone would walk out the house in the middle of the night, leaving her purse and its contents, get into the car they do not use, and drive off into the darkness. Everyone knows that a lady does not ever, never ever leave without her purse. At this point, there seemed to be more questions than answers to this mystery.

The next steps were the normal actions of the check boxes on the missing person investigation form. Detective Buford made sure the lady and her car were entered into the national and state law enforcement computers. This would allow that if any officer in the United States of America checked on Diane or the car, the system would tell the officer that they were missing and to contact the investigator. He also posted local bulletins so the deputies and other officers in our county would know that she was officially listed as a missing person. With the proper actions accomplished, he then updated his supervisors who also became concerned about this unusual case. When the sergeant discovered that the victim left her purse, he assigned additional detectives to the investigation. As the sergeant indicated his wife, his mother, his girlfriend would never leave her purse anywhere; the purse is permanently attached to the lady. Of course, he then corrected himself defining the girlfriend as being before the marriage to his wonderful wife; yep, that must be correct.

The detectives interviewed members from both sides of the family, neighbors were contacted, business associates, and friends were all interrogated concerning this case. They also issued subpoenas for bank records and telephone calls while conducting all other actions to locate some information on the missing lady. With all of this accomplished, they had put together a story that continued to power the concern for alarm.

The investigation revealed that since the marriage, Diane had three major problems occur in her life. Three years prior to the disappearance, Diane had taken an overdose of medicine in an attempt to commit suicide. At that time, she was very depressed as she has often been during her lifetime. The second incident happened about a year before this when during a fight with her husband, he beat her to a point that required medical treatment. This incident resulted in Tim being arrested and Diane refusing to prosecute her dear loving husband. The last problem arose within the previous months prior to this incident when her mother passed away causing Diane to be very depressed over the loss of her mother. They also discovered that this quiet couple kept to themselves while they drank their bottles of scotch together in their quiet mobile home.

When Diane disappeared, Tim was in the process of being demoted at his current job. The demotion would cause him to be transferred from his supervisor position in the other town to a salesman at the local office. With this, it also caused Diane to lose her job as Tim's secretary at the old location. Most believed that this was all a benefit to both of the couple as they would not need to travel as far to work, and Diane would have some time for herself. With all of the other information, the investigators could not determine any facts on the location of the missing lady.

It was now time to sit down with Tim and have a more detailed conversation with the missing lady's husband. With that interview, Tim continued to repeat the story that he went to bed, and she was gone when he awoke. He added that they may have had more than a few drinks of scotch that night. When he was asked if there was a firearm in the house, Tim stated they had a single barrel one shot 20-gauge shotgun. On viewing the weapon, the detective was told that it would smell as if it had been fired recently because his son shot the weapon a week prior to the incident. At that time, the young man was showing his girlfriend how to shoot a gun. With the answer to every question, there was always an explanation, except for how to find Diane. Detective Buford then asked that special question about taking a polygraph test. The response was that he had been waiting for that request and was ready and willing to take the examination. Arraignments were made, and the test was scheduled so the husband could be cleared of any wrong doing or not.

With a polygraph test, the certified examiner creates a list of questions to be answered by the examinee. They create questions unrelated to the incident that they know will be answered truthfully and mix them among the questions concerning the investigation.

These base questions could be similar to asking about the day of the week or the person's first name. The other questions in this test covered if he knew the location of his wife, if she was alive, if he had killed her, and several others directly associated to the investigation. The results of the test indicated that Tim had been untruthful about all questions concerning the location, actions, or status of his missing wife. Mr. Bright maintained that he knew nothing about this incident insisting that his wife simply vanished from their home.

To assist him with proof of innocence, they offered another test to determine the truthfulness of his statements. This stress evaluation test weighs the physical reactions of the human body when one responds to the questions. The questions are established in the same method as the polygraph test. With his reactions to these questions, the persons blinking, twitching, breathing, and time for response all allowed for a final conclusion. This test also showed that Tim was untruthful concerning his knowledge of the disappearance of Diane. He told the investigators that he had no information about his wife, and that both of the tests were wrong. Mr. Bright also told the detectives that he would not answer any other questions and stated that he would hire a lawyer to protect him from their allegations because he had no idea of Diane's location.

As these tests are not usable in a criminal prosecution, the information could only be used to assist the investigators. With their opinions and beliefs matching that of many of Diane's family and friends, there was a strong belief that Tim was involved in his wife's departure into the night. Opinions are not probable cause, the information that is required to legally justify an arrest.

With all the evidence and all the interviews, there was still the one main question of this investigation; where was Diane Bright? With her husband being silent and no information as to what may have occurred and of course without locating Mrs. Bright, the investigation was at a standstill. The case file was packaged together and placed in the Open Case file cabinet to gather dust as we waited for some new information. It was Benjamin Franklin who said that "three can keep a secret, if two of them are dead." As the investigation still contained secrets, the investigators were concerned and frustrated with this unsolved outcome. With the file in the storage cabinet, the calendar moved forward through the years.

Some three years later, Detective William was investigating a case where an unidentified lady had been found murdered and abandoned in the woods. The local news media had broadcasted the general description that had been published by the Sheriff's Office to help identify this woman. Based on the general physical build, Beth, the daughter of Diane Bright, believed that it could match the description of her missing mother. This caused Beth to immediately go to the Sheriff's Office and meet with the investigator. After a short discussion, it was determined that Diane had never had any dental work, and that the current victim had a wide variety of dental actions. On reviewing the information, Detective William determined that this was not Diane, this lady was another victim of a terrible crime.

With this being over three years from the time of her mother's disappearance, it is easy to see the concern and the anguish of the family left behind. Detective William is a man who is very dedicated to helping other people; even when he can do nothing, he still tries to do something. When the situation would require one step, William would take twenty steps to assure that everything was done to help the other person. William is one of those good people we all want to know and who was also a great investigator and high-quality Deputy Sheriff. When William retired as a major, he recalled all of the times we had worked together as partners and as him being my supervisor. He told the entire room that surviving the gun battles over his career was easier than dealing with me which of course caused most in the room to join the two of us in a very boisterous round of laughter over that opinion.

Detective William advised Beth that he would take a look at the cold case and determine if there was any information that could be developed at that time. All of the steps of checking and every methodology of case solving were conducted by the investigator. He was able to determine that there was no new information as to the location of the missing mother. After several weeks, Beth was updated on the review of the case and went home to continue her frustration and concerns for her lost mother.

## THE EMOTIONS FROM A BADGE

We now need to move forward almost three more years, that is five years after Diane disappeared from their home. I was just six days after what would have been the fifty-first birthday of Diane when we reach the next chapter in this story. During that time, Tim, who was still living in the same place, had recently been very depressed for no known reason. On that morning of early April, one of Tim's daughter's, Alice, had spoken to him but was not able to reconnect with him that afternoon. With his recent depression, Alice was concerned and drove over to her father's home. When she got inside, she discovered Tim sitting on his bed with his shotgun between his legs and a gunshot blast wound to his chest. She immediately called 911 to report the emergency.

The deputies were able to determine that Tim was cold to touch, and rigor mortis of the body was in progress. This stiffening of the body, temperature, and body colors helped the investigators determine that the shooting occurred earlier that morning. The body and weapon position indicated that as Tim sat on the edge of the bed, he held the shotgun between his legs and placed the barrel up to his chest. Slightly bending forward with the gun pressed to his chest, Tim pulled the trigger and shot himself to death. The shotgun was the same one that Mr. Bright described to Detective Buford as the only firearm they had in the house. Tim had gone to his grave without ever saying anything about the disappearance of his wife; Diane was still missing from our world.

Now let us put another wrinkle is the case by moving forward this time by just twenty days. Look careful at that word days as we see this six-year-old case jumping up twice within the month. Earlier that year, we had a very strong storm that could be described as just short of being a hurricane come through our area. This storm had stirred up many things including items underwater in the local bypass canal. The Sheriff's Office Underwater Recovery Team was conducting tryouts so they could add additional members to that dive team. One person trying out that day was Sergeant William; yes, the man who three years earlier had taken a second look at the missing case of Diane Bright. During the tryout that day, the group located a vehicle in the bottom of the canal that had been brought from the deep mud by that recent storm. To resolve this abandoned vehicle at the bottom of the canal, they met the duty requirement of removing the car from the water. Once the vehicle was sitting out on the edge of the water, Sergeant William, the old homicide detective, looked in the backseat where he saw a human skull. The diving operation stopped, and the criminal investigation began.

While the homicide unit was en route, Sergeant William felt that the car was familiar to him from one of his past cases. The vehicle tag registration was obtained with the notification including this was a car being driven by a missing adult Diane Bright. Everything came back to him striking him like a bolt of lightning. A short time later, the uniformed deputy securing the crime scene documented my arrival at the location. After a quick briefing, or with Sergeant William an oration of a saga, we began the next step in the investigation.

The vehicle had indeed been the car that went missing with Diane Bright. It was apparent that the car had been submerged in the water and the mud for many years. While trying to pull the car from the water, the vehicle turned upside down and was pulled out of the water on the roof. This caused the roof to be smashed down to the level of the hood and the trunk. There was a small crack between the two allowing one to see inside the vehicle. It was obvious that there was a human skull and a body in the rear seat of the automobile. With the damage to the car and the saturation of the mud, we decided to move the car to the evidence parking lot to conduct the crime scene processing and the recovery of the deceased person. As it was now late in the evening, we had a wrecker take the vehicle to the secured lot and waited for the next day to process the car.

The next morning, we met with the crime scene technician and the medical examiner with a debate on how to process this evidence. The easy answer was to request the local fire department to respond to our scene. This fire truck had a new firefighter with them that needed some experience in using the power saw to cut apart a wrecked car. We all agreed with this training requirement, and that young fireman took out that powerful saw and cut the roof right off of the mangled automobile. When we lifted the detached roof from the car, the human remains were more visible than when we peeked through the cracks. To the amazement of the medical examiner Dr. Charles, this body was in a state of adipocere that resulted in a total saponification of the body. This was very rare for a death in our tropical Florida weather usually occurring in the frigid weather and waters located very far to our north.

Slow down just a minute and let me explain some of those big fancy words that were just used in the previous paragraph. Believe me those words were not in my vocabulary prior to this investigation. The adipocere procedure is a process where a dead body is buried in a very damp or wet location and is enhanced by a very cold location. This cold and wet condition slows the process of the decomposition and forms a corpse wax. This causes the fat within the body to deteriorate in a different fashion compared to the burning away in the hot sun. With this action, the human body changes into a state of saponification causing the skin and muscle to have an appearance similar to powdered soap that is damp and sticking together in a clump. In this condition, the entire body retains its shape and looks like a rock sculpture of that human being. Our victim had this condition with only her extremities of the hands, feet, and head being only bare skeleton bones.

The next step in the investigation was to transfer the body to the Medical Examiner's Office and process the vehicle. We went through the messy muddy car and were looking for everything and anything. We eventually took a water hose to the vehicle and sprayed the mud out of the interior. With all of the work, we found a few bones and a ring, a very unique ring.

The viewing of the autopsy was a sight that none of us had every experienced before that day. Even Dr. Charles who had read about this type of condition never had dealt with this situation in his career. The most interesting part was that this kept the body intact which allowed us to better review the corpse for any damage. The review indicated that there were no signs of injury to the body. We could not locate an area of a gunshot wound, a stab wound, broken bones, or other damage that could cause the death. With the lengthy investigation, we still had a lot of information but no answers on her death. The other question, and the most important of all, was if this was truly Diane Bright.

With a criminal investigation, one will always have opinions about the case. These opinions cannot be used in the investigation as we can only use proven facts to resolve a case. To provide a name to our recently discovered deceased lady, we brought in a forensic odontologist. Here we have another one of those big words that were never taught to us in our high school English class; when we actually went to class, let's just keep that statement between us. So with this definition, it explains that in the field of dentistry, the doctor is certified to have the ability to examine teeth, teeth marks, or other dental information to identify a person or bite mark and testify to his decision in a court of law. With the most recent photograph of Diane Bright, we provided the local expert Dr. Richard with the opportunity to examine the victim and compare to the photograph. Dr. Richard was also amazed at the condition of the body considering it was recovered in the Florida climate. We had to remind him that he needed to look at the teeth and not the body. Based on the unique twist to the front upper teeth in the victim's skull and the same teeth matching in the photograph, Dr. Richard confirmed that the deceased was our missing lady.

With this information, we met with the victim's daughter Beth to discuss our recent information. During that discussion, we asked her if she had ever seen the unique ring that we found in the car. On seeing the ring, she started to cry as she identified her mother's special ring. With the doctor's identification, the ring and the car, we made the next-of-kin notification concerning the death of this sad lady. She told us that she knew all along that her mother was dead, but it was something she did not want to accept until she was found. When you work hard and find a solution to a crime, it is not always the answer that everyone truly wants to hear.

With all of these many steps, we were not yet finished with the investigation. Dr. Charles certified that he was unable to determine a cause of death and would not be able to determine this as a natural, accidental, or homicide death. On meeting with the State Attorney's Office, the decision was that they would not be able to prosecute anyone over this incident. Even if the husband were alive, the medical examiner could not determine the method or cause of death.

With the victim located, we cancelled all of the missing person alerts for the good lady. The missing person case was closed as we had located the lost lady. With the husband dying twenty days before she was recovered, we were not able to bring him in for another round of questioning. The medical examiner and the state attorney could not provide a ruling based on the lack of answers to the way she may have died those nearly six years ago. With all of this, we closed the death investigation as an undefined death with no additional leads. The one action that was accomplished was we finally let the family know where their mother, who had vanished over five years ago, had gone to on that dark evening. It is very hard to bury a loved one, but it is even harder to not know where they are or if they are even alive.

Mr. Bright took to his grave his own deep dark secrets. We will always have to wonder if the secret inside him ate at him like a vicious cancer. Just six days after his wife's fifty-first birthday, with him being fifty-eight years old, was the five long years of secrecy and the memories of that November evening his wife disappeared become the cause of his own death, was that his own death sentence?

We will never know how Diane Bright died or will we ever know why Tim Bright killed himself, still we will finally and forevermore know the location of both of these individuals. May they both and each rest in peace.

# Swear They Are Dead

Here comes another story were I once again misbehave, just a little.

Recently, a circuit court judge reminded me of her first autopsy that she had attended with a very crazy homicide detective. At that time, she was an assistant state attorney working as a prosecutor that had just been transferred to prosecute homicide cases. With this new assignment, she wanted to view an autopsy so she could better understand the information presented by the Medical Examiner's Office in the courtroom. One day at a homicide crime scene, she requested that I notify her so she could attend the autopsy procedure for this case.

She was a wonderful and pretty young lady who was raised locally in a real good family. The horrors that she was witnessing with the murder cases were nothing like what she was used to observing in her pristine life. When she entered the morgue that afternoon for the autopsy, it was obvious that for her, there was a definite and complete stay way back zone. From her position, she would have needed binoculars to see the body and the procedure. My partner whispered to me to behave myself; it is obvious that his comment would not work.

Continuing to talk to the young prosecutor about the ongoing procedure, we helped her move closer and closer to the body. When she got close enough, I asked if she was ready to perform the validation procedure. With a stunned look, she asked me what was the validation procedure? I told her that as a homicide prosecutor, she must know what I meant as it was required by law. We discussed if they may have a different term that is used in the legal field from the law enforcement side to define the procedure. She insisted that it made no sense to her and again inquired for an explanation. I told her that being at the autopsy, she would need to be able to swear and avow to the court that the victim was indeed deceased. Providing this sworn testimony to validate the death requires the person testifying to have touched the dead body allowing one to swear under oath that the victim is indeed dead. She simply stared at me, and with determined speed started backing away. She advised that she would not in any way, now or ever, touch a dead body. I reminded her it was the required legal action defined in case law to validate the death. She insisted she knew nothing of such law, procedure, or even the term.

With her having a Juris doctorate and working as a prosecutor, her opinion of the procedure of course was correct. When I told her that it was a joke, she once again started to breathe. She continued through the process to complete her first autopsy, learning a great deal about the procedure and of course never touching the body. The only body she touched that day was mine with a large legal pad by slapping the back of my head to show her excellent method of communication. I came to a complete understanding of the matter and of course sustained her objection.

# Firebomber

Within each of our lives, we will all face an experience that will be the very best time of our entire life, and also one that is the very worst time. I want to tell you about the most dreadful investigation that I ever had to conduct out of my many horrible cases—yes, sadly, there is the one that is the most terrible. In this story, I will break my rule and tell you the real names of the victims as they each and every one deserve the honor of remembrance. I will also use the real name of the killer so that no one will ever forget the so very disgusting criminal act of this abysmal killer. With respect for the survivors of this awful event, I will continue to keep their true names from being exposed with the publication of this most reprehensible tale. This is a difficult story to tell and to cope with due to the emotional trauma to so many people including myself, so I will offer you my apology now knowing this tale will most surely also upset you.

This early Saturday evening was like so many of the midsummer season in the south as we yearly celebrate the holiday that honors our great nation the United States of America, that is correct, the Fourth of July without a doubt Independence Day. On this day in 1983, the weather was a typical warm evening with occasional thunderstorms creating strong winds and a damp and muggy atmosphere. With the holiday being on Monday, many people were preparing for the start of their three-day weekend for a conclusion with a family barbecue and a grandiose fireworks show to top off the holiday celebration. Everyone was busy and simply enjoying the fun weekend.

## THE EMOTIONS FROM A BADGE

On that afternoon, Leigh Ann Carter went to her job as a cashier at the grocery store near her home for her evening-shift assignment. Leigh Ann was a recent graduate from the local high school and was attending a local college while also working this job to assist with those college expenses. She was an eighteen-year-old young lady from a good and loving little southern family. This nice girl was a very good and very well behaved person, the wonderful daughter who was so loved in that family of four. When she arrived at work that day, the boss advised the employees that he was overstaffed, and that another nearby store was shorthanded for the evening. When he asked for volunteers to help at the other location, Leigh Ann, who was always ready to help others, raised her hand to offer her assistance. Within a very short time, she had traveled to the new location and opened up Register 6. Throughout the evening, Eli would be the bagboy who would help Leigh Ann and her customers with their purchases. She, of course, had called her parents to let the family know she would be working at the other store that evening; she was a good child.

At sixteen years of age, Eli was still in high school and working at the grocery store that was a few blocks from his home. He also was a fine young man who was helping the family by working while he went to school. Eli was another good and dedicated employee who was helping to keep things going on this busy holiday weekend.

It was about six o'clock in the evening when one of the local residents observed a strange individual in the county park that was one block south of the grocery store. The strange person was wandering around the area carrying a five-gallon bucket; this stray was known to most in the community as John William Ferry, Jr. Billy, as most called him, was a very odd-looking person while he wandered and lived on the streets. He had long hair, a full beard, raggedy clothing, shod in large rubber boots, and was total unkempt and messy; and by the way being so filthy, he also had a very foul odor. Billy was a very nasty and aggressive-looking person who would most likely be grungier looking than a person shown on television shows as living in the backstreets of a megatropolis. With his wandering around and rambling comments, it was not a concern that this often seen scamp was out on the street that evening, like so many evenings, it was just Billy.

Within an hour, Billy showed up at the convenience store that was on the north side of the park and directly across the street from the grocery store. As usual, he bought a soda and a Twinkie and then stood outside to consume his evening meal. After a short time, he came back into the store, and again as usual, complained that his half-finished soda tasted funny and demanded a replacement. The clerk knew it was not worth arguing with Billy and allowed him to obtain a replacement drink, which to her great desire expedited his exit from the store. On finishing his meal, Billy returned to the clerk and prepaid for $4.60 of self-service gasoline. With the gas pumped into his five-gallon bucket, Billy walked away to the rear of the store.

After about thirty minutes, Billy showed up in the grocery store across the street from his recent gasoline purchase. Wandering the store for a few moments of shopping, he then headed to Register 9, the quick lane attached to the office, to conduct his purchase of one can of sardines from Gina the cashier who was also prepared for his routine visit to this store. With groceries in hand, Billy walked past the other registers on his way out of the exit door. One of these was Register 6 where Leigh Ann and Eli were busy working; neither of the employees noticed the foul-smelling tramp as he left the building. They both held true to their dedication to the job and made a terrible mistake by continuing to perform their work.

With the busy weekend, there were twenty employees at work to help the over forty customers shopping in all areas of this typical grocery store. This store was one of many in a well-known national chain of quality grocery stores. It is just like the store that you go to shop for your groceries, where your friends shop, your family just like anyone. We all know that shopping for groceries is a normal need and is in no way a dangerous act, never a risk. We should outlaw the use of the word "never."

Billy took his can of sardines and went back across the street again disappearing in the rear of the convenience store. A few minutes later, he came from the rear of the building while carrying his bucket full of gasoline and walked back across the street toward the grocery store. His appearance was not unusual for the community, so there was no need for anyone to have any concerns or to take any action as everyone knew that Billy would never do anything wrong, that is right, that erroneous word "never."

With the store busy and full of shoppers, the register lanes were full of customers; and of course, Register 6 personnel were working hard to help those consumers. Leigh Ann was ringing up the purchase for Martha Vance a twenty-four year old mother who had her four-year-old daughter Jenifer next to her helping with the purchase. Behind this group were two more young ladies twenty-seven-year-old Melody Darlington and her seventeen-year-old niece Misty McCullough who were in the process of transferring their items from the cart to the register's conveyer belt. As Leigh Ann went through the purchases for Martha Vance, the items were packed by Eli as he stood there with his back to the door.

Now usually telling a story, one would go into a detailed background of each of these individuals who were listed above. It is hard to tell you about them because they are each your average person like your friend, your family, and your neighbors. Leigh Ann had been a greeter when she was in high school to help new students adjust to the new school. Eli had just returned from Boys State where the high school students go to the state capital and perform a mock session of the legislative body. Melody and Misty were very good church members who had made a last-minute run to buy some food for the baby at their house. Martha and Jennifer, who always wanted to be with her mother, were making a shopping run for the holiday weekend while leaving dad and the other child at home. These were all just good people, good family, and good neighbors. Each and all were taking care of some obligation to help themselves and others have a better day. Even with the dark of night and the rain shower, they all know that it was not dangerous to grocery shop. The good folks were having a nice evening.

With the hard working employees helping the busy shoppers, the clock showed that it was five minutes past eight o'clock that evening when the exit doors opened from a person approaching from the outside. As the winds blew in from the open door, Gina, the cashier in Register 9, looked up to see her previous customer Billy Ferry walk into the store entering through that exit door with a five-gallon bucket in hand.

Once in the store, Billy took the bucket and threw the gasoline on the people around Register 6; as the gasoline splashed on them, Eli looked around and saw Billy standing there with a lighter burning in his hand. Billy, with that lighter set for full length of flame, ignited the gasoline. A large explosion occurred around the area of the register that engulfed the employees and the customers. With the gasoline being thrown and the winds from the recent storms coming in from the open door, this caused the gas to have both a large area of fumes as well as the liquid that struck the people standing near that register. The fumes created the fiery explosion that covered nearly a ten-foot circle and the liquid that drenched the victims continued to burn their entire body, burning even after the explosion. Everyone screamed, everyone ran while some inhaled the smoke that filled the store from the explosion and from the fire as the store merchandise and structures continued to burn, continued to burn just like many of the people in the store.

Laughing and cussing, Billy ran from the store past several people who were standing outside the building at the time of the crime. As he passed one group, they heard him state "that will show those crazy bastards," he must know what that nasty word means as he had just proven that he himself is one. The felon continued to run from the scene being chased by one of the bystanders to a neighborhood to the west of the store. The citizen lost sight of the culprit in the area of Billy's parent's home as the firebomber disappeared into the dark night.

As many people went to aid the victims, the tragedy continued to unfold as the fire trucks were screaming to the scene while being raced to the location by Deputy Sheriffs. One man saw a small child completely on fire from head to toe running from the store and screaming in total fear, panic, and pain, she was four-year-old Jennifer Vance. The bagboy, Eli, had escaped the explosion of the fumes but had a large splash of the liquid strike his back creating his entire backside from ankle to head to be on fire. Martha Vance,

Melody Darlington, and Misty McCullough, all of them were on fire because they had been inside the circle of the explosion and were also drenched in fuel; they were all fleeing from the burning building as they too with flames from their body continued to burn. All of these poor people were helped by the bystanders to extinguish the fire on their bodies as the fire rescue personnel were arriving; the fire was out, but the pain and fears from the injuries continued with intense pain, extreme, and horrible agony. Of the sixty people that had been in the store that evening, eighteen people were injured by smoke and by flame injuries that required the need for treatment at the hospital. Out of this large number of injured people, five of them were being treated for the most serious of burns to their body several of which had 100 percent of their body burned by the flames. Then in the middle of all of the chaos arose the concern that nobody could find Leigh Ann; she could not be found at the smoke-filled and fire-charred scene at that moment she was lost.

    The victims were all treated at the scene as best could be done by the highly trained paramedics from the county's fire rescue personnel, who are more than excellent people and professionals, who also showed their human side by being visibly upset by the sights of that terrible incident. Several of the injured victims were transported by fire rescue vehicles with lights and sirens clearing the roadways en route to our local trauma hospital that includes the regional burn unit. That evening was very hard for those tuff and brave people from fire rescue and the Deputy Sheriffs; it was very hard on all of them.

    The deputies started the investigation and continued the search for the firebomber. The callouts were conducted for all of the bosses and of course the homicide detectives. When in the middle of dinner with a group of friends that evening or at any time, the beeping from my pager was always a bad sign. On calling the communications center, the supervisor advised me of the ongoing event. At first, I could not believe the story that was being told to me; this was more than horrible and difficult to believe for even this hardened investigator. That evening, I was at a location that was near the hospital that contains that regional burn unit, so as I rushed to the scene with my lights and siren clearing the way, there were ambulances rushing toward that hospital, one then another and then more. It was obvious that this was going to a very long, a very bad night.

On arriving at the scene, it was easy to see that this was a huge incident and a total mess. The numerous fire trucks having extinguished the fire were still treating the minor injuries and containing the scene. Sheriff's Office cars filled the parking lot and also saturated the area seeking to locate the fleeing criminal. My first step was to determine my requirements for this case by matching up with my supervisors the lieutenant and the sergeant who had already been at the location establishing a game plan for the investigation. Both were eager to provide me with the news that I was to be the case investigator for this crime; remember the lead detective is responsible for the investigation. This may have been their way of paybacks for the troubles I so often caused each and both of them, but Sergeant Randy told me that Major John and the sergeant himself wanted this case done right. That was quite a compliment from those two most honorable supervisors.

By the time I started to view the crime scene, a man totally confused and in a total state of panic arrived at the location. The deputies were trying to console him but could not provide any help to the gentleman who was so concerned; he insisted on speaking to an investigator. On meeting the upset man, he advised that he saw the incident on the television news and responded because his daughter was working at this location tonight; since the crime, he had not been able to contact his daughter, a cashier at the store, her name was Leigh Ann Carter. I advised him that she had not been interviewed at this location, and that the injured had been transported to the hospital; and with a gracious thank you, the father rapidly left the scene for his trip to the hospital. It was now time to process the crime scene.

On entering the exit doors, it was easy to see that the registers areas for number 6 and 7 were the center of the fire. This location was charred and black from the results of the explosion and the flames burning the structure of the register kiosk and the items for sale displayed around the burned area. Directly above that space, in the white-tiled ceiling, was a circular burn area that covered nearly a ten-foot diameter, this defined the location of the explosion. On further inspection, I discovered something that no one wanted to see, a human bone.

Carefully inspecting the area around the bone and removing other objects from around that site, I was able to determine the location of our missing girl, Leigh Ann had been found. At the time of the explosion, she had been in the center of the blast as the toss of the gasoline had been in her direction causing her to also have a large amount of the flammable liquid on her body. As she lay there on the ground, she was formed in a partial fetal position with her hands and knees coming toward one another. Her entire body was so badly burned that it was hard to identify her remains as a human body; the blackened body looked more like a mummy from and ancient tomb than a girl who was alive an hour ago. Only a few straps of melted cloth from her polyester uniform remained on her body. The scraps were obviously the uniform of an employee of the grocery store, and with only her being missing, it was enough to believe this was that young lady; the burns were so bad one could not identify her by looking at the scorched remnants of her face. As the fire department was still in the store with their hoses containing the hot ashes, it was important to keep the victim intact, less for the investigation than for the dignity of that lady. We wrapped her burned and damaged body in a sheet and removed her from the scene. The victim was placed on the sidewalk wrapped securely in the sheet to provide her privacy from the view of everyone. A short time later, I saw her father return to the scene again talking with the deputies advising them his daughter was not at the hospital. It was now once again my turn to go and speak to the man with this time being much more difficult; it is not easy to tell a parent that their child is dead, no matter the age of the child. This would be only the first death notification for this investigation. That good man, the loving father fell totally apart as his tears even as many and strong still could not define his grief. We made sure he got home safely that evening, safe to the home of a family now of only three.

The investigation that evening was a very simple step-by-step process right from the Investigations 101 methodology causing the location to be photographed, measurements taken, evidence impounded, and interviews conducted of the many victims and witnesses. With so many people witnessing the crime that was committed by a person known to so many of the witnesses, the establishment of probable cause was quickly resolved and a warrant issued for the arrest of Billy Ferry. The only problem in the investigations that evening was that Billy had disappeared from the scene and from the investigators, hidden by the dark and rainy night. With the local and national news coverage, most of the community knew that we were looking for Billy; and the search was on, everyone was looking for the criminal, the good deputies were all hunting for Billy. During that search, a deputy discovered some graffiti painted on the entrance wall to Billy's family neighborhood that read "Billy can't take it no more—fire," now there had been that fire.

As my actions at the scene were complete and a warrant issued my next stop was at the hospital to check on the other victims. The families of the victims were in the waiting room struggling for updates on their loved ones and on the investigation. We sat together as I explained the ongoing investigation and expressed my sympathy and concern; there was so little that I could really say to help this group deal with their tragedy. Having been briefed by the medical staff prior to the family conference, I was told the victims were burned on at least 99 percent of their bodies which required the medical staff to provide a pain medication that was to a level of being just short of an overdose of the medication allowed the patient to barely being conscious. As I spoke to the families that night, we could still hear the patients, my victims, their family members back in their rooms screaming from the pain that was so far beyond being able to describe with any word in any language. Their pain was so intense with the excessive medicine being unable to provide relief; their bodies were so dreadfully damaged that even this experienced homicide detective had trouble looking at the mangled person as they lay there screaming in misery, my victims' screams ripped my heart. It was time to call it a night and prepare for the long day of tomorrow.

Tossing and turning in bed as I tried to sleep that night, I remembered a story of the Soviet leader Nikita Khrushchev as he dealt with the Cuban Missile Crisis. As the Soviet ships were steaming toward Cuba, he thought of the statements made by President John F. Kennedy indicating this could bring the two nations to war. Comrade Khrushchev remembered that during World War II, he was at a location after a battle where he could smell the bodies of so many people on fire and burning from that conflict. The horrible and disgusting smell was beyond his tolerance or that of any human being. That grotesque memory is claimed to be part of the reason he called the ships back to their home ports. All that night that same smell of my burned victims stayed in my nose; to this day, that smell still returns whenever I recall that night of agony suffered by those innocent people. In a short time, I arose as the alarm went off, and that smell also stayed on.

With the horrible smell being beyond the comprehension of so many of the good people in our society, we should consider the other part of this injury, the pain. We have all been the recipient of that small burn, picking up the hot pot from the stove, the touching the hot grill of the oven, and so many other ways that we feel so stupid for taking the action that creates that burn. Now imagine that is a first-degree burn that may put a small red spot on our skin that stings and hurts beyond our human tolerance. The next step up in severity is defined as a second-degree burn that will cause the skin to have a bubble and create a pain that makes the first degree seem like such a minimal pain. With the third-degree burn, the skin is burned through a layer of skin causing the surrounding skin to convert to stiff leather consistency; and with a pain level that as described before even with pain medication, the victim still screams in unbearable pain. Now my description in this paragraph speaks of a small burn to one's body, my victims' burns covered up to 100 percent of the body most covered with the highest level of burn. With their body damaged and the skin burned away while overdosed with pain medicine, my victims continued to scream in pain, excruciating pain. During my career as a homicide investigator, I never discovered an injury that was more painful than a burn. When one is shot, stabbed, choked to death, drowns, or dies from any other method, the pain cannot reach the level of a burn. Any suspect who would face me with a weapon would cause me to negotiate with them unless the weapon was fire, that person would be immediately shot.

With this being a major news event by Sunday morning, everyone in our town knew of the crime; and with the published photographs of Billy, we were all looking for him, the citizens, the deputy Sheriffs, everyone wanted him off of our streets. This would be accomplished when just before noon, a citizen saw Billy walking down the road and enter into a convenience store that was in an area about three miles from the crime scene and separated from that area by a major highway and a bypass canal. That good citizen called the Sheriff's Office where the dispatchers relayed the location to the patrol units; this was not the normal dispatch as the information created many of the deputies to rush to the scene determined to capture the rabid animal. Sixteen hours after he walked into that store and burned so many people, the clock struck 12:00 noon as Billy was cuffed and stuffed into the backseat of a Sheriff's Office caged patrol car. This time, the beeping of my pager was not to deliver bad news; this was great news informing me that the firebombing maniac was off the street.

With the criminal in custody, he was transported to the Sheriff's Office to allow me to conduct an interview with the suspect. As the many deputies brought him into the building, he began to fight and struggle while screaming at the uniformed deputies. The local media was filming the scene as one of these good deputy Sheriffs who was struggling with Billy was kicked in the head and knocked to the ground by one of Billy's big rubber boots. Billy was obviously out of control, well, obviously in front of the news media. Once inside, he was placed in an interview room to allow for my intense interrogation of this felon. Sitting in the room with the messy and smelling firebomber, a man that everyone thought was crazy, a man that was obviously out of control, the first step was to advise Billy of his constitutional rights to remain silent and to have an attorney present. Without anyone else watching this wild beast, he sat there like a professional businessman and advised me that he would not answer any questions as he requested a lawyer. At that moment, he looked like he knew exactly what he was doing raising the question was he truly crazy or an award-winning actor?

The paperwork was completed, and we gathered together to march the disgusting-looking smelly mess of an animal out to the caged marked patrol vehicle to transport him to the county jail. As we walked down the front steps of the Sheriff's Office, I was on his left side marching the killer past all of the news cameras. That evening, the video was broadcasted on the national news stations and into the living rooms of our citizens, including my cousin's home in another state. As they sat there watching me on the news, strutting out with the arrested bad guy, they screamed with great pride to their friends in the room, "Look, that's our cousin!" The friends looked at them with great surprise and total disgust when my family realized the miscommunication and said, "No, the guy in the suit, not the killer." Everyone in the room seemed to be much happier with the updated information. This detective was still not happy.

On that Sunday afternoon of the holiday weekend having the killer in custody and creating safe streets for our citizens, the investigation was not anywhere near complete, it was just starting. We went out to the location where Billy had been arrested and discovered his secret hideout in a patch of woods south of the location of his arrest. The campsite was a small tent that within and around was covered with trash, dirty clothing, nasty and obscene reading material just overall a grimy mess. One would have to wonder if living in a jail would not be a better environment than living at his private abode.

That afternoon, I went to the first autopsy, the medical examination that determines the cause of death. Standing there in the cold room, I observed Leigh Ann lying on the table; she was so badly burned that it was difficult to look at the charred and scorched remains and see a human being, a sweet young lady. The large mass on that table looked more like the large pieces of wood and ashes that remain in a fire pit on the morning after the burn. With this sad sight, it was easy to determine that she had died as a result of total body burns, this was to 100 percent of her body. With this type of injury, she was fortunate to die at the scene rather than to suffer, as the others were still suffering as they screamed from their terrible pain at the burn unit of the hospital. That afternoon, my reports were brought up to date, and I went home to finish the weekend; it was not a good holiday.

On the afternoon of the Fourth of July, my pager again gave me another beep requiring me to contact the Communications Center supervisor. That call was the next step in the many days of bad news; Martha Vance had died from her burns. We now had two people murdered by the commission of this stupid crime.

With the holiday over, it was time to get back into full motion. Normally, the majority of the assignments would be nearly finished at this point in the case; this was not a normal investigation. From the definition of the crime and the actions of the criminal, it was obvious that the defense in this case could be based on insanity. Major John told me, or as I keep saying per him asked me, to find out every bit of information on the background of the suspect. We also were assigned to contact every business in the shopping center that was the location of the grocery store. Major John also "asked" that we do everything else that we could think of doing to strengthen our investigation. We headed out for our many tasks for the day.

One of our tasks that day was to attend the autopsy of Martha Vance, the second murder victim. At the autopsy, her body was not as destroyed as the Leigh Ann's; but instead, the outer skin was burned off exposing the next layers of the body red and raw from the burns. This was another quick process to determine the cause of death was total body burns to over 100 percent of her body. This fine lady lived two days in pain before her death ended the life of the mother of her four-year-old daughter, the little girl who in great fear was still suffering and screaming in the burn unit. That did not last for long as we were notified after the procedure that Jennifer Vance had now died from her injuries making the crime a triple murder.

The rest of that day, we contacted each of the businesses located in the shopping plaza and many of the key witnesses who had been the scene at the time of the crime. The information was stacking up along with the paper documents that were also continuing to pile up. The step-by-step actions were being completed as we continued to create a solid investigation for the prosecution of the crime.

## THE EMOTIONS FROM A BADGE

The following day required me to attend the autopsy of Jennifer Vance, our third homicide victim. The young little four year old took up such a little space of the steel table. Jennifer was also burned over her entire body, another 100 percent victim, with the skin of her chest creating the appearance of dried brown leather. These horrible burns caused the skin to lose its flexibility forcing the doctors to cut large incisions across her chest and stomach to relieve the pressure, thus creating her body to have an appearance similar to the slashes on the top of a baked ham. Her face was burned to the point that you could not recognize the cute little girl who had so happily gone shopping with her mother. She no longer looked like her picture of that pretty little girl wearing her little red cowgirl hat. This little lady lived three days of the pain before she went along to once again be with her mother. Each of these autopsies were a gut-wrenching task that are required for the job duties, sadly a small child is so much harder than an adult. Her damaged face and marred body always comes into my mind first when I remember the smell of my burned victims, those good innocent people. That was one of those moments that make the difficult job even harder. At least, once again, the little girl was with her mother.

As the days passed by and the investigation continued, the court proceedings started to become the priority of the case. The state attorney, the leader of the prosecutor's office, himself took a personal interest in this event and became the chief prosecutor of this case. Mr. E. J. took the allegations to the grand jury and obtained indictments for three counts of first-degree murder and one count of arson. Being charged with these offenses, we went to the courtroom to take the next action in this process. At that hearing, the public defenders were representing the defendant on his accused actions or better said were the attorneys for the guilty criminal. The ruling on that day involved the judge declaring the defendant to have a mental instability that would prevent him from assisting his legal representatives from providing him with a proper defense. The judge ordered him to be transferred to the state mental hospital to be held until he was mentally able to work with his legal team. So Billy was shipped off to the state prison funny farm while several more of his victims still writhed in pain in the burn unit. Billy who was not quite right could still play the system better than most would ever believe.

Over the time that I had contact with Billy Ferry, he was usually in a jail cell. When I would sneak up to the cell without him having knowledge that anyone was looking, he had the calm and comfortable appearance of most anyone sitting on a park bench. Once he realized he was being watched, he started shaking and rambling to fulfill the requirements and the actions for a person with mental problems. This has always forced me to wonder if Billy is not as insane as he wants others to believe; not that he doesn't have problems, but the problem is much less than his award-winning performance.

The next phase of the investigation was to investigate Billy Ferry, anything and everything about his past. This went from his birth to his arrest for the firebombing to enable us to paint a picture of his entire life. The search for this information enabling us to create his biography was launched, and moving forward with another interruption, our fourth victim died in the burn unit.

The following day, I attended another autopsy that of Misty McCullough, the seventeen-year-old girl who had been shopping with her aunt. Her cause of death was due to 95 percent of her body receiving the deadly burns. The good-looking high school girl also had her top layer of skin burned from her body, that red and raw look of the horrible damage to the body of this young lady. Poor Misty had lived thirteen days of pain before she died from her horrible injuries. She should have known not to take that dangerous risk of going grocery shopping with her aunt. Misty was the second child and the fourth victim to be killed by this pathetic firebomber; it was just so not fair.

As the investigation continued, I compiled more and more information about the life of Billy Ferry showing that whatever he did, the outcome was for him to quit. With my job, I had an obligation to the victims and their families; there was no way that I would quit. As we moved forward, we were again hit with bad news; Melody Darlington had died becoming the fifth murder victim.

At that autopsy, we saw the same horrible damage to her body as we had seen on the other ladies with the damaged layer of skin having the red and raw appearance. Melody had fought for twenty-seven days before she died from the 98 percent body burns. Finally, all of the homicide victims were out of their misery, and their families could leave the agony of the screams coming from the burn unit of the hospital and return to their peaceful homes. Even today, these families still have trouble dealing with the empty bed or for some more than one bed in their peaceful home. This was now a murder of five innocent ladies.

The other very serious injury was to Eli the bagboy who stood behind Leigh Ann the night of the crime. With him being the closest to the door, the wind blew the fumes from the gas more toward Leigh Ann and the other lady. Without being in the plume of the explosion, he was only burned by the gas that struck his body, 50 percent of his body, his entire back side. He would endure the incredible pain and recover from the burns allowing him to move forward with his life. Eli today lives his life with theses forever burn scars coving the entire back side of his body. For his fortune, he was the only one of the six people who were the target of the thrown gasoline who survived the crime. The five ladies did not have that luck; those five ladies were killed by a mass murderer, a firebomber.

Out of the eighteen people injured in the fire that night, only one died at the crime scene. The other seventeen victims went to four different hospitals throughout our community where the four additional good ladies suffered and later died from their wounds and where five more victims were treated for their critical burns. The bag boy Eli was one of the critical with four of the customers, an adult woman and three children, being the group of five that sustained the most serious nonfatal burns. The children were two twelve-year-old girls and one seven-year-old girl, three innocent little ladies who had to deal with this terrible tragedy by suffering with their own unbearable burn pains. Only eight of the eighteen victims were treated and released from the hospitals on the night of the fiery terror, all eighteen of the blameless and innocent victims did not need to ever suffer this horrible catastrophe, the horrendous pain, the appalling murder.

In September, Mr. E. J., the state attorney, returned to the grand jury and updated the criminal indictments against Billy Ferry.

At that time, he was charged with five counts of first-degree murder and one count of arson; Billy was facing the possibility of five death sentences. Sadly, if convicted, the execution would not be burning him at the stake.

The biography that I had compiled on Billy Ferry showed that he was born and raised in our town growing up in a neighborhood that was in walking distance of less than half a mile from the crime scene. If one were to sneak through the back way, it would be measured in yards. The irony is that Billy was born in the same hospital where I came into this world just two years to the month after his delivery. The patriarch of the family was a good man who worked as a refrigeration mechanic for a large restaurant chain with the mother being a housewife raising their four children. With Billy being the oldest, he had two sisters with the first three children joining the family each a year apart. The youngest is a brother who arrived nearly twelve years after Billy and was just eighteen years old at the time of the crime.

Billy's path through the local school system took the normal course of the elementary school that was located near his home and across the street from his junior high school both of these being just behind the convenience store where he purchased the gasoline to commit his blazing crime. From there, he moved over to the high school that was in the small community just east of his neighborhood. During his sophomore year, Billy had grades of As, Bs, and Cs with his junior year dropping a level for each of the grade averages including a failing grade. Halfway through his senior year, he cited personal and family problems requiring him to drop out of high school just short of obtaining his diploma. As he did so often, Billy quit rather than to complete his obligation and fulfill a need for his high school education.

With our main city having an international port, Billy went to work as a laborer for one of our local supply companies at the docks. During his time of employment, he achieved his first of many arrest, this one for breaking into a vehicle. Both he and his accomplice served their probation in such good standing they earned an early release from the probation and moved on with their lives. Of the two, only Billy's accomplice ended his life of crime.

Over the next four years, his working assignments went from one type of job to another. Billy worked as a crew member on a tugboat, picking vegetables at a local farm, and even as a "wiper" on a tugboat. The "wiper" is the term used for an apprentice who is beginning training as a mechanic for a tugboat. During this training, Billy was released from employment with the company determining that he was "unwilling to perform his duties." None of these jobs lasted over a year or less indicating that the firebomber is not willing to complete an obligation.

During the same four years, Billy again achieved another arrest this time for armed robbery. These charges were quickly dismissed preventing his prosecution for these alleged crimes, a simple misunderstanding. With this and many other actions, the Billy Ferry biography moved along with an entry each and every year.

Moving forward in time, he again went back to work on the tugboats where he was injured by a metal line and shackle striking him in the upper torso and the head creating an ongoing injury. When he returned from medical leave, he continually complained of being unable to work due to the recurring pain from that injury whenever he was aboard a boat. The next injury he claimed was to have slipped on oil that was on the deck of the boat. With his continual complaints of the pain from these injuries and the problem of him being accused of not being able to get along with his crewmates and also that he was stealing money from his shipmates, none of the boat captains would allow him to work on their craft. Once again, he lost another job being terminated just after his one year anniversary. Just over a year later, he was awarded $10,000 from his civil lawsuit against the company. He learned about the civil law from this moment in his life.

With no longer being able to work at the docks, Billy continued to go back to the tomato farms and work at the processing plants of those companies. At one of these businesses, Billy claimed he was injured on the job and filed a worker compensation complaint. The manager of that company sent Billy to a doctor who diagnosed the poor lad's problem as "compensationitis," that's right, no injury, just a desire to file injury complaints. With that medical opinion, the manager informed Billy that his claim was unsubstantiated resulting in Billy threatening to sue the company. That response resulted in Billy being terminated from yet another occupation.

By the end of the month of his termination from that last job, Billy was once again arrested for one of his many worthless check crimes. This was a failure to appear in court warrant for one of these many white-collar crimes which required him to sit in jail for a month before he could plead guilty to the charge and receive probation for the crime. During this time in jail, he was able to celebrate the Fourth of July holiday just three years before he would commit his most disgusting crime.

Over the next few years, Billy is continually in and out of jail for his worthless check charges. Most of those crimes were from our county, but a few are originated in a county to our north that contains a very large national park. During these years, Billy was continually going back and forth between the two counties. The only time he was out of his normal tends was for an arrest in Dallas, Texas based on one of our office's bad check warrants. This was the only time we were able to show he was out of this local area, and we were never able to determine why he was out in Texas; the Lone Star state was more than elated to send our Florida native back home.

As the calendar moved forward, Billy was beginning a life where he was often found out on the streets of our big city. The area where he was living has many flophouses, and these streets were a well-known place for drug dealers and gay prostitutes to sell their product. On one evening, Billy was found passed out in a flower bed of a bar well-known for the clientele of the aforementioned prostitutes. With his appearance and unkempt condition, I am more than positive that he was not involved in any of that activity; no one would want to be involved with that odiferous mess.

In the year prior to the firebombing, Billy went to the same grocery store that he would some fourteen months later set ablaze. At that time, he complained that he had purchased some sour cream from the store, and the item being molded caused him nausea and discomfort. The store refers him to the company that produced the nationally known brand of the sour cream product. Through his battles with both companies, Billy demanded a settlement of $1,200; and eventually during the haggling, $3,000 dollars to cover his loss of wages. That was strange as we do not show him working during the time of his injurious claim. Both companies refused to compensate him for the claim, and he ends all correspondence with threats to take civil actions against these businesses, once again civil actions. With all of his steps in this complaint, Billy never told anyone why he ate cream cheese that was covered with mold, as most of us would not eat that damaged product.

Over the next year, Billy continued to increase his aggressive and unusual actions. On one occasion, he was stopped by the local police for throwing rocks at vehicles and people in one of the major intersections in town. After that problem, he was stopped in a major retail business as he was seen to be pouring flammable liquid over items in the store. On being confronted, he engaged in a struggle with the security personnel at the store that resulted in no arrest for this incident. The next incident was at a convenience store where he was seen pouring ammonia on the coffee counter of the store. We move on to another charge of disorderly conduct where he is charged with the minor crime and released at the scene. Finally, Billy is seen at the Food Stamp office pouring ammonia on the floor from a small jar while making the statement he was going to blow up a store. Each and all of these were considered minor events being created by a goofy person who was not really a danger to others. With the systems and techniques of law enforcement at that time, there was no method to allow one officer to discover the other incidents had ever occurred or that Mr. Ferry was earning frequent flyer points for his offenses. Each of these incidents in the first six months prior to the Fourth of July holiday were handled in the best legal fashion for that moment in time; the outcome of that information would change in a very short time.

Along with all of these incidents was one that occurred just seven days before the crime when Billy was in the grocery store that he would set afire; that is correct, just one week prior to the crime was the date of this comment. While paying for his items, Billy told the cashier that he had recently witnessed a grocery store clerk being covered with gasoline and set on fire. When the cashier questioned him about the statement, Billy simply walked out of the grocery store, the future crime scene. Would this make you believe that the crime of arson and the murder of five innocent people were premeditated and not a momentary mental lapse of sanity?

Before we finish our biography of this fine young man, we need to speak of another strange time in his life. From sometime in 1965 through 1980, Billy had a common-law wife whom he lived with during a continually rocky relationship. The two of them lived in the poor side of our town but mostly lived up in the national forest where that other county continued to issue worthless check warrants, and other minor crimes were committed by this criminal. During their life, they had a child together; a boy who would end up being raised by Billy's parents as a result of child abuse complaints on Billy and his lady; her own two daughters from a previous marriage were also taken from her. This soul mate woman was Susan Elaine Hallowell who, being three years younger than Billy, had continual physical confrontations with her good man, the arsonist. While living in the forest, they stayed in a small trailer that had a wooden room attached to one end of the structure. The property was owned by Billy's parents providing these two their own private residence. The conditions of this location were once described in a newspaper article about this crime with even that reporter, a professional writer, having trouble finding words to define that bad environment; Billy's tent at the time of his arrest may have been cleaner. After many arguments and fights, Susan left Billy and went back to her mother's house on the east coast of our state. One day in May of 1980, Billy met up with her so he could give her a ride; it was the last time she was ever seen by her family or anyone. To this day, nobody knows where she may be or if she is even alive today. The county of the lovely couple's home site has her listed in an active investigation as a missing person, still missing even after searching and digging around their home without locating a single clue.

## THE EMOTIONS FROM A BADGE

Over the years, I have attempted to locate this missing woman based on information from her previous arrest and reports from the various law enforcement agencies. This missing lady has used the names of Susan Hallowell, Susan Ferry, and Susan Miller; while during the time she as Susan Miller, she had two daughters by the same last name. With all of my searches over the twenty-eight years since the crime, these investigative request for information that should help locate the woman have always come back with blank answers leading one to believe that she no longer exists. If you know this lady, or if you are this lady, please get in touch with your local law enforcement agency so we can close that active missing person investigation. Let us all hope that she survived that trip with Billy to that wide open and thickly wooded national forest.

The investigation was finally complete with the evidence processed at the lab, interviews completed, crime scene documented, and the life of Billy Ferry all combined into a very large report; and with everything finished, the entire documentation was all placed on a shelf at the office. Billy was alive and well but still locked up in the state mental hospital with all of us awaiting the medical approval for his return for trial. The five young ladies were each buried in a closed casket ceremony because their bodies were so grossly distorted; their loved ones could not bear to see the remnants of this vicious crime. I am sure that their families still display photographs in their homes, especially the one with that little girl in her bright red cowgirl hat. The great frustration of wearing a badge is often the impatience while waiting for the arrival of lady justice.

One year later in July of 1984, the mental hospital ruled that Billy could be returned to the county jail as he was mentally able to assist with his defense. The court process was then in motion allowing only nine months of legal arguments before the new judge would issue the order that Billy Ferry was competent to assist with his trial. Finally, we had the great news of a date being set for the trial to begin, a date that would be over two years since the night of the burning crime.

With all of the other twist and turns of this investigation, we have to look at the next little interruption for the prosecutors in this case. During the election previous to the trial date, our long-term state attorney Mr. E. J. had lost his seat to a new group of previous federal prosecutors. In some ways, this was a big loss to our community as Mr. E. J. had been an excellent prosecutor and is an outstanding person. Many people and several investigators from numerous law enforcement agencies, including federal people, believe Mr. E. J. was associated with some of the historical members of our local organized crime organizations that date back to the Roaring Twenties, some even believe he has been involved in criminal wrongdoings. With my involvement in more than one of these investigations into corruption and with my several generations of family living in this area creating a wide knowledge of the people and their history in this community, I know that all of these allegations are totally unfounded especially based on the other investigators adjustments of the truth and on their incompetent investigations. When Mr. E. J., now an appellate court judge, stands next to the local Catholic bishop, I can assure you that he is even a better man than the outstanding bishop, Mr. E. J. is a man of honor.

With the change of command and staff at the State Attorney's Office, there was not a single person with knowledge of this ongoing investigation. The new state attorney Mr. Bill decided to assign his longtime associate in federal prosecutions and the new assistant state prosecutor Mr. Lee to prosecute this case; Mr. Lee had a lot to read to get caught up to date on this major investigation. In federal courts, the chief investigator of the crime is allowed to stay in the courtroom during the trial to assist with the prosecution in contrast to the state law that requires the investigator, like all witnesses, to remain out of the courtroom during trial; Mr. Bill was going to have me stay in the courtroom to help with the prosecution. Wow! I would sit in the courtroom as my investigation was presented to the jury, which very rarely happens in my state.

The first step in this process was to decide how the case would be presented to the jury. To my surprise, the first decision was for Mr. Lee to be the only prosecuting attorney so that he would present to the jury the prosecution's case was so outstanding that only one person was needed to present the tribunal. The presentation, or maybe the casting for the Broadway show, was in the beginning of the steps that would create the methods that would be used in the courtroom. The trial would now begin in August of 1985, just over two years after the crime.

At the beginning of the trial, Mr. Lee presented to Judge Manuel the need for this detective to be allowed to stay in the courtroom to assist him with the case. Over the objections of the two public defenders, Mr. Craig and Mr. Wayne, the judge ruled that based on the recent changes in the State Attorney's Office and the short time to prepare for this major case, there was a need for me to stay in the courtroom. In this and only this case, the judge allowed me to sit with the prosecutor and witness a trial of one of my investigations, what an education.

The first step in any trial is to pick the jury. This is done by bringing in a group of citizens that have shown up for their call to jury duty, so the prosecutor and the defense attorney can each ask the potential juror questions to determine their eligibility. When you have the citizen responding with answers of how every killer should be executed or they knew he was guilty because they saw the news reports, they can be dismissed with cause. Other possible jurist can be dismissed if the attorneys present a reason that the judge will allow the dismissal such as a person who has worked their entire life as a cashier at a grocery store. Each side also has a number set by the judge of how many prospective jurors they can decline without justification. So if you do not like a person simply by the way they dress, you absolutely do not want a man in a purple suit and white socks to serve on a jury, he's gone. With the process completed, the jury consisted of twelve peers and a couple of alternates so that if the need were to arise, one could replace a main juror. Now we need to expand on the definition of the word peers for the defendant Billy Ferry; as we all know, this would require a very lax and wide definition as these peers were good citizens, fortunately not many people are like him. With the jury seated, it is time for the next step.

To start the trial, each attorney has to stand before the jury and give their opening statements. As in all trials, the prosecutor will tell you how horrible the terrible criminal was to have committed the outrageous crime, and that this treacherous criminal should be found guilty and punished for this unforgivable wrongdoing. The defense attorney will give you the information of how the poor misunderstood and unjustly accused person should not be held responsible for an error of judgment as we must forgive any and all mistakes so we can continue to live in our perfect world. The presentation from the defense almost made me feel sorry for poor Billy having to endure this unjust prosecution until the photographs of the charred victims resurrected the smell of the burning flesh. After instructions and rulings and various other legal actions, it was now time to present the testimony and the evidence.

The prosecutor, Mr. Lee, was an experienced and very intelligent lawyer who had come to our state from his hometown up in Michigan to work as a federal prosecutor. He knew his stuff and did a good job as he presented the information to the jury. The defense attorneys, Mr. Craig and Mr. Wayne, were also very experienced and very good attorneys. With this case, they were prepared to show everyone that Billy was mentally insane and could not be held responsible for this crime. With Mr. Lee being the rough and gruff prosecutor demanding justice and freedom while Mr. Craig and Mr. Wayne seemed the warm and friendly neighbors who wanted to help the poor man with his challenge. The old statement that all the world is a stage sure came alive during this trial, and each and every one of the lawyers should have received the Oscar award for best actor that year. They are all three, and each one is a very good person and a high-quality attorney.

Now with the defense team looking at showing that the defendant was not legally sane to be held responsible for this crime, we had to prepare to fight the McNaughton rule. At this time, you must be asking everyone, the what? Well, this is a rule in the legal community that was based on the first famous legal test for insanity that came in an 1843 trial when in that case, an Englishman Daniel McNaughton was trying to kill Prime Minister Robert Peel of the United Kingdom when he shot and killed the secretary of that British prime minister. This act was based on Mr. McNaughton believing that Prime Minister Robert Peel was conspiring against him. The British courts acquittal of McNaughton was defined as "reason of insanity," then sending him to a mental institution to live the rest of his life. The outcome of this case caused a public uproar that required Queen Victoria to issue orders for the court to develop a stricter test for insanity. With the many adjustments and changes of this law by the courts and the legislators, and probably even rulings of some social organizations and bingo clubs, the law as always has been continually adjusted for centuries. With all of these changes throughout history still to this date, the basic tenet of this law remains the mental ability for one to know right from wrong at the time of the offense. In this case, one would have to ask if Billy did not know right from wrong when he fled from the burning crime scene; why would an insane man run and hide from his capital felony crime?

The next action that should be mentioned is that when a defendant goes to trial, the attorneys go out of their way to make sure the accused is dressed up and cleaned up to look like a good law-abiding citizen. This often changes the motorcycle gang member by shaving his beard, cutting his hair, and covering all of his tattoos, some that praise Satan, to look so much like the choir director from your church. Let us remember that Billy's attorneys were using the insanity defense in this trial. With that approach, Billy kept his wild long hair scattered above his full beard while dressed in his jailhouse denim blue uniform that would alone make a person look a little different, maybe even crazy and downright scary. It shows another smart move by those high-quality attorneys on his defense team.

The next stage of the trial has the prosecutor presenting his side of the case with everything indicating the defendant is guilty. Mr. Lee moved forward with the employees and customers that were at the store on the night of the fire. The victims and the witnesses each and all testified that Billy had entered the store, threw the gasoline, lit the fire, and committed the crime before he fled from the scene while the building and the people burned. Even Eli who had half of his body burned in the crime, who recovered in the burn unit as he screamed in pain and watched the other victims die from their burns testified about the crime. The fact that Billy committed the crime was not a difficult task to prove to the jury. When the prosecutor would finish with his witness, the defense would question that same person. The defense did not attack the witnesses or victims during their examination of these people. Many of the questions again were directed about how crazy the defendant acted while committing the crime. When the defense is complete, the prosecutor has the right to once again question the witness. The aggressive Mr. Lee took great care in moving these good folks through their appearance in court.

One point that was raised by Mr. Lee was the incident where Billy bought the molded cream cheese. When Billy tried to obtain benefits through this complaint, neither of the companies were willing to help him; he could not profit from this allegation of a bad product. When he lost that battle, Billy threatened to take civil action and maybe retaliate for the lack of concern. One of the witnesses repeated the statement that Billy said as he fled the burning store, "That will show those crazy bastards." Mr. Lee made many wonder if this might be the reason he attacked this store; was the firebombing an act of revenge?

Another witness called by Mr. Lee was a nurse who worked in the jail in that other county where Billy lived in the forest. She told the story of Billy being in jail and acting out and misbehaving during one incarceration. Eventually, he complained of medical problems that prevented him from walking. This required Billy to have a wheelchair for his weeks in detention. When the notification came that Billy was to be released, he stood up from the wheelchair and walked unassisted out of the facility. It was just another miracle cure.

Within the trial, the expert witnesses of law enforcement, fire rescue, crime scene, and lab technicians moved forward with all of the correct answers and little controversy. The battles began when the prosecutors called their psychiatric witnesses to the stand. When a defendant is evaluated for their mental stability, the court usually appoints three psychiatric professionals to conduct the appraisal of the subject. You can bet your life savings that one of these doctors will swear the patient is totally insane and more that completely crazy. One of the others will tell you the defendant is perfectly sane and in no way could ever be crazy. That third person will break the tie, and you will never be able to guess which side this one will ride with for the mental stability of any defendant. For this trial, the prosecution and defense provided their own experts to define the sanity of our individual. We must now remember the McNaughton rule of knowing right from wrong in contrast of our own opinion of the sanity of a person who burns five people to death, just because the act is wrong does not mean legal insanity.

In the prosecution presentation, Mr. Lee called several psychiatrists to the stand to provide their opinion of the sanity of the defendant. All of the doctors for both the prosecution and the defense agreed that Billy was an acute, chronic, paranoid, and schizophrenic person but were split on their opinion if he was legally sane at the time he committed the crime. Dr. Gerald said that Billy was very well aware that the crime was wrong and therefore was legally sane at the time of the crime where he fled the scene to avoid arrest. During Dr. Gerald's examination, Billy told him on more than one occasion that he would not answer any of the questions; he would only talk to his attorney or his own doctor. Billy must have thought it would be wrong to discuss with this good doctor his criminal involvement in a terrible felony arson that killed five people.

During the trial, several psychiatrists testified about the mental condition of Billy at the time of the crime. Each of these doctors provided their own individual opinion of Billy's sanity at the time of the murders based on that McNaughton definition of the law. By the time this entire group had testified, they all agreed that Billy was as stated before an acute, chronic, paranoid, and schizophrenic person; and on his status at the time of the crime, they each had a different opinion. Based on their testimony, it was about a half and half opinion on his knowledge of right from wrong when he committed the crime, the crime where he ran from the burning people to escape into the dark night to prevent being arrested for these murders.

The most interesting psychiatrist to testify was Dr. Emanuel who was from another state. When he testified for the defense, he insisted that poor Billy had no idea that his actions at the time of the crime were wrong. Mr. Lee was concerned about this good doctor evaluating the defendant in our good state resulting in him asking the doctor if he was licensed to practice medicine in our state. The good doctor explained he was licensed in three other states with Mr. Lee again asking about our state. The doctor answered that he was not licensed in our state, and the objections took over the moment. After many disagreements, the judge allowed the prosecutor to challenge the doctor's right to be conducting business in our little town. I was a very good show in the courtroom that day.

During the trial, I took the stand on several occasions to testify about information that I knew about the crime. One piece of evidence was Billy's bucket that the state lab stated it tested positive for having contained gasoline. The main point was my testimony about the lighter that had been recovered from Billy at the time of his arrest. This was one of the typical plastic lighters that can be bought at the counter of so many stores. These lighters have the ability to adjust the length of the flame, allowing a person to ignite an object at a close or long distance, depending on the length of that flame; on striking the lighter, it showed the jury that long length of the flame. With this lighter being set at the longest length for the lighter's flame, it would create a distance that would place the person holding it at the furthest from the point of ignition. This would provide a safe distance from igniting maybe a cloud of gas fumes and liquid without that person being engulfed in the explosion. A person who had worked in the engine room of a tugboat, around the fuel stored on the boat, maybe they would know that the person who lit the fire would need to be at a safe distance from the ignition. This could be a person who would surely know right from wrong when he burned those five young ladies to death.

With the prosecutor completing his presentation of the guilty person, it was now time for the defense to present their side of the how this pitiful man needed help and understanding for his simple mistake. Let me tell you that these attorneys Mr. Craig and Mr. Wayne were more than good; they did an outstanding job with their presentation to the jury. They displayed themselves as warm and respectful gentlemen who were desperate to help everyone comprehend the problems that forced the defendant to have a deep mental problem that prevented him from realizing that his mistake was wrong. It was a trophy-winning presentation.

They brought their psychiatrists to the stand to counter the prosecutors, one was the doctor Mr. Lee attacked, and told the jury of Billy's mental problems based on the doctor's professional opinions. Mr. Craig was so humble with his own professional presentation that as he moved forward, one could only begin to feel sorry for little Billy, the murdering firebomber.

The defense brought on the members of the Ferry family to testify about the problems and changes in the defendant's life. They talked of the injury to his head on the tugboat and how he was different since that time. Billy often spoke of how the Russians were secretly poisoning the people of America through food, drinks, and other chemicals. Billy felt that everyone wearing red was one of those Russians that had a secret room hidden in the grocery store that he set on fire, the store with a red in color logo.

With all of his aggressions and arguments with the family, they tried to get help through law enforcement and mental health officials. They were told that Billy was not a danger to a point that they could force him to undergo any treatment for their concerns. On one occasion, they talked Billy into going to a mental health facility for an evaluation of his problems. That counselor told Billy that he could leave for the night and return the following day, as Billy claimed a job interviewed was scheduled for the following morning. The family was again advised they could not force Billy to stay followed by his father telling the facility that Billy would not ever return, and Mr. Ferry was correct; Billy never came back for the help.

Another witness for the defense was Billy Ferry himself, ready and willing to tell his side of the story. As he sat on the stand, wiggling, smiling, and often belching, Billy told the jury that the Russians were contaminating America, so this forced him to spread radioactive particles throughout the community. These particles would destroy the dangerous chemical agents being spread by our enemies. Billy knew that the contaminants were being spread in our food and our drinks, and that by eating, this would chemically castrate him, his family, and everyone. Billy knew that if you wore red, you were one of these Russians who were so dangerous to everyone. With all of this, he could not take it anymore, so he firebombed the grocery store stating that "war is hell," and he dealt the Russians a blow they would never forget. Billy told quite a story as he sat there showing all that watched that he was a very crazy man, or was he.

Eventually, the defense presented an excellent case that Billy was not a normal person and was out of his mind on that horrible night. They never argued that he had committed the crime; their entire presentation was that he was not sane at the time of the offense, therefore innocent by reason of insanity. With the defense finished with their presentation, it was time for closing arguments.

When both sides have completed their presentations, each is then allowed to make a closing argument, or a speech, to explain to the jury what has been presented by both sides. These are truly well-presented orations by the lawyers to help convince the jurors that they are correct, and the other lawyer is wrong. Mr. Lee spoke of the bad killer who committed the horrible crime against the innocent victims, ending with their obligation to find the killer guilty as charged. Mr. Craig wore his little old man sweater as he and Mr. Wayne expressed the sad story of how poor Billy should be forgiven over his mistake because he was insane at the time he committed the crime that he did not know was wrong; the jury had to find Billy innocent by reason of insanity. If the presentations had been judged at a gymnastic event, each attorney would have all scored a ten for their routines.

With all of the talking completed, the judge then instructed the jury on their requirements based on the law. With these instructions, the group was sent to the jury room and sequestered until they can reach a final decision. The discussion by the peers on the jury was now in progress.

The trial had taken eleven days to present the evidence to the jury, and that jury took two hours and fifteen minutes to decide the verdict. With the courtroom full of family members, those of Billy and those of the many victims, and so many other people interested in this case, the verdicts were read for the five charges of murder and the one count of arson, he was guilty on each and every charge. While the verdict was being read, Billy, now a convicted murderer, sat quietly in his chair at the defense table stretching his arms and yawning. His response was a display of boredom, the reaction of the victims to his crime was much more painful, much more deadly.

With a capital felony conviction, the next step requires a penalty recommendation hearing. During this phase, each attorney presents their case on the need for a recommendation of execution or the need for forgiveness and preventing an execution. Each side has to face the challenge by convincing the jury that their side has the best answer, life or death.

The prosecution presented some witnesses that testified to the condition of the victims burned in the fire. Mr. Lee's first witness was this detective who described the mangled body of Leigh Ann Carter at the crime scene. This detailed description of the morbid sight was as difficult to state as it was for those in the courtroom to hear; then the photographs of the victims were presented to the jury. The second person to testify was the nurse from the burn unit who treated the other victims of the crime. Her description was a story that contained such a disgusting description of the injuries and pain from the burns. The nurse also told how Jennifer Vance, the little four-year-old girl, kept pulling the medical tubes from her body, as if the little girl wanted to die. The objection to that statement was overruled by the judge.

With the completion of the prosecution's presentation, it was now time for the defense to provide their side of the story. Several psychiatrists again testified about the mental stability of the convicted murderer with all agreeing on his severe mental problem. The best action of the defense attorneys was a videotape of the nine-year-old son of Billy Ferry talking about his father. The boy testified that his daddy was as good as he could be to him with the attorney requesting what he meant by that comment and receiving the reply of "since he is so sick." The next statement was that he wanted to be able to visit his father. The comments from the little boy abandoned by his father, requiring his grandparents to raise him, were not as touching as the screams from the four-year-old girl as she ran out of the store fully engulfed in fire and then died after several days of suffering.

The next witness was Billy himself telling the jury that the Russians were trying to kill them with poison that causes stomach cancer. He told them they had made the biggest mistake of their lives, but that he understood that they were helpless because the Russians were controlling them with electronic actions. Mr. Craig and Mr. Wayne did a very good job of displaying a person who was crazy, the question for the jury was how crazy.

After the attorneys give their closing arguments, the jury again returned to the private room to provide a recommendation to the judge. It was once again time to wait for an answer from the jury. It was not a very long wait for the jury to return with their recommendation for the punishment for this horrible crime. This jury voted six to five to recommend life sentences for these vicious crimes; this action could prevent the defendant from receiving a death sentence.

A date was set for a sentencing hearing, and the court was adjourned for this difficult procedure. Judge Manuel would now have to wait for the presentence investigation before making a final decision for the sentencing on this case. Many were upset about the jury's decision prompting a drive for letters to be sent to the judge concerning the sentence on this offense; over a thousand letters reached the judge.

Between the trial and the sentencing hearing, a local television station had a half-of-an-hour talk show about the future sentencing. The local reporter had three guests to speak about the crime and to offer their opinion of the final decision. One of the guests was a state senator who had recently adjusted the state's death penalty law after a United States Supreme Court ruling on the death penalty. The good senator had very little to say about what should happen, only what could happen based on the law. The second person was Eli, the young bagboy who was now eighteen years old. We need to remember that as he stood there bagging groceries, he felt the gasoline splash on his body and saw it strike the five women; he looked back to see Billy ignite the lighter and set them all on fire. With his scars from the burns, the memory of the tragic deaths and the horrible remembrance of the pain he believed that Billy should receive the death penalty. The third person was one of the jurors that had delivered an unbiased opinion as to the crime and the recommendation for sentencing. During her presentation that day, she made the statement that she was and has always been against death penalty; and with that opinion, she would not recommend that ultimate punishment. A jury should be a group of one's peers that does not have a preset opinion on any of the factors of the trial, the crime, the defendant, or the punishment. If she would never vote for a criminal to be executed, why did she not tell the attorneys so she would not have been qualified to serve on that panel? Based on her statement, her prejudice against the law created an injustice for the outcome of this trial. It is shameful that an American citizen would have such total disregard for our laws. We should always wonder if her shameful misconduct altered the outcome of this most serious violation of the law, the violation of murder of five murders.

With the calendar reaching the date for sentencing, Judge Manuel prepared for that hearing to complete this case. From the bench, the judge advised that he had received a large number of correspondences containing many opinions for the resolution of the sentence all of which would not be considered for his final opinion. The judge did have these letters made part of the official record of this trial. The next action was to allow the victim's family members speak to the court where they expressed their grief while begging for the defendant to be put to death. The statements and some similar opinion letters were included in the presentence investigation. That information would be used to justify the judge's final decision on the sentencing.

The prosecution made a statement requesting the death sentence that included a petition with 1,300 signatures demanding death for the criminal. There was very little else that could be presented to the courts; the desire was to send the defendant to death row.

After that presentation, the defense provided their information to prevent that death sentence that was a statement by Billy Ferry. The ramblings began with Billy claiming that Ronald Reagan, the current president at that time, was a communist who was poisoning the country with stomach cancer; that the convenience stores with red signs were hypnotizing Americans, also all beer has been poisoned and causes brain cancer, and that he was the victim of monitoring of his thoughts. When the court started to announce the sentence, Billy interrupted the judge advising the Russians were coming on strong in a different and new color—blue. Though his comments were strange what should be the punishment for such a horrible crime.

It was now Judge Manuel's turn to decide; he spoke with the confidence and conviction of a dedicated judge as he adjudicated Billy guilty on all six counts and sentenced him to death on each of the five murders and to thirty years for the arson. To many in our community, the judge had made the proper decision to put this vicious and rabid animal to death, a death that would be less painful, less horrible, less terrible than each or any of the fine young ladies who suffered from those extremely painful burns that destroyed their bodies. Lady Justice had balanced her scale for this crime; it was now time to wait for her to use the sword. Justice is not swift in our great nation.

Billy was sent off to death row at the state prison to wait for the next of many actions that would result from the order to execute him. The next step in any death penalty case is for the defendant to appeal the horrible injustice inflicted upon them by the court. This was of course filed within the next year of the conviction by a public defender from another county that was appointed to assist Billy on his appeal of this case. The public defender noted seven violations of the court procedures that should be considered for the judgment to be overturned and a new trial granted to correct these errors. The victims were not able to appeal their own death; there are no appeals from a grave.

The first complaint was that Billy under the Sixth Amendment to the Constitution had the right but was not present during the selection of the jury. His absence from the courtroom was with his own agreement to be out of the court so that he could rest when the attorneys were debating about the jury member who was to be selected from the jury pool. When this occurred, the judge received acknowledgement from the defense attorney indicating the defendant wanted to leave the courtroom.

Item number two was that the psychiatrist Dr. Gerald had testified that Billy would only speak to his own attorney and his own doctor. The law does not allow the jury to hear that a defendant invoked their rights to remain silent based on the Fifth Amendment to the Constitution; was this a statement to a doctor or an invocation of his rights?

This takes us to the third objection that Mr. Lee the prosecutor should not have attacked the psychiatrist Dr. Emanuel for not being licensed in our state. The challenging of the state license was damaging to his professional evaluation based on his qualifications.

Step four resulted in the court not allowing the defense to address the statements of the prosecution witnesses during the rebuttal phase of the trial. These witnesses testified that Billy often appeared to be faking his medical and mental problems. The defense was sure these needed to rebut the rebuttal, or easier said argue some more.

Finally, it was my presence that should require the Supreme Court to overturn this case with the fifth objection being that the case detective, a witness who would testify in the trial, was permitted by the judge to stay in the courtroom during the procedure. This is not the normal course, and even though by law the witnesses cannot stay in the courtroom, this can be allowed by the judge based on necessary justification as defined under the state law. With the new prosecutor walking in on this case at the last moment, the judge did allow me to stay to assist the attorney.

The sixth objection was that the jury should have been selected in a process where only one potential juror was present at the time of questioning. This was raised based on one of the potential jurors asking if Billy was really crazy then he could have just thrown water on the people. The defense claim was this tainted the other prospective jurors who may have heard the statement.

The final complaint was that the judge overruled the life recommendation of the jury with a death sentence. The objections indicated that this could only be done if the judge could "provide facts suggesting a sentence of death should be so clear and convincing that virtually no reasonable person could differ." This public defender did not feel that Judge Manuel had sufficient grounds when he stated in the sentencing hearing that this crime was a deliberate act with the appeal stating that "deliberate acts are not necessarily cold, calculated, and premeditated acts without any pretense of moral or legal justification." The attorney must not have felt that viciously burning to death five innocent young ladies who risked their lives by going grocery shopping would be a "cold, calculated, and premeditated acts without any pretense of moral or legal justification. Even though the trial judge did not, the jury could have realized this in reaching its life recommendation. " At this point, I should apologize to you for allowing you to become aware of the irrationality of our legal system; it seems the paper on which the Constitution of the United States of America was written continues to fade based on the actions and rulings of our Judicial Branch of the government.

It was April 30, 1986 when our state Supreme Court issued a ruling on the appeal from Billy's attorney, nearly four years after the crime. The court addressed the issue of Billy not being in the courtroom during the discussions over the selections of the jurors. They decided that the absence of Billy was a voluntary waiver of his right to be in the courtroom and recommended that a judge obtain a stronger documented statement in future cases. The second part was for the objection of Dr. Gerald telling about only talking to his lawyer and his doctor. This opinion was that this was a harmless statement that did not affect the verdict by the jury. The other objections to the actions within the initial phases of the trial were ruled "meritless and unworthy of discussion." The conviction of the five murders and the arson crime were all upheld by the court ruling.

The final step in the court ruling was the validity of Judge Manuel issuing the death sentence for the murders. The court ruled that the jury's recommendation of life was a reasonable recommendation based on the "valid and mitigating factors" described in the transcript. They included in the order that "reasonable people could differ on what penalty should be imposed" on this horrible crime, so the override recommendation by Judge Manuel was an "improper" action. The Supreme Court vacated the death sentences and ordered that the defendant should be returned to court to have life sentences imposed in accordance to the recommendation of the jury. Billy would not be executed for the five murders; this ruling would place him in prison for the rest of his life. Over these years, many people made decisions on how Billy would live the rest of his life; only Billy decided that five innocent ladies should burn to death for grocery shopping.

With time moving forward rushing toward thirty years since the crime, the Fourth of July holiday always brings back some bad memories. Had it not been for this crime, Leigh Ann would be a college graduate celebrating her forty-sixth birthday while she was raising her own family. Martha Vance and Melody Darlington would be in their mid-fifties continually shopping at the local grocery store as like us all preparing to celebrate every holiday. Misty McCullough would also be in her mid-forties out of high school and through college to celebrate the holidays also with her own family. Little Jennifer Vance would have grown up to be in her mid-thirties with a family that would have made her mother Martha a grandmother. By this time, that little red cowgirl hat would only be remembered when someone dragged that old picture out of the closet. None of these people not a single solitary one should have been the victim of a murder. They should not have had to deal with the terror, the fear, and the pains from those horrific burns to their bodies. These ladies all deserve to and should be alive today; grocery shopping should not be a fatal risk.

During these years, many things have occurred that have a connection to this offense. Leigh Ann's mother never recovered from the shock of her daughter's death. The emotional trauma changed her into a person who could barely speak as she starred with such a blank look. She and her husband have both now passed away leaving their son as the only family member who is still alive and who is still angry over the murder of his sister.

Eli has grown up to create his own family and continue to be a very good citizen. On one of the many anniversaries of the crime, he was interviewed by one of the local news stations about this terrible offense. The grocery store has moved to another shopping plaza, but as he stood in the old parking lot of the crime, he spoke of the incident. He stood there very strong as he answered the reporter's questions explaining how he has moved on and does not care now that Billy was not sent to death row. The important thing to him was to move forward with his own life with his family. While watching the interview, I looked into his eyes; it was easy to see the sorrow and pain were still within his body; the body with a back that is still covered with the burn scars.

The many other victims that lived through this atrocity have all moved forward with their own lives and have continued to overcome this tragedy. The loved ones left behind by those five young ladies have also moved on with their own lives still missing their ladies. No matter the outcome of this horrible crime, nothing can relieve the anguish of these people. Even the death penalty causing an execution of the criminal would not give them the only relief that would help these fine people; the only relief would be the return of their loved one.

The Ferry family has also suffered when people in the community made false allegations against his young brother. The crimes were investigated, and eventually, he was cleared on any wrongdoing in these reports. It was sad to have his brother attacked for the problems that Billy had created on his own. The brother has grown up to be a good person who has his own business and his own family. The whole family has moved forward as best could be expected for the problems they had to face.

The young son of Billy has his own problems that would cause one to wonder if there is a need for intervention. In February of 1991, almost eight years after the firebombing that sent his father to jail for 125 years, the fourteen-year-old boy was arrested in the same area of his father's crime carrying a bottle of gasoline that contained a fuse. The juvenile court resolved this to the best benefit of the young lad. Now in his mid-thirties, just a few years older than Jennifer Vance would be if she were alive today, the young man has been arrested five different times for driver's license violations, domestic violence charges, and of course just like dad, bad check offenses. Looking at his booking photograph, it is easy to see the father's face in the young man.

After many years had passed, I had the opportunity to meet with Major John after his retirement from the Sheriff's Office. As we set with numerous friends and some relatives by marriage, we chatted about several of our cases as we sipped on a large cup of Cuban coffee, strait, strong and dark coffee. Major John told everyone that after the arrest of Billy Ferry, he made sure that I was never involved with transporting the suspect at any time to any location. My response was to question why he would not allow that action with his answer being that he knew that my involvement would definitely cause Billy to be shot and killed while trying to escape. The response to his answer was again to ask why he did not allow that to occur; the good man jumped from his chair and expressed to everyone you see it was obvious what I would do just exactly that to the killer. The major made one mistake in his entire career of over thirty plus years in law enforcement; he should have allowed me, the SWAT team trained sniper, to transport that disgusting criminal.

At the beginning, I told you that this would be a horrible story that would most likely upset you based on the horrors and the outcome of this crime. To me, this was more than the worst of crimes as the victims were not doing anything that should have caused them to be a victim. These ladies were not working a dangerous job, partying with a group of armed drug dealers, committing a crime, or out in the wee dark hours of the night; the risk taken by each and all of us was they were grocery shopping at eight o'clock in the evening. These poor victims were not simply murdered; they were tortured to death by the horrible and continual pains from the fire that destroyed their bodies. Death came to these girls at an early age not allowing them to live the good life that each of them would have obtained if they had been allowed to continue with their life. Billy Ferry did not even face his victims to challenge them to a fight; the dirty coward snuck up behind them and threw gas on them as they were trapped in the area of the cash register kiosk. In the end, he did not offer a justifiable reason to destroy and kill these innocent people.

Today, Billy Ferry lives in the state prison. The conditions of his cell are cleaner than his campsites; the food is better than his can of sardines. He is serviced for all of his needs at the tax payers' expense. His daily routine in prison is a better environment than what he had on the streets living in the dirt. Nobody can argue that Billy is not a person who has some mental problems. With all of his actions, it is easy to see that he may not have the severe problems that he displays when he knows that someone is watching him. Knowing the whole story, one would have to wonder if Billy did not plot and plan to achieve an easier life in prison than the harder one that he struggled with on the streets. With this approach, the challenged man did not have anything to lose, just a large benefit by living in prison. In the end, did Billy pulled a scam on all of us by killing those fine young ladies only for his own benefit?

Remember to give a big hug to your family, your loved ones, your friends because we can never know if they will ever have to face a most ghastly event. Let's take a breath and maybe get a refill on what you are drinking before we move on to the next story. By the way, let us never forget the victim of a horrible crime, keeping their memory alive in a smile is the best for all of us left behind.

# An Expert Witness

Please let me throw a little tangent in here to add to these wild stories.

Now on this one day, it became obvious that it was going to be a very busy day for this homicide detective. The court had ordered that the serial murder be taken out for a medical examination to evaluate if he had a medical condition which caused him to kill his ten victims. Well, I guess that if you are a serial murder, you are a very sick person. It is too bad they do not use the best medical treatment to immediately heal this horrible condition, a lethal injection.

Well, several detectives and other deputies formed a group to transport this very dangerous killer to the required medical assessment. We went to the jail where he was being held in a very secure location separated from the other inmates. The serial murderer was in a special group of three cells that were detached from the general population.

The guestbook at this jail block showed the serial murder was residing in the middle cell of the line of three. On one side of his cell was an inmate who was involved in a major smuggling operation. That was the investigation where we had to live in freezing weather in an orange grove on a stakeout for several days while his group landed over twenty tons of marijuana in our county. On the other side was the firebombing criminal that I had also arrested for the mass murder. The very grungy, nasty caveman looking individual who threw gasoline on the customers of a grocery store and lit them on fire. We need to remember that in his crime, about thirty people were injured by the flames, five of which suffered and died from the extremely painful burns. These three county jail guests were not participating members of any church social groups.

As I watched the serial murderer being dressed and chained for transportation, I could hear, "Psst, psst, Mr. Cribb," coming from the firebomber's cell. As I looked in his direction, he wiggled his finger in a motion to have me come to talk with him. I walked over to his cell and was greeted by my other previous customer. The mass murderer pointed at the serial murder and said in a low voice, "That guy is crazy!" Now would that not be a person, a firebombing mass murderer, who could be certified as an expert court witness on being crazy. Geese Louise!

# Family Dispute

Now let us get ready for another rough story about a family tragedy. Yep, a refill on our drinks before we go into this amazing tale.

History has shown that every family will occasionally have one of those moments where they have a disagreement; some may even grow into an argument. As a family, we must always remember the most important ideal of *familia prima*—yes, that is my little knowledge of Italian saying family first. The main thing that I have learned is to simply tell my wife, "Yes, dear, you are correct." That got me in trouble one time when she asked, "Correct about what?" Without having paid any attention to her first statement, my answer to the second proved that I was not listening to her. That more than proved she was correct, and this man was more than wrong; my great wife resolved that concern immediately and completely forever. Well, let's talk about the other people in the world rather than this foolish man.

Throughout my career, the response to the many domestic arguments was a continuous task. The important resolution is to correct these problems in a manner that prevents any one side of the battle killing the other. This resolution of arguments requires the incident to be investigated by the homicide detectives. On this one special day as the summer season was rushing to an end, just one day before the autumn equinox, it was time to investigate one of these dreadful incidents.

While sitting in the office completing some paperwork, the receptionist transferred a call to me from the FBI Memphis,

Tennessee office. The special agent on the line was inquiring about a multiple murder that had occurred in our county on the previous day. The response was a simple answer of we did not have a multiple murder yesterday, did we? The FBI agent told the story of their office receiving several telephone calls from a man in Tennessee. The gentleman has told them that his brother-in-law is on the run from Florida and is driving northbound to his family in Tennessee. The reason for the flight is that he killed several family members down in a small town in Florida. The agent then told me the name of the town; as best as he could translate, the spelling was W-h-y-m-a-o-m-a, spelled Wimauma. The agent was corrected with the pronunciation of y-ma-ma and informed that was a community in our county. The informant stated that the relative's last name was George, and the only address that he had for the crime scene was a post office box number and no physical direction to the home. My response to that statement was that would be the correct information for that community, the agent saw no humor in my remark that it had to be a real big post office box to commit a murder in, not a single giggle from that man. With the information documented and phone numbers exchanged, we both moved forward to continue our investigations.

Let us start with some history and a description of our small community of Wimauma. Way back in 1902, a gentleman decided to start in small community out in the distant woods of our very large county. This location was on the Seaboard Air Line Railroad track about halfway between Bradenton, Florida, and Turkey Creek, Florida. That narrows down the location for you as there is no doubt you know exactly where Turkey Creek is located in the beautiful Sunshine State of Florida. To help you a little, Turkey Creek is just up the tracks from Edison and further down the rails from Bradley Junction, so there you go, you have the exact concept of longitude and latitude coordinates for that location. Anyway, this good man decided to name the town after his three daughters, Willie, Maude, and Mary, by taking the beginning of each name to create WiMauMa. The town started with a grocery store, a post office, and a train station. Later in history, my father would be the telegraph operator at that little Seaboard Railroad station. To this date, the town of Wimauma is still way out and a far place further than anywhere; it is a very rural and serene community.

After briefing Lieutenant Richard and Sergeant Randy, we started to follow up on this news from the Volunteer State. One of the patrol deputies working that southern isolated area was a friend of mine, a good person who would one day become a homicide detective himself, was contacted to help us locate the residence. Deputy Kenneth contacted the postmaster to determine all that could be recovered from the federal documents of the United States Postal Service. The card for the post office box rental indicated the owner was a Tommy George who lived in the community. The directions to the home stated that the owner of the grocery store knew the location of the home, welcome to Wimauma.

At the grocery store, Deputy Kenneth was able to determine that the new owner had no idea how to locate the George residence. This did not stop the diligent investigator from contacting other residents who eventually gave him directions to the home. Deputy Kenneth followed the information by going that far bit down the road, just after the railroad track but before that place that sells them flowers and located the small dirt road to the south. This path took him to an old wooden home with a tin roof that was covered on the front with an open porch. On the front door was a handwritten note stating that Tommy George was going to kill himself. We were all heading south to this little house in the woods.

When we arrived at the residence, we discovered the house was locked up and secure. The note on the door was a confusing and concerning little document with some rambling about Tommy George possibly preparing to kill himself. On searching the yard, the nose of this little detective discovered some little red dots in the dirt, it was obviously blood. With the blood on the ground, the information from the FBI and the note on the door, we knew we had to check inside the home to see if anybody was injured and needed assistance. We immediately forced our way into the residence. For the three ladies found on the living room floor, it was too late to provide them any help. We did a quick search of the house to make sure no one else was hidden away that needed any help or were hiding to become a danger to our group. This search was negative for anybody else; the home appeared empty.

We contacted the Memphis FBI and were able to update one another. The news from up north was the suspect was barricaded in a relative's home with hostages, one of them being another brother-in-law who had also been shot at our crime scene. Then the worst news was provided indicating that the seven children who had been at the shooting scene were all missing. The call ended and another immediate and more detail search went through the entire residence. The good news was that none of the children were found at this scene. Later, we discovered that all of the children were safe and sound up in Tennessee; it never hurts to have a bit of good news pop up in a murder investigation.

At this point, we had to stop our investigation as the law required a search warrant to allow our entry into the crime scene. The original search was justified to verify the health and well-being of people who could have been trapped in the residence. After we discovered the three deceased victims and no living victims, we had to step away and get the legal right to enter the crime scene and conduct the investigation. We simply waited as the legal document was created, approved by the state attorney, and signed by a judge for the final serving of the warrant. The steps were completed, and the search warrant was served on that little old house in the woods.

On searching the residence, it was easy to determine that the victims had been placed in the living room after their death. All three of the ladies were lying next to each other, with their bodies aligned, indicating that the placement on the floor was after being moved from the original location. The first two bodies had a slight portion on top of the other person. The third was barely under the other two indicated she was placed at that location first. The bodies were covered with blankets and then pushed further together with a large rug around the three bodies. With the time of death being over twenty-four hours prior to that time, the lividity was enhanced with the internal blood settling to the lower portion of the bodies. This condition created the appearance of a very large bruise on the lowest part of the body. The hot and humid house that had been locked closed was also adding an environment that caused the swelling and rigor mortis, the stiffening of the body, to be moving quickly through its normal progress. The bodies were also starting the internal deterioration that when moved caused obnoxious gases to escape the bloated carcasses. The examination created an easy answer to the cause of death, multiple gunshot wounds.

The first body that had been brought into the living room was that of Carol George, the thirty-three-year-old wife of Tommy George. On her body were two bullet wounds with both being to the front of her body. The second lady, slightly atop the first, was Mary James, the fifty-four-year-old mother of Carol George and the mother-in-law of Tommy George. The body of Mary James contained seven bullet holes to the left side of her body and back. The dirt on the front of her body indicated that she had fell facedown into the dirt. The third body, again slightly atop the body of Mary James, was that of Janet Banks; she was the sister of Carol George and daughter of Mary James. This would define Janet as being the sister-in-law of Tommy George the shooter. Her body contained six bullet holes to the right front and right side of her body with an additional shotgun blast to her vaginal area, a total of seven shots. This last shotgun blast could be better understood knowing that Janet Banks had a family nickname, Cougar. That moniker could be used to best describe her personality. It was apparent that Tommy George was not fond of his sister-in-law.

The remainder of the scene was on the exterior of the residence in the area of the blood spots located earlier in the day. These spots were in the area where tire marks indicated a vehicle had been parked at that location, possibly at the time of the crime. With the night having already stolen the sun on that very long day, we decided to seal up the crime scene and finish processing the following day with Detective Lee being assigned that duty.

With the clock nearing midnight, we had determined that the Cumberland County Sheriff's Office in Crossville, Tennessee had taken the killer Tommy George into custody. His brother-in-law Donald Banks, who had been shot in the side and the arm, was in the local hospital; and all of the children, each and all not injured, were staying with relatives in the community. It was now time for some sleep, a power nap.

That following morning, my assignments covered the autopsies and the communications with the multiple agencies involved in the investigation. All of the people and the guns were in Crossville, and the vehicle used to flee the scene was in Forsyth, Georgia. The information was coming together, and the reservations were also completed for my trip up north. We should note here that part of the background check on Tommy George was very easy to accomplish by retrieving his employment application to become a detention deputy with our Sheriff's Office, he was not hired to fill that position.

That next morning, it was time to jump on an Eastern Airline flight to Atlanta, Georgia. That was an easy trip since my mother worked for Eastern as I was growing up, or say getting older, where we flew to the four corners of the globe. This one-and-a-half-hour flight was just the start of a long day of accomplishing very little in the investigation. The stop in Atlanta caused a two-hour layover before the one-hour flight left for Knoxville, Tennessee. It took just four and a half hours of flying that day. This created the next step of renting a car and another hour plus of driving to Crossville. Now Crossville is a small friendly town in the middle of a triangle of the cities of Knoxville, Nashville, and Chattanooga, not as small as Wimauma. With the long day of travel, it was a late afternoon arrival in this town nestled in the rivers and lakes on the mountainside, the middle crossroad of east meets west Tennessee. It was a quick meeting with the Sheriff to make arrangements for the events required on the following day.

During my many, many and more interviews on that following day, the stories were all used to complete a single tale. To make things easier, let us not go through each and every interview. The reason for this is based on the fact that so many people became involved as the events progressed during the time from the murders to the surrender of the killer and the travels through the many states. As the situation continued, many more relatives and friends became involved in trying to help everyone else. Remember now this is the mountains in the Volunteer State of Tennessee, so that is like everyone is some kind of relative.

Before we lay out this saga, let us define a few more people involved in this tale. There are two of Tommy George's sisters, Cindy and Sandy, both living in Crossville; and Cindy has a husband Bobby who also becomes involved in the story. The family outsiders will be the attorney Mr. McIntyre and of course the local Sheriff Billy Joe Hobson. The final group is the seven children who were at the home on the night of the murders. These were the four George boys: Adam, age fourteen; Brian, age twelve; Chuck, age ten; and David, age nine, along with the group are the two James girls: Big Holly, age five; Little Holly, age two; and finally, Donnie Banks, age eight. The James girls were family members that were being raised by their grandparents, with Carol James being grandma. Now stop right here and take a look at those ages from fourteen to two years of age, the witnesses of a tragedy. Children should never have to experience such a heartbreaking experience. So with this group defined, let us move on with the whole story.

It was early in the evening hours of that Sunday of September 19, 1985; that day was the thirty-fourth birthday of Tommy George, when Carol called her mother Mary James asking her to come over to the house. Apparently, they had no electricity, and she needed help moving food from the refrigerator. Mary told Carol that her sister Janet and her husband Donald were at her house, so they would all bring the three kids with them and help with the problem. On arriving at the house, the electricity was working because Tommy had been able to convince the electric company to turn the power back on, and he would pay the bill the very next day. With this financial problem, the argument between Carol and Tommy started to grow.

The seven kids were in and out of the house as they continued to play and have a good old time on that nice afternoon. The adults continued to argue with Mary and Janet jumping into the event totally agreeing with Carol and loudly arguing with Tommy. As the shouting continued, Carol decided she was going home with her mother and taking the boys with her. Tommy disagreed and said he was taking the boys with him and moving back to Tennessee. Donald was moving around the house avoiding the most current difference of opinions.

As they stood in the front yard, Mary told them that she was going to take the car, an AMC Hornet station wagon, that Tommy was buying from Mary's husband and drive her family to her house. With Tommy having the keys in his pocket, Janet went over and became physical with him while trying to remove the keys from his pocket. Tommy pushed her away and walked into the house with the keys still in his pocket.

By this time, the children were all in the parent's room watching television; the ladies were on the side of the house at the car, and Donald was closer to the front of the house. Tommy came walking back out of the house; he was carrying two guns: a rifle and a shotgun. It is it hard to define which lady was shot first, but all three received some of the projectiles. Carol was near the rear of the car when she was shot twice, with Mary exiting the driver's seat receiving seven bullets, and Janet closer to the rear of the driver's door where she was shot six times with the rifle. After that, Tommy fired the shotgun blast into Janet's vaginal area, with that shot appearing to express his anger toward his sister-in-law. As Donald was trying to go up to the porch, Tommy fired the two bullets that struck him, one in the side and the other in the elbow. Neither of the bullets that hit Donald was fatal, yet all of the women died from their wounds as they lay there in the front yard of that little home tucked away in the woods.

For a short time, Tommy seemed to wander around the front yard in a confused state. When he finally walked over to Donald, he said, "What have I done? What will I do now?" Donald did not know how to answer those questions; his response was asking if Tommy was going to kill him. The fortunate answer for Donald was that Tommy told him that he would not kill him. At this point, Tommy told Donald to go inside and wait.

While the shooting was in progress, the oldest George son, Adam, left the bedroom and looked out the window toward the car. By that time, the fourteen-year-old's mother was already on the ground, and his father was finishing the shooting of his grandmother and his aunt. He went back to the bedroom and told the other kids to stay in the room. After sending Donald into the house, Tommy came and got Adam to help him with the next step.

The two of them went outside and picked up Carol to bring her inside the house. While carrying his mother, Adam thought she was still alive. They went into the living room and softly placed the lady on the floor. As they went to bring in the grandmother, the second oldest boy, twelve-year-old Brian, came out of the room to check on his mother, where he determined that she was dead. At that point, he went out and helped his father and brother bring in their grandmother and then their aunt. This young lad was sure that all three of the women were dead before they were moved to the house. After they were all on the living room floor, they covered the bodies with the sheets and the rug. The fourteen and twelve-year-old boy had helped their father moved the dead bodies of their mother, grandmother, and aunt. What a terrible task for such young children.

Tommy wrote a quick note to leave on the door and moved to the next step of everybody grabbing some clothing and loading up into the Hornet station wagon. This was an older vehicle that was in poor mechanical condition and had several windows broken out of the car. With the house secured, the two adults and the seven children loaded into the very small car, and the nine survivors were headed north. After a short distance up the road, Donald became aware that Tommy also had a pistol with him as well as the rifle and shotgun. With his injuries, he was afraid to try and fight with Tommy out of fear that it would cause his son Donnie, the two girls who lived grandma, and the George kids to be in danger or even be killed during the tussle.

While traveling north, Tommy would stop every so often and call his sister Cindy to coordinate a meeting point. On the first call, he asked Cindy if she loved him; then she had to help him, no questions, no hesitation, she had to help her brother. With that agreement, Cindy was to meet with Tommy between Wimauma and Crossville as he knew his car would not make the trip. They agreed that every hour, they would call back to her home where her husband Bobby could help them with their locations and finally meet up.

Cindy went around town trying to find a car that could make this trip. She finally borrowed a cousin's car and with her sister Sherry headed out on the trip. Every hour, they made the calls before finally matching up for the meeting in Forsyth, Georgia.

After traveling the 418 miles to Forsyth, the nearly seven-hour trip came to a halt for the little Hornet stuffed with the crowd of quiet people; it seemed that no one wanted to talk on that trip. With a little searching, the sisters met up with the brother in the parking lot of a convenience store at the interstate exit. The troops in the brother's car all grabbed their belongings and jumped into the sister's car. The new car was not much bigger than the original, and this new arraignment contained eleven people in yet another compact vehicle. A few hours up the road in that overcrowded car while on the north side of Atlanta, they decided to drop off Sherry at a hotel, and two of the children would stay with her. This would provide more room in the car, and another family could drive down and give them a ride home later that day.

As they continued up the road, Cindy stopped for some gas and refreshments. At that time, she was very tired and wanted to stop for the night. While everyone was in and out of the car, she finally was able to see Donald in the backseat, the first time within an area of light. That is when she saw that Donald had been shot, and she saw the rifle and shotgun on the floor of the backseat. She loved her brother and decided not to ask any questions; she loaded up the car and was determined to reach Crossville. That was just another 252-mile portion of the 670 miles trek from Wimauma. These almost five hours passed quickly with her new determination to get to her mother's home.

While Sherry was in the hotel with Adam and Brian, they were all getting ready to get some sleep. The boys were watching the television when Adam said, "She's dead" and started to cry. As the boys sat beside each other, they were both crying and not wanting to talk about what happened back at the house. With her pushing the boys to talk, Adam finally looked straight at her and said, "They're just dead. Granny, Cougar, and Mom, they're just dead." Finally, she made the boys tell her the whole story of that horrible day; through their tears, they let her know the whole horrible story. With her hearing this terrible information, she got in touch with her brother-in-law Bobby to tell him this unbelievable story. Now, Bobby was in total fear for his wife; the lady who did not know that her brother had killed three people before she got in the car with him to drive him home to his mommy's house. The story was beginning to spread through the family.

It was now Monday morning with the sun rising as they finished the long trip to the mountain home. On their way through the town, they were on the main roadway and passed by the police station. When they passed the building, Cindy made some comment about the police, and all of the children gasped and shrunk down into concealment; this seemed a bit strange to her. By this time, Bobby had informed all the family members in Crossville, and many more were becoming aware of the story. When she met up with the family, she now discovered the reason for the trip; she was beyond shock.

With the family gathered around, Tommy was threatening suicide now that the kids were with his family. Tommy walked around with the pistol saying he was going to turn himself into the police; then he decided to run, and finally, his own death was the solution. This conversation continued to circle through those three options, round and round they went; that wheel just kept spinning. They finally got him inside the house, so they could all find the best solution for this calamity.

Meanwhile, Bobby was calling the Memphis FBI office to get law enforcement involved in this situation. At first, he was hesitant with the limited information out of concern for his wife and her family. As the day moved forward, he provided more information to allow the FBI to help in locating the murder scene and to have the Cumberland County Sheriff's Office to locate the criminal. By that time, the killer was barricaded in his mother's home with his family and an attorney, Mr. McIntyre, who was helping resolve this dilemma.

Sheriff Billy Joe Hobson had a broken leg and could not respond to the scene, so he sent his chief deputy and his Deputy Sheriff to that location. With two members of the three-man agency at the scene, the situation was totally under control.

While the negotiations were in progress, Mr. McIntyre created documents for the four George boys to be placed under the guardianship of Tommy George's mother. The other children would be taken care of by the George family until the James girls could be returned to grandfather's house in Florida, and the Banks boy would go with his father. With this done, Tommy was ready to surrender to Sheriff Hobson, and Donald was able to be transported to the hospital. The tale of the tragedy was now complete, and the investigation was continuing.

So now let us go back and talk about some of the interviews that helped put the facts together. After my morning breakfast, well a cup of coffee, up in Crossville, it was time to start my all-day investigation. By the way, by that time the family had been to Georgia and back to provide Sherry and the boys a ride to Tennessee, everyone was now in town. That morning, Mr. McIntyre brought the George boys into the Sheriff's Office to complete an interview with each of the lads. The George boys did not want to talk about the nasty little family secret. To me, it seemed that the good attorney had encouraged the children to not speak to me. With the other youngsters, it was difficult to conduct interviews with these very young children. The meetings were very limited and more so very delicate with these little ones; remember the youngest was only two years old.

The other interviews went very well during that long day. At the hospital, Donald gave his details, and a large number of relative were contacted at Tommy's mother's home. The interesting point here is that the George boys were back with their grandma in the afternoon. Both of the older boys were anxious, eager, and willing to tell the detective the story; the change seemed strange now that the attorney was not there.

With the several long days, it was time to find a nice little diner with some mountain cooking and head back to the hotel. On checking in with the bosses down south, the updates were exchanged on this ongoing investigation. The Forsyth County Police had recovered the abandoned Hornet at the convenience store. The State

Laboratory would process the car and ship the evidence to our office. All was accomplished on that short trip, except for an interview with the killer.

The next morning, I met with Sheriff Hobson at his office. We made arrangements for the evidence, or better stated the guns, to be shipped back to my office. Then it was time for the interview. Out of professional respect, the first action was to contact the suspect's attorney to ask if he wanted to be present during the interview. The good lady at the office advised that Mr. McIntyre was not in town that day. With a gracious thank you, the phone call was complete, and it was time for the interview.

The first step in interviewing a person who is suspected of having committed a crime is to advise the person of their rights. After completing this step, Tommy George told me he wanted to say two things. The first was that he loved his wife, and second that he did not intend to do anything that day. His eyes told the story that he was the person who was the most upset with Tommy George. After his two comments, he stated that he would not answer any of my questions on the advice of his attorney. That was not the first time a suspect had ended my interview with that statement. While leaving the room, this grumpy detective had to stop and look back at Mr. George, the killer who had generated so much damage to his family, his children, and himself. How can anyone make such a senseless, foolish, stupid mistake?

With the completion of my first trip to Crossville, it was time to head back home. The road trip, the airplane ride, the layover, and another flight got me back to my town. It was another long day to move forward with, but not complete this investigation.

With evidence packed and sent off to the labs, paperwork completed, and all of the investigative actions resolved, it was time for our next step. With my testimony before the grand jury, they returned an indictment for three counts of capital murder and one for attempted first-degree murder. The warrants were issued, and it was now time to complete that next step.

With the lawyers and the courts, all the legal steps were accomplished for the next move in this case. The defendant waived his extradition, and we had to make arrangements for his return to our jurisdiction. This resulted in a meeting in the conference room because Major John did not have a large enough office to include such a large group. It did not seem a reasonable approach to have a detective take an all-day trip with a rental car and two airplane flights to return a triple murder suspect to our county; you think the flight attendant would be comfortable with those passengers. The group also felt that a twelve-hour road trip on the interstate was not the safest answer to this transportation. The final decision was that the Sheriff's Office plane would be used to retrieve the criminal. This was going to be another interesting action in my career.

The office travel agent set up the trip, and the flight plan was filed for our little jump to Tennessee. Now let me explain the Sheriff's Office airplane was a Cessna 206, single engine, propeller driven, six-seat aircraft. With this design, there are two seats in each of the three rows. The size of these closely joined seats is a bit smaller than those on a commercial airliner, about half the size of first class. So with it now being middle October, and I am not joking it was on my birthday, we loaded up that airplane called SO-Four at Vandenberg Airport and departed on Runway 36. The pilot was Deputy Edward who, prior to being a deputy, owned an airport and flight school; he was an excellent pilot. In the front right seat was Detective Gerald from Intelligence who was sent with me to assist with the prisoner. This gentleman had served in the U.S. Navy prior to joining with the Sheriff's Office. By this man's height of just less than seven feet and having a build that looked larger than a football player, his huge hands helped one believe the story that he was his naval fleet boxing champion; no one wanted to fight that pleasant deputy. In the next row back was this young detective on his way to retrieve another murder suspect.

So let us take a moment to talk about this airplane ride. When we left Florida, the airport is a spot that is just twenty-two feet above sea level. This was a nice and pretty morning with the Florida sun lighting the beautiful horizon. Now in an airplane, we have to move up above the land, so if we flew, say a thousand feet above that airport, we are really 1,022 feet above sea level. Our flight was going to take us to the Crossville airport that is located about three miles west of that town. That runway is located at 1,881 feet above sea level, so to be 1,000 feet above it, one would fly at 2,881 feet above sea level. So think about the fact that these flatlander Florida cops are flying up into the mountains, the Rocky Top of Tennessee.

With flying an airplane, there are two methods of controlling one's flight plan. One is by Visual Flight Rules (VFR) and the other is by Instrument Flight Rules (IFR). With the VFR, you can look out the window and see where you are going. With darkness and weather, one cannot always use VFR to fly. With the IFR, one uses the instruments and the Aviation Flight Center controllers to follow the flight plan. With IFR, the pilot does not even need to look out the window—well, kind of like that.

On this particular day of our 571-mile trip lasted just over four hours of travel time. The problem arose when we discovered the Crossville Airport was completely covered with fog, sound that fog horn. Flying through the mountains and engulfed in the fog, we could not see outside of the airplane. The fog was so thick; it was as if the windows had been spray painted white. We were definitely flying IFR. As we neared the airport, Pilot Edward asked us to be very quiet as he had to communicate with the controllers to land the plane; as we tried to look outside, we wondered to land the plane where? Neither of the detectives made peep. We went straight, we turned this way, then that way, we slowed down, we dropped lower; it was obvious we were heading to the runway, that long strip of pavement that we could not see. The moment finally happened as we cleared the fog at the same moment the tire touched down on the runway. The fog cleared at about ten feet above the ground. When we reached the parking place, the detectives both told the pilot that he had done a great job and how scared we were with that blind landing. The good pilot Edward replied with the statement that he was the most petrified person in that airplane. The detectives did not even wait to find a church to offer their thanks to the good lord.

That afternoon, the legal actions were resolved, and the preparations were completed for our group to take custody of the shooter that next morning. At that time, his attorney presented me with a letter instructing me not to talk about this crime with his client. The letter was accepted with Mr. McIntyre being informed that any discussion with me would be the decision of his client which would not need the good lawyer's approval; Mr. McIntyre did not seem to be happy with my attitude. Now the pilot supposedly slept well that night, but the detectives had trouble putting the white bed sheets over our heads. That white cover reminded us of the challenging landing; it was a bit foggy in our memory.

With the morning sun, we got together with Sheriff Hobson and got the criminal out to the airport. As we looked toward the sunny blue cloudless sky, we were much more comfortable with the scheduled departure compared to the previous days' landing. We put handcuffs and leg irons on the prisoner and loaded up the aircraft. The pilot and Detective Gerald were again in the front row with me in the middle and the killer in the last row. We taxied out to the edge of the runway where Pilot Edward made his final inspection and then set up for the takeoff. When he stopped on the runway, I requested everything to stop. The pilot and Detective Gerald looked back as I turned toward the prisoner, reached back, and several times opened and closed the door next to his seat. Mr. George asked what I was doing with a reply that if he acted up while we were flying, I wanted to make sure I could open the door and push him out. His response was a solid promise that he would not cause any problems for this little detective while we soared through the sky. I turned around to see the smiling faces of the front row, and then it was SO-Four departing Runway 8. In four hours, we were landing back home at the local airport. On that day, the sky was clear, that made for a much easier landing.

Over the next eight months, the legal system moved forward with the final resolution of this case. Mr. George did not want his children to be brought back to Florida for fear the grandfather would seek custody. More so he did not want to put his children through a trial where they would have to testify against their father on his killing their mother. It was obvious that after the crime, he wanted his children to live a safe and quite life in Tennessee. The defendant made a deal to plead guilty to all charges. The three murder cases would be reduced to first-degree murder, and he would receive a life sentence on each murder. On shooting the brother-in-law, he received twelve years for the attempted murder charge. The man would spend the rest of his life in prison.

The good part of his final decisions is that he did everything he could to protect his children. Even his frantic trip north was to help his kids stay with his family. Through all of the terrible mistakes, he did man up and try to take care of the kids. It was most likely not an easy task; in the long run, it was the best solution.

With this being twenty-seven years since the murder, we would have to calculate the ages of the George boys to now have a range of forty-one to thirty-six years of age. The James girls would be thirty-two and twenty-nine years old with Danny Banks at thirty-five years of age. That gaggle of kids stuffed into that little Hornet and rushed up the road are now all grown up. We can only hope that they grew up to become some good citizens and to have created their own loving families. The question would always be how the older boys who carried their dead mother, grandmother, and aunt were able to cope with that horrible situation. Most probably, they each and every one do all they can to prevent an argument with their own spouse. The wedding vow of "until death do we part" is not a definition of how to end one's marriage.

# *Oops!*

We need to hold on for a minute and look back at the other story. In that last story of the triple murder, the lieutenant in the story was very new to homicide investigations. Throughout his career, he mainly worked on the narcotics and vice side of law enforcement never before seeing the grotesque sights of his new assignment. When someone begins working in the homicide unit, it exposes them to very difficult and horrible visions. It is very challenging to deal with these terrible conditions of the crime scene and the horrific conditions from injury and decomposition of the human body. Your emotions have to be held down, but still, your mind ponders how these deplorable acts can really happen to anyone. Each investigator finds their own way of how to deal with what they have to see and endure.

In that multiple homicide case, Lieutenant Richard and I were standing near the three murder victims who had been rolled up together in a single large rug since the time of their death. This crime had occurred many hours prior to our arrival at the crime scene, and the bodies were starting to deteriorate and to decompose over that time span. As required by my assignment, I went over and rolled the three ladies out of the rug resulting in an explosion of the very large, loud and terrible gas to expel from the deteriorating bodies. This is normal for this condition as the deterioration of the body parts changes the solids into a gas which is retained in the tightly wrapped rug over the confined bodies. With the release of the pressure from the rug, the gas is expelled and produces a sound similar to someone passing gas. Yes, in this case it sounded just like a very loud mega "fart." This also allowed the release of the overly disgusting stench from the rotting body gases from the three ladies. Immediately, I held my fingers to my mouth displaying a very embarrassed expression and said directly to Lieutenant Richard, "Excuse me."

Oh, my gosh, the lieutenant went ballistic as he started yelling and screaming at me ranting that I was disgusting and sick and then stormed out of the house. Of course, my sergeant, who was much more prepared for my offbeat personal actions, looked to the ground and shook his head without saying a word. After all, he was a bit more—well, I guess a lot more prepared for my jovial attitude at a crime scene. Would "jovial" be the correct word for that action?

That poor lieutenant had a very hard time with the views and the smells of the assignment and did not last a year in homicide. At the end of the good man's long career, he moved up the ladder and eventually retired at the rank of major. Later in the day of that murder investigation, I went to his office telling Lieutenant Richard that I was very sorry, and that I did not mean to upset him with my questionable humor. I hoped that he would forgive me for my error and simply let this whole incident just "pass." Yep, he immediately and with loud, strong, and short words threw me right out of his office. Well, excuse me!

# Olympian Killer

As you would remember on my date of commission as a Deputy Sheriff, I became the first teenager to wear the star badge in my county. Being so young, I had a different approach to the young people in the local community. Driving around the town, many would wave at me and stop to have a chat. Of course, there were also those that would wave with only one finger. Overall, I developed many friendships that covered the total gambit of the ages of the residents. Today, I often swell with pride when during a conversation, someone brings up my name, and one of the group will tell a story from many years past of how I helped them. My greater pride is how many people remain my very good friends to this date.

One family, a clan of Sicilian ancestry, is my very special group that contains six sons. I could not tell you which of the eight family members would be my best friend for each as an individual, and the family overall is at the top. Now, the father would tell you he, without any doubt or competition, was the top of the list while the mother would stand in the kitchen cooking pasta and smiling. The mother, who we all believe is a saint or angel sent from heaven, has a good chance of being the true leader. Of course, she would not allow that title and abdicate it to which every son would be the nearest at that particular moment. The whole group, I being the most, takes pride in me being their adopted son and brother. The best part of this association is their introducing me to their cousin. This wonderful and perfect woman is now my wife who is a very special blessing for me that goes beyond description.

## THE EMOTIONS FROM A BADGE

Through this clan, I met up with many other families in our little community. From the parents, and the school personnel, and the students while attending many of the local football and baseball games and other local events, I grew to know so many of the townsfolk. As a deputy, I was also aware of many of the hangouts and secret activities that continually occurred within the town. I did my best not to overstep my bounds as a Deputy Sheriff to prevent myself becoming a tyrant. Whenever a real problem would occur, I immediately stepped in to prevent that concern from becoming a catastrophe. Many a young person got sent home early in the evening before the fight or for some other bad decision that could create one of those regrettable errors.

Our community also had great pride in another local establishment that was an internationally known training facility for divers and swimmers. One excellent coach came to town every summer for training sessions instructing his students to a level where they became competitors in the Olympics. Several had won many of the various Olympic medals, a few even the gold medal. The son of that coach, a well-trained diver himself, was one of the silver medal winners in the previous Olympics. Once again, he was in town for summer training to prepare for his competition in the next Olympic Games. His training, abilities, and dedication would make anyone believe that he was on his way to win those additional medals, especially the gold.

During my career, I realized that a college education was a requirement for improving my life within and after the Sheriff's Office. After graduating from high school, I attended the very best university in the United States of America. During that time, I learned that to earn a degree, one is required to actually attend the classes and learn what is being taught. This bit of knowledge struck me way too late creating a return to my home with grades requiring my departure from the school. The times had changed, and I had moved forward to that point in life of recognizing the need for that college degree. As a detective, it would be difficult to be a student and investigator at the same time, so it was time to plan and more so plot to achieve that task. The detective division had a requirement that there should be a detective on duty during the evening shift.

There was a need for only one to resolve the regular daily needs and only if required additional personnel would respond to the crime scene. This was an excellent method to manage the work product and usage of the division personnel. With this concept, we would rotate the assignment on a monthly basis to always have a person on the night shift. Without having to go into a deep explanation, you can be assured that nobody liked the night duty. A young detective had convinced the division major to permanently assign him to the night shift so he could attend college and eliminate the rotating night shift, a well-received suggestion. When that detective was finishing school, he wanted to return to day shift allowing me to persuade the major that I should fill the night position. With my excellent presentation, I was appointed the night detective and also became a college student. The first detective had been very good in making the major believe the permanent night detective was a great idea. After all, that brilliant detective was eventually the Sheriff at the time of my retirement.

Now I have explained several different concepts in the first part of this story that seem to have no connection. Let me try to make sense of the above paragraphs and bring the stories of my friends in the community, the swim school, and the night detective all together into this one tale, a very heartbreaking story.

With my continuous schedule on the night shift and my days of colleges classes, all was moving along so very well until there arose a night of tragedy. It was a Monday evening, the first day of August, with the end of the summer break racing toward a new school year and with me patrolling the area as the night detective. During the evening, the local teenagers would gather together at the "Spot." This was the dead end of a long empty road that went to a location of a construction site for a future subdivision. The surrounding woods created a very private, dark, and empty area for the kids to meet, greet, and of course drink a little brew or such. Mainly, this was a quiet little location where they could gather together with their friends. As like almost any night, several cars were parked on either side of the roadway; some of the teens were standing around the cars, others in the roadway and some in the middle of the road.

## THE EMOTIONS FROM A BADGE

A set of headlights were approaching down the road like many vehicles that would come and go from the location to join up with their friends. This car was a small two-seat sport car with three occupants, all of the three were divers involved in the training at that local pool. The driver was that twenty-five-year-old silver medal Olympian with his twenty-three-year-old girlfriend, the third a twenty-two-year-old male friend. They were headed down the road to drop off the twenty-two year old at his home a quarter mile or so north of the "Spot."

It was just before eleven o'clock at night as the car was getting closer to its destination. The Olympian was driving down the two-lane road at a speed estimated to be around ninety miles per hour, or even more. He missed the stop at his friend's house and continued to fly down the small dark roadway not seeing the crowd gathered at the end. The Olympic diver became aware of the group as he hit a car on the side of the road causing the sports car to bounce back into the roadway where he ran over one person and then a second person standing in the road. The driver yanked the steering wheel to swerve away from the two he had just struck and ran over three more young people sitting on the curb. Within the group on the curb, there were two more people standing who were also struck as the vehicle continued down the road. The speeding vehicle then struck two other cars parked on the side of the road and continued down the road before coming to a spinning stop and facing almost 180 degrees back to the initial point of impact nearly a hundred yards from the start. Finally—yes, finally—they had come to a stop.

The radio alert tone sounded as the dispatcher announced the multiple injury traffic crash involving several pedestrians at the "Spot." Without a hesitation, my blue light and siren were turned on as I roared toward the scene. A marked unit arriving first on the scene was on the radio demanding immediate assistance with a tone of voice that alone could describe the terrible scene. I was the second deputy to arrive at the location. The group of teenagers was in a total state of shock. Many stood there in a daze; some tried to provide medical treatment to others, and some were searching for other friends whom they could not find. Approaching the scene, I walked up to the first pedestrian that had been hit; I stopped and looked down.

He was a seventeen-year-old male who was within a few weeks of starting his senior year of high school. This man was someone I knew from the community. Even though we were not friends, I did not need his identification to know his name. The hardest part of the identification resulted in the extreme damage to the young man's body. His entire body was horribly torn apart with pieces lying around in the large pool of blood. I moved forward to the next body.

When I stopped at the second body and looked down, I was even more shocked at this horrible sight. This nineteen-year-old boy had just graduated from high school and was so anxious to go to college that he had already started classes early at the local university. The young man had been a good player on our town's high school baseball team. I knew him because he was good friends with one of my future cousins. The two of them along with several others were in a group that was always hanging out together and having a good time. That relationship is how this man became my own friend. His body was smashed, shredded, and torn apart lying slaughtered on the ground. Each arm and each leg was ripped from the body; his head was partially torn from the shoulders with pieces of skin helping to keep the body parts close together. Completely stunned, I stood there in a daze looking at his very severely damaged face, the face of a good friend. I was standing there frozen and could not say a word; the horrible description is still beyond my ability with words.

As more emergency personnel began to arrive, their vehicles lit up the scene bringing me back to reality. I could see another friend of my cousin who was also in that same group of friends, treating the injured people who had been run over while sitting on the roadway curb. Three had very major injuries to the legs and torso, but they were still alive. Two more had less serious injuries but needed emergency treatment and transport to the trauma center. The treatment this young man provided prevented at least one of the victims from bleeding to death. The extreme injury to the almost severed leg created a wound that was gushing blood; his actions with a tourniquet helped slow the bleeding and save a life. When I asked him about where my cousin might be, he replied that he did not know but thought he had been there earlier but was not sure. I looked up to see the other deputies searching the darkness for missing people.

At that moment, it felt as if my heart had come to a complete stop. I ran to my patrol car, grabbed my cellular phone, and called the family home. His mother, that wonderful lady, answered the phone. To this day, she will tell you that she has never heard me speak to anyone with such a stern and strong voice that I used on that tragic night. I asked if the young man was home with her answering that he was in his room. I asked if she was looking directly at him receiving her reply of no that he was in bed. I demanded that she immediately go to his room and verify that he was there. She asked why. I told her to do it and to do it right now! When she looked in the room, he was there in bed fast asleep. I calmed down and started to breathe once again. After apologizing for my attitude, I explained to her what had occurred, and of course, she started to cry. I told her I had to get back to work, as always, she told me to be strong and that she would say a prayer for those who were hurt and a special one for me. Her many prayers have surely kept me safe and alive, and probably sane, more than once over my long and dangerous career.

Knowing that my future cugino, Italian for cousin, was safe, I returned to complete my work at the scene. I walked past the dead bodies and the injured being treated to the far end of the road. There in the middle of the road was the vehicle with damage and blood all over the car. Off to the side of the road was the Olympic diver. He was wearing a tank top, a bathing suit, and flip-flop sandals squatting with his feet flat on the ground. His elbows were on his knees with his head in his hands. He was crying. I had to stop, completely come to a stop. I wanted to approach him and to fix the problem right then and right there as my growing anger was starting to control my thoughts when another deputy called my name. Fortunately, hearing my name brought me back to reality. I had to walk away immediately to prevent myself from making a major mistake.

Walking away caused me to again walk past the body of my friend. I stopped and stared at the mangle person splattered on the road. It is the job of law enforcement to "serve and protect." That night I had done neither, I felt totally worthless.

The Olympic diver was charged with two counts of driving under the influence with manslaughter, two counts of manslaughter, and three counts driving under the influence with serious bodily injury in the traffic crash. While the trial was pending, he continued to practice and try to qualify for the Olympics. During this same time, we had funerals for the dead teenagers. The others were trying to recover from their wounds. Some have never fully recovered from these wounds, both physical and emotional. Still, the Olympic diver, the drunken killer, went on with his life.

The irony of the Olympic diver driving while drinking was a chapter from his own biography. When he was eighteen years old, he was the passenger in an automobile that was struck head on by a drunk driver. He received very serious injuries that included breaking all of his facial bones, his left leg, a torn knee, lacerated liver, and the removal of his spleen. The doctors had to rebuild his mangled face damaged in the nearly fatal collision. One would think that he would be a strong advocate against drunk driving; instead, he had become a drug addict and an alcoholic. Some stories claim he was using cocaine up to five times a week, smoking marijuana, and drinking fifteen beers at a time.

The story of his drinking that day indicated that the three in the car had gone to a local bar having a few beers while playing pool. This had been near noon creating several hours of a gap between leaving the bar and killing the victims. They never explained nor was it proven where they were during the missing hours. There is a rumor on the street that the group had gone to the home of a friend. The friend was an older man who, along with his roommate, were coaches at that swim club where all three of the car occupants trained with them. Both coaches also had their regular jobs working for the county school board. One was a teacher, and the other was an administrator in one of the local high schools. The young man who was the passenger was a close friend of the administrator who had once been arrested but not prosecuted for child molesting and went on to retire as the principal of a high school. The rumor is that they drank all day at this house of the diving coaches', the residence of a school principal and a school teacher, before leaving to go straight to the passenger's home. The Olympian drove away with an alcohol level that was later tested to over twice the legal limit.

While the diver continued to work on his eligibility to compete in the upcoming games, some of the teenagers who had been at the "Spot" that night would go to the diving meets and protest his presence. It seems that his mind and spirit were not with him during this time in his life. With the pressures and the protest, he was not able to obtain his qualification for the Olympic team. Eventually, the court date had arrived, and the prosecution was ready to proceed with the horrible case.

The community and the media all crowded the courthouse on the day of the trial and with the courtroom packed full to the walls the prosecution called its first witness. After the very graphic and horrible descriptive testimony of this witness, a Deputy Sheriff, to everyone's surprise the Olympian stopped the trial and changed his plea to guilty to all of the charges. He did not want to relive the events of that night of tragedy and have the horrible pictures displayed to the public. He indicated to his attorneys that he did not want the families of the dead teenagers to have to go through any more of this terrible event. The judge ordered him to immediately be taken into the custody of the county jail.

Three weeks later at his sentencing hearing, the Olympian changed his plea from guilty to no contest to improve his position in the multiple upcoming civil suits. The stern hanging judge with a history for very strong sentences showed a rare side of sympathy and ordered a sentence of seventeen years in prison and fifteen years of probation. This was much less than the sentencing guidelines would have suggested for these dreadful crimes. The requirements of probation included acts of restitution and a permanent and forever revocation of the Olympians' driving privileges. The time had finally come for his punishment for these crimes sending him off to state prison. He won no medals for this action.

As with any case, we all know the killer did not spend that entire time in prison. Within five years of the accident and about four years in confinement, he was released from prison. During his time in prison, he moved from jail cells to a halfway house and eventually to parole. Within the prison, he began a drug and alcohol rehabilitation program. Since his release from prison, he has remained clean of the drugs and alcohol that plagued his life. Some of his treatment has been his involvement with community service hours ordered by the court. This required him to attend meetings where he would tell others they should clean up and move forward with their lives by describing how this incident damaged his own life. I wonder if during his talks, he includes the stories about the other people who received permanent injuries and those who died and how it changed or ended their lives.

The last news was that the Olympic diver, a convicted murderer, is a working man who is a teacher coaching divers and swimmers at a high school in his community. That is correct, the killer is a high school teacher. His marriage and raising three children has created a requirement for him to have his driving privileges restored for the benefit of his family. A judge in his home state recently ruled in his favor granting him the privilege to once again be a licensed driver to operate a vehicle. With all of my anger, I must say that the Olympian has also suffered with this tragedy. He is trying, and we should all hope and pray for him, to continue with his own life even though he cannot clear that evening from his mind or from mine. Still, at this writing, we have moved forward twenty-seven years with him being in his fifty-two years of age. My friend only lived to be nineteen years old the night of his death, splattered on that dark road by a drunk driver.

The young folks who were injured as they sat on the curb have also moved forward with their lives. One young man still requires medical treatments and wears a brace to support his leg. He is doing well raising a family of his own. One of the girls has moved away from town and started her family. Several years after this incident, she was a witness to another fatal drunken driving accident that killed the drunk driver and seriously injured the other driver. She stayed with the injured driver talking with her and holding her hand as fire rescue cut that victim from the wrecked vehicle. In her mind, she remembered how important it is to have someone talk to you when you are so very scared, just hearing a voice helps. Maybe this new tragedy made her into another special hero with her actions of an angel.

Driving down the road, alone in the car, I will sometimes stop by the cemetery. As I go back into the lot, I have to stop by the graves of my father-in-law and my mother-in-law. With a quick check on these wonderful people, with a prayer and humble thanks for my wife, I blow a kiss and shout out a "chao!" as I move on to the back. Once at the plot of my friend, I stand by the grave and wonder why we lost such a good person. As I look across the cemetery, I see so many headstones of people I know. Some of these many people died when they were grandparents, some as babies, and so many others at ages in between. I feel as if I am looking at the good people while so many bad people are alive in the state prison or out on parole. Still, I can always look back at the grave knowing that the good young man would snag that baseball flying across the infield and with a toss to the first baseman throw out a runner, yet with his own turn at bat, he would hit the ball and place himself on that same base. It was, no, I should say, it is a great honor to be his friend.

When we bury a friend, we must always remember that it is only the body in the crypt. Wherever their beliefs take them, part of their spirit will always remain within our own heart.

# Drop the Gun!

After the last story, we should take a quick break before moving on to another little tale. Now with your drink in hand, let's drop back to an earlier part of my career, way back when I was a brand-new Deputy Sheriff patrolling the streets of our big county. Back then, the criminal activity and the number of calls were not to the high volume that we have today in our growing town. But on this one quiet little Saturday morning many years ago, I was about to meet my first major challenge as a law enforcement deputy, to serve and hopefully to protect.

It was early in the morning, so of course, I was just leaving the drive-through with my second cup of morning coffee. The short little road that I was on curved around and ended with a stop sign at a T-bone intersection. The other road was a larger road that connected some neighborhoods to the major highway in the community. As I sat at the stop sign, a sharp-looking sport car came to a screeching halt right in front of me; the driver was an off-duty Deputy Sheriff. This young man had been the leader of the Sheriff's Office Explorer Post before recently being hired as a Deputy Sheriff; he was a dedicated cop and an outstanding person. Deputy Ron leaned out the window of his hot rod and screamed that there was a fight just up the road, and a person was armed with a pistol. As he looked up the roadway, he pointed to a pickup truck that was driving southbound on the east side of the road through the front yards of the residences on that road. Deputy Ron looked back at me as he pointed at the truck and yelled, "That's him!"

## THE EMOTIONS FROM A BADGE

With that truck coming at the passenger's side of my marked patrol car, it was time to take action. The blue lights went on, and I exited toward the back side of my car. That fleeing felon came to a stop and opened his door. The front of his truck was just a few feet from the side of my patrol car while I was near the back corner of the marked car placing the suspect and me within maybe ten feet of each other. The next requirement was to draw the old .357 magnum revolver and take control of the armed criminal. The gun was aimed and ready to fire as I ordered the suspect to show his hands and exit the vehicle. He held his hands out strait away from his body forming the look of a cross as he shuffled sideways away from the truck. He kept moving until finally, his right hand cleared the door and showed he was holding a pistol. It was obvious that this was the old World War II military pistol that was a .45 caliber semiautomatic firearm; the history of this weapon defines a deadly weapon.

At this point, I am yelling, screaming, and demanding that the suspect drop the pistol. During these multiple shouts, the suspect is turning the barrel of the gun in my direction. As his weapon is moving toward me, I am squeezing the trigger on my double-action revolver. The hammer is coming back as the cylinder is rotating and locking into the firing position. Again and again, my order to put down the weapon is ignored as my trigger pull is in the process of firing my revolver. My demand continued as I set my sights in position; the front post between the sides in the open square of the back sights and both sights flat across the top aiming right at his center chest. With the very short distance between us and my abilities with my pistol, there is no doubt that the .357 magnum bullet will strike the suspect in the center chest; the hollow-point projectile will poke a small entry wound in his skin and then expand as it rips trough his body, creating a very large exit wound. The tunnel that will be created within the body will cause various body parts, including the heart, to be torn and destroyed as it creates the death of an armed assailant. That stupid criminal would not drop the gun; the idiot was in the motion of aiming the gun at a Deputy Sheriff, that fool was about to die. Then it finally happened.

As I looked back and forth at the pistol and my sights, my mind told me the real description of the assailant's gun. This was the same BB pistol that I myself was an owner, not a .45 caliber firearm. My trigger pull was relaxed just a quick moment before my gun was discharged. Had I not owned that same BB gun, had I not recognized that this was not a real gun, then that young man at that very moment would have positively been shot to death. Coming that close to killing an idiot who would not simply obey the order of an armed Deputy Sheriff to drop his gun was a bit upsetting to me.

As I moved toward the suspect, my firearm was holstered, and the subject was now ordered to drop himself to the ground. He stood there looking at me and told me he just want me to see it was a BB gun. Once again, he disobeyed the lawful command of a law enforcement officer, so it was my turn to help him. Once he was facedown on the ground, the little BB pistol was physically removed from his possession. Then it was time to talk, well maybe yell at that idiot who almost had me kill him over a BB gun. Do not ever argue with a Deputy Sheriff who is pointing a pistol at you; obey every request immediately and precisely. Live to later tell the story.

You can imagine at that moment this young deputy was having a bit of an anger management problem. After helping him off the ground and continuing to discuss the matter, eventually, the young man was able to slide down the side of his truck back to the ground as he started to breathe in a much less-restrained condition. By this time, we had determined that the incident up the street was a group of friends playing around; he was not trying to argue but wanted me to see it was a BB gun, not a real pistol. He explained that he had learned a very valuable lesson and would never make that mistake again. He was overly and more that extremely apologetic. This young man also realized how fortunate he was to be alive; he was rather happy not to have been shot to death.

It had become obvious that the gentleman had learned a very valuable lesson from his irrational mistake. With this great knowledge, there was no need to arrest the youngster for his blunder; one with a lesson well learned. The good little boy was assisted back into his truck, provided with his now broken BB pistol, and sent out to enjoy the rest of the very beautiful day.

Deputy Ron was amazed that I did not plug the suspect with my powerful pistol. He was still in a state of disbelief when it was explained that I recognized the BB gun as one like my own. He stated that he did not own one like that; Ron would have shot the gunman. We were both very happy to have the good outcome.

Deputy Ron worked his way through a very good career with the Sheriff's Office. When he had left the Explorer Scout as the major of that program and on leaving the Sheriff's Office, he also held the rank of major. To this day, he reminds me that he would have shot that kid with the gun; overall, Ron is a very good man.

So let us each and all remember one little bit of advice, whether you are right or wrong, whether the law enforcement officer is right or wrong, obey the orders demanded of you by any cop, especially if they are pointing a gun at you! The final outcome can be decided at a later time, in a nicer environment, not the morgue.

# Murder for a Car

Now let us jump back to one of my many murder cases that everyone seems to be more interested in than some of my other rambling tales. This one happened in the early part of February when the weather is sunny and cold. Well, for this area of the world, it may not seem that cold; but for the four days of this investigation, the temperatures went from as high as 70 degrees all the way down to 37 degrees, now that is really cold in the Sunshine State. On this particular day, the cool weather with a bright sun shining, it was a great day for our residents to enjoy the State Fair. That great day was about to change when the dispatcher called my radio number. The dispatch was to a location south of town where a dead body was dumped on the roadside of a major U.S. highway that travels through the county. It was time to get to work.

When I arrived at the scene, there were several other detectives mingling with the uniformed deputies. Sgt. Randy was already on the scene welcoming my arrival with one of his large smiles as he assigned me as the case detective. This would be my murder to solve.

The first action of the investigation was to take a look at the crime scene. There on the ground, lying on her back, was a nice-looking young lady. Her head was pointing to the west with her feet closer to the edge of the highway. The boy was over 150 feet from the highway in an old parking lot that was being demolished, both the lot and the buildings. This poor girl looked to be in her late teens or early twenties and was dressed in a pair of blue jeans and a white dress shirt that was covered with a denim jacket. The clothing all had labels of some of the more expensive of clothing lines that were enhanced by several pieces of quality jewelry. This young lady had the appearance of a high-class person who had been dropped off in a less than high-class portion of the community. Some interesting bits of evidence were the drag marks that indicated that the victim had been dragged about thirty feet from the location where a set of tire tracks were barely visible in the damp sand. Positioned on the back, with the dress shirt open to the stomach, one could see that the victim's belly button contained water. This odd situation indicated that the victim had been dumped at the location prior to the morning rain.

As with any murder, it is a primary action to determine the cause of death. This examination made it rather easy to reach a decision on that part of the case. On the lower left side of the shirt was a small hole surrounded with powder burns. On looking under the shirt, the entry wound of a small caliber bullet was located in the left side near the lower portion of the ribs. There was no sign of an exit wound to the body.

While searching the pockets of the young lady, we discovered a very important piece of evidence; her driver's license. Fortunately, the photograph on the driver's license matched with the young lady. This is often a difficult task to identify the victim and can create delays in the time-sensitive investigation. With this data, we now knew that the young lady was Lynn Harold, a nineteen-year-old girl who lived in very high-class area near downtown. As others processed the scene, it was time for me to move on with my part of the investigation.

With little to go on the first steps of the criminal background checks, driver's license records, and other basic actions were the actions in my work product. These all showed little or nothing, indicating that she was a good lady who had a tragic night.

The next stop on my travels was a visit to the Medical Examiner's Office to take a second look at the victim in the morgue. At this cleaner location, we were able to recover the lady's clothing, the sheet that she had been wrapped in for transportation and other pieces of trace evidence, including a strand of hair that appeared to be different from hers. Oh, yes, the little pieces of evidence that can solve the crime.

With the all afternoon search for her relatives being unsuccessful, we now made another attempt to locate a next of kin. It was nearly six hours after finding the victim, nearly eight o'clock at night, when we climbed the steps of the elegant historic home. The mother of the victim responded to the doorbell to greet the two detectives at her door. Even before my badge was displayed, Mrs. Harold recognized me as a homicide detective. This lady was an owner of a business that provided court reporters to the county court system. These reporters are the one who type transcripts of court actions, depositions, and other legal actions. Mrs. Harold had been a court reporter on some of my previous cases. As she looked at me, she screamed and fell to the ground in tears; I felt like the Grim Reaper. We were able to calm her and place her in a chair before we made the official notification of her daughter's death. At her request, we contacted some friends and her son to come to her home; she needed to be with someone.

After calming the good lady, just a little bit, she was able to give us some background on her daughter. Within the previous two weeks, the victim confessed to her that she was a lesbian. Since that time, they were having several arguments concerning this new disclosure about her personal life. The young lady had separated from old friends and began to socialize with people who were not known to her mother. Even though she had recently quit college and was bouncing between jobs, the young lady did not have anyone who would want to kill her. The mother had no idea who would have killed her little girl. The only new friend that Lynn had spoken about was a girl who works in the legal field. During her recent jobs, Lynn had worked with the lady at one of the lawyers' offices. She believes that the girl is Angela Piles and was able to provide a telephone number for the girl. She continually stated that she had no idea who would do this; no one should have done this. Mrs. Harold said that she last had seen her daughter at midnight as she left for the evening. That would be some fifteen hours before she was located on the side of the road, tossed away like a piece of trash by a worthless killer.

# THE EMOTIONS FROM A BADGE

As we were finishing the interview, Mrs. Harold asked about the victim's car. The response to her was what car? This information indicated that the victim drove a newer model BMW 320I that is registered to the mother. Paperwork was completed and documents resolved, and the stolen vehicle was entered into the National and Florida Crime Information Center computers listing the car as stolen during the commission of a murder. All law enforcement officers were notified to search for the wanted car.

With the mother having family and friends by her side, I made her a promise to find the answers to this horrible crime; this case would be solved. We then packed up and went off to complete the difficult task of solving the crime. Alerts were sent to all local agencies to search for the stolen car. My agency broadcast that alert once every hour, each and every hour. The first step for me was to search the area of a local gay bar that was the favorite place for Lynn to socialize with her friends. The area was searched, block by block, each street each avenue and every alley with the final results of not finding the stolen car. The radio cracked again to advise me that the friend of the victim, Angela Piles, was at the Sheriff's Office requesting to meet with this investigator. With the office located in the same old neighborhood as the gay bar, it was a short trip to meet with yet another person who could help solve the crime.

This interview would take me to nearly midnight to obtain the information that I would hear over and over again. Angela Piles told me that Lynn was a nice person who recently had come out as a gay person. Lynn did not do any heavy drugs; she did not drink very often to a point that she was rarely if ever heavily intoxicated. She advised of several friends and locations that she would visit but had no idea of anyone who would want to even hurt her much less kill her. This was a story that this lady could not believe could happen to my victim.

Before heading home that night, the Aviation Unit supervisor advised that they had searched the area of the crime scene and the bar without locating the missing car. With my great appreciation, he agreed to my request for a second search after the morning sunrise. It was now time to get some sleep and wait for the next day to arise.

That next day included the autopsy and continual interviews of people who knew the victim. The interviews were each and all the same as the one with Angela Piles; no one had any idea of who would do this to the good lady.

At the autopsy, we were able to determine that the victim was killed by a single gunshot wound to the left side of the ribcage. The bullet had traveled through the body and ripped through the liver. The small .25 caliber bullet was recovered in the body. The interesting bit of information that we were able to determine was the victim had no other injuries. No scrapes, bruises, cuts, or anything similar. This would indicate the victim did not resist, did not fight, and did not struggle with her killer. The autopsy easily defined that as she sat there in the car, the killer simply or more so maliciously shot her to death.

After the long day of interviews, I was lucky enough to get to bed by midnight on that evening. So during these first thirty-three hours of the investigation, we had been able to determine that a nice young lady had been killed and dumped on the side of the road. We also knew that nobody had a clue on who would have committed this horrible crime. As I climbed into bed that night, all of that lack of information would dramatically change in just a few short hours.

Usually when the phone rings in the early hours of the morning, it is to deliver bad news. This morning, the call had me up and moving where at three o'clock in the morning, I was standing next to my victim's automobile. The tag was different as it had been stolen from another vehicle and placed on the stolen car; this new tag had not been listed as stolen. The vehicle identification number had been partially scratched off but was sufficient to determine this was the victim's car. The main point, and the item listed in the alerts, was a bumper sticker. On the rear bumper, the officers saw the joke sticker that stated this was a CIA vehicle so "you better not ticket this car." When the city police officers tried to stop the car, all of the occupants jumped and ran; they more that ran with each disappearing into the night.

What a great present for an investigator, the undisturbed stolen car. We kept everyone away from the car, sealed it up, and towed it to our evidence garage. That great piece of evidence was processed inside and out and then the rest of everything else. We knew this was going to be the solution to this crime. Fingerprints were recovered from the interior and the exterior of the vehicle. One set of prints looked as if a subject had stood up through the open moon roof and placed his hands on the roof. Other fingerprints were found that did not match the ones recovered from the roof. The one other piece of important evidence was located under the gas pedal; this was a .25 caliber shell casing, the casing that fired the deadly shot.

Based on the fingerprints recovered from the car fingerprint analyst, Royce had searched for suspects who would match these prints. The description of the suspects fleeing the car at the time it was stopped helped to reduce the search. The other action that helped was locating the victim's checkbook in the glove box. Several checks had been written to the same subject, Daren Long. Mr. Long was very well-known to local law enforcement for any and every crime of theft. If you could steal it or forge it or scam it or in any way cheat a person out of anything that of course was a crime, then Mr. Long who was now just three months after his eighteenth birthday had committed that crime, more than once. Fingerprints on the car matched to Mr. Long, and the search was on for the suspect.

Without being able to locate Mr. Long, the other fingerprints were also examined to determine the others in the vehicle. It was now Sunday morning when Mr. Royce provided me with the additional information that indicated a second suspect. This second person was Cy Regions an eighteen year old who had a single previous arrest. This previous violation was the crime of stealing a bicycle; that is correct, not even a felony. Without being able to find the notorious thief, it was now time to locate the single error subject who might help us solve the crime. Steps were taken, and those actions located this man at his grandmother's house. A quick meeting allowed an agreement for Cy to come to the office to speak with the detectives.

At the office, we sat down with Cy Regions and advised him of his constitutional rights and started a consensual interview. From all of the history of the two suspects, we believed that the longtime criminal was the killer who had driven the innocent bike thief around in the stolen car. We were ready for Mr. Regions to give us all of the needed information to arrest that big thief. Things were about to change.

The first part of the story was that Mr. Long had stopped by his house in the stolen car. During that time, he never entered the car. How about your fingerprints in the car? The story changed that he had taken a ride in the car with other friends. They all traveled across the state to visit others and were out of town until the police stopped the car. Then why did you run? Well, Daren did say the car was stolen and that is why they ran. What about the murder, did he talk about that? He looked at me, straight into my eyes, when I demanded the truth. His eyes went down to the floor as I insisted on the truth.

At that point, he looked back to me and gave us the true story. Very early Thursday morning, he was standing near the car that was parked on a dark street near the gay bar. The young lady was walking up to the car; she was alone. Once she was at the car, he stepped out, pointed a pistol at her, and forced her into the car. He had planned to steal the car and some money from the girl. As they drove down the road, she was telling him of the changes in her life, she begged him to let her go, she told him to take the car and just let her go. He reached an area on a big highway that he was not familiar with. The girl pulled out a knife like a steak knife and tried to stab him. He shot her and stopped the car. She asked him to take her to the hospital, but he simply pushed her out of the car and drove away. A short distance away, he realized he should have taken her to the hospital, so he turned around to find her. Because he was unfamiliar with the area, he could not find her. From there, he went on to meet up with his friends.

When he was confronted with the body being pulled nearly thirty feet, no signs of a fight by the victim and no knife being located, he was not able to defend his statements. He was insistent that he was the one who committed the murder. We inquired about the other people, and he insisted he was alone on the crime. The others only rode in the stolen car. We asked about Daren Long, and he insisted that he was not involved in any of the murders. That statement made me perk up requiring about "any" of the murders; English class taught me that was a plural not a singular statement. That is when he told us of two more murders and a kidnapping that he and a group of other friends had committed within the city limits. The call went out, and the city homicide detectives arrived at the office.

As the day progressed, Cy gave information on the two other homicides and the kidnapping that the city police were able to clear. As he gave us information on the others involved in those crimes, the criminals were scooped up by the city cops and brought to our office for interviews. Some of these criminals were so young that as they sat in the chairs waiting to be interviewed, their feet did not reach the floor. I told Sergeant Bobby from the city that it looked like they had broken up the gang of killers; forever to be known as the lollipop gang. The good sergeant did not laugh.

Before the evening was over, Daren Long showed up at the office with his mother. Daren told us that he wanted to be interviewed about this crime spree. Once again, we started an interview with the reading and waiving of the rights. We were a bit shocked when Daren told us that he has and would steal anything as he has done all of his life. He insisted that we look at all of his arrest and note that none of them had involved a crime that physically hurt anyone. He would not ever do any crime that would hurt a person. He also told us that Cy Regions had the car and confessed the murder. It was amazing that a notorious criminal was a thief but could not injure another person. This was a real twist to the mind of a very callous detective.

After nearly eighty hours, the case or should I say the cases were solved, and the criminals arrested. I met with Mrs. Harold to let her know that her crime had been solved, and the criminal was in jail. My promise to her had been completed; it somehow seems to be a very shallow resolution.

With all of the evidence, we were able to show that the gun used in the city murder cases was the same pistol used in our murder. All of the evidence simply strengthened our case and provided a great case to prosecute. The prosecutor was a man who had been a friend of mine since elementary school. The defense attorney was a lady who had defended several of my previous clients. It was a quick and simple trial to determine the guilt of the murderer.

At the age of eighteen, Cy Regions was sentenced to life for this murder. The kidnapping and the robbery each resulted in fifteen-year sentences. To this date, Cy, now forty-five, has spent twenty-six years in prison. The bike thief who increased his actions in violations of the law will spend the rest of his life in prison.

To this day, Mrs. Harold starts to cry whenever we see each other in the community. Sadly, Lynn Harold never lived to celebrate her twentieth birthday. While out for an evening of fun, she was murdered by a bike thief. We should each and all have the ability to simply walk to our car without having the fear of being a murder victim.

# Hunted

No break right now, let us jump into another story that will probably upset you. During my time in homicide, there was this one investigation that was very different, just down right creepy, from all of my other cases. This story will seem like one of those horror stories that are so often told during Halloween, just a crazy case that went on forever; at the time it seemed as if it would never end. More so we feared that if there was an end, that it would be a very traumatic and horrible conclusion. To help resolve the unresolvable problem, all that could be done was to continually fight the battle, so remember to keep track of the time span of this continual hectic tale. So mount your horses, draw your swords, and let's fight this forever battle.

It was the day after my birthday in October of 1982 with one of my assignments that morning being to investigate a bomb that had been attached to the vehicle of the victim John Williams at the southern portion of the county. The device had explosives wrapped in a brown paper bag and was wired to the ignition of the truck. Apparently, the device had not been wired properly and did not explode when Mr. Williams tried to start his truck. With this problem causing the truck not to start, this required John to fix the problem where he needed to look under that hood. With the hood opened and the discovery of the explosive device, Mr. Williams changed his approach to fixing the car. The deputies responded, the Explosive Ordinance Team disabled the device and the crime scene technician (CST) processed the scene for evidence. The best step taken by the

CST that morning is the impounding of the brown paper bag that contained the bomb.

My first interview with Mr. Williams was with a man who was very nervous and concerned about his close call that morning; no, I did not sneak up behind him and scream, "Boom!" The very professional interview showed that he had no enemies or ongoing battles that would cause anyone to want or need to murder him. He was a man with no prior history of trouble, not a gambler or alcoholic, just a hard working good employee who was engaged to marry a nice young lady. There was nothing in his background that would make one believe that anyone would want to kill him.

While speaking with his fiancée, Dina Garland, they both indicated that recently, another man had been showing interest in the lady. The gentleman, Donald Rose, is employed as an automobile mechanic at the local telephone company where Dina is the administrative assistant at that location. The office is located across the bay from the location of the crime scene. This would place Miss Garland living about halfway between her office and the crime scene, the home of her boyfriend, and on the same side of the bay as his abode. Mr. Rose lived near the office and on the opposite side of the large open water, and having no reason to be near the crime scene. These locations created a good distance between all of these sites.

Dina started to tell her story of how she started her job in January of that year. She worked the day shift in the office, and that Mr. Rose worked the evening shift in the garage. Their schedules and work sites allowed them to meet each other, but the job's assignment would limit that contact as their shifts overlapped by about an hour. Since starting the job, Mr. Rose went out of his way to befriend her and to provide her with gifts.

This started with Mr. Rose coming to work early and having another employee set up a lunch with the three of them. The meeting was similar to any group of employees going out to lunch, just the normal gathering that we have all had at work. As time progressed, the gentleman would leave small stuffed animals, flowers, greeting cards, and other such trinkets on her desk. As time continued forward, Dina became more evasive to Don's actions as he continued his persistence; then he met her fiancée. The company had worked out a promotional deal with the local soccer team to sell group-priced tickets to the employees. These tickets were all in the same section of the stadium. On hearing of that opportunity to see our local team in action, she bought tickets for John and her to attend the game; Don also bought tickets for both him and his wife. On the night of the game, John and Dina were sitting together when Don arrived for the sporting event. Sadly, Don, who strangely was dressed in his work clothes, advised that his wife was not able to make it to the game. They sat together and enjoyed the local team win another of their many victorious games. It seemed as if Don was a bit cold to John that evening while enjoying the time with Dina.

The month before the bomb was placed onto John's truck included the day to celebrate Dina's twenty-eighth birthday. On that day of, she received a gift from Don of twenty-nine roses. This also included some other items including a ring, a diamond ring. With this surprise gift, she had a friend who is a jeweler give an estimate on the ring. The value of the ring would be $995.00, nearly a grand for a simple gift. She returned the ring and the other gifts to her fellow worker and admirer. This action was not received well by Mr. Rose who increased his notes and letters to her. During this time, the roses continually came to her office and to her home, the rose forevermore.

With this information being the only unusual event in the life of either person, it seemed like a good lead to follow. The next day, I met with Don at his home to prevent any problems at his employment. At the residence, Mr. Rose was very evasive and very uncomfortable talking about the incident. He especially went out of his way to remove the conversation from the presence of his wife. As we stood in the driveway, he denied any involvement or knowledge of the crime. He even stated that he thought Dina was a nice lady, but the stories of his infatuation were an exaggeration by the lady. He insisted that he did not commit the crime as he had never committed a crime. The gentleman was left in his driveway as the suspicious detective drove away to continue the investigation. Dina received more roses that day.

On my return to the office, the first action was to obtain a criminal history on my good gentleman. This is accomplished by a computer check that will search the FBI files of people with prior criminal arrest in the United States of America. This examination showed that Mr. Rose lied to me when he sated he had never been arrested in his entire life. When Don Rose was eighteen years old, twenty-five days after reaching that age, he was arrested in Rawlings, Wyoming for breaking into a small store. This meant that his fingerprints were available to compare to any latent prints obtained from the evidence.

On contacting our CST concerning the evidence recovered from the crime scene, we had a wonderful bit of news. Fingerprints had been located on the brown paper bag that contained the bomb. Without even having to ask, you are absolutely correct the request was made to obtain the fingerprints of Mr. Rose from the FBI to compare to the ones recovered from the paper bag. The investigation was on hold waiting for the answer to this very important question. As we waited, Dina received more roses.

It took just one month before my fingerprint examiner called me to provide the results of the requested evaluation. The expert advised that the latent prints on the brown paper bag were a match to those of Donald Rose; we now had the identity of the mad bomber.

My next steps were to initiate an arrest affidavit, obtain the approval of a prosecutor of the State Attorney's Office, and have a judge sign the warrant for the felony crime. With warrant in hand, I once again crossed the bay to our neighboring county. With the assistance of those deputies, we met Mr. Rose at his place of business and served the warrant, another criminal in custody. Now let me surprise you with the outcome of the arrest Mr. Rose immediately denied any involvement in this crime. It was obviously a conspiracy against him by everyone else because he did not commit this crime, any crime, never a crime. So the question arose as to how his fingerprints got on the bag; the answer was that he wanted to speak to his attorney.

With the arrest of the criminal, my involvement in this story was suspended pending the trial of the defendant. Even though the felon was arrested, this did not stop his desires for Dina, or the roses.

With the arrest and the internal investigation at their place of work, Mr. Rose continued to send gifts and roses to Dina. The return of the ring was a continual battle with Dina refusing to accept the item and with Don continually returning the jewelry to the lady. It was nearly daily; certainly not a full week went by without Dina receiving a gift, a rose or a note from the criminal who tried to kill her fiancée. Eventually, Dina discovered that Don was following her, seeing him many times on her way to or from work. Even on her days off, she would see him sitting in a parking lot across the street from her apartment complex. The stress was building for Dina, and the gifts continued to arrive.

By this time, Dina's employer was becoming concerned over Mr. Rose's actions at the job site. This led to a situation where just before Christmas, Mr. Rose resigned from the company that he claimed was harassing him. That day he went to his locker and removed several very large Christmas gifts that he loaded into his truck before he departed the premises. On returning to her home that evening, Dina discovered the Christmas presents, a note, and of course some roses on her front doorstep.

Three months after the arrest, a suppression of evidence hearing was conducted concerning the fingerprints on the paper bag that contained the bomb. We gathered in the courtroom of Judge Angeles who listened to the defense attorney, Ron Booker, who presented that the fingerprints should be suppressed as the prints could have gotten on the brown paper bag before, and that someone else used that brown paper bag containing Mr. Rose's fingerprints to construct the explosive device. Once the defense offered their argument, the prosecutor from the State Attorney's Office, Daniel Perks, offered no objection or argument to the presentation by the defense. Based on the request of the defense, Judge Angeles ruled the fingerprints were not allowable as evidence and that without that information available to the prosecution, he dismissed the case. Without an objection from the State Attorney's Office, the case was tossed out, and the suspect was released to be a free and innocent man. On confronting the prosecutor, Mr. Perks would not speak to me about the results of the hearing. A man who was always been cordial and communicated so well with me prior to that day would not talk to me about this issue, not then and still not today.

To the surprise of nobody reading this story, you know we have to jump off on a tangent after that last paragraph. For several years, there were investigations into criminal wrongdoings at the county courthouse. During this time, several assistant state attorneys were arrested for use of drugs. Other portions of the investigations caused some of our judges not to seek reelection; one of these judges was Judge Angeles. As for Mr. Perks, he resigned his public position to go into private practice. As for Mr. Booker, we have a much more interesting story.

While working with the federal government on courthouse corruption, we obtained information that Attorney Ron Booker could fix your case for the right money. One of our informants was willing to prove that it was easy to pay the "extra" money to resolve the case. Based on a federal court order, we went to Mr. Booker's office and surreptitiously entered the barrister's office. Within the office, we installed a hidden video camera and a microphone with the judge's instructions to observe only our informant's visit. That next morning, we sat and watched as the attorney and the informant talked about the case. As things progressed, we were excited as the conversation was obviously headed in the direction of wrongdoings. Then it stopped, came to a complete and total halt, for some unknown reason, the attorney changed the topic and the entire direction of the conversation. The meeting was completed without any evidence of wrongdoing; the attorney showed his total perfection. This story has always left me with many questions without being able to obtain the many answers; those answers are there, unspoken and hidden. After several years of absence, even Mr. Perks returned to the State Attorney's Office. Well, let us just get back to the original story.

With the court ruling and the trial, my investigation was complete, thus ending my involvement in this bit of foolishness. That would change to being an interruption rather than an end to my involvement. In November of that year, Major John advised me that we were both being summoned to the Sheriff's Office. Neither of us could figure out what I had done wrong this time or better stated what I had been caught doing this time.

The meeting with Sheriff Walter was not about me, for a change, but concerned the problems that Dina Garland was continuing to have with Don Rose. The Sheriff had been contacted by the parents of Dina who were people he had known for years. After hearing the ongoing story, he decided to have me look into the issue with his request being to fix the problem. The major was told to give me free rein and all assistance to resolve this concern; it was like one of those old pink phone messages from those days in SEU.

After just over a year, I was again speaking with Dina at her apartment about the concerns about Don Rose. During this last year, Mr. Rose continued his persistent tracking of Dina. She would receive letters and roses left at her front door. On one occasion, two small boys brought flowers to her door. At the door, she could see Don in the parking lot below watching her as she talked with the young lads. Every week, sometimes every day, she would have some type of contact with him. She would see him waiting on the side of the road while she drove to work. He had sat across the street from her office and watched her when she left the business. Corporate security had been in touch with him while he sat across the street. The investigator was informed that as he was not on their property, he could stay at that location. With the civil suit in progress over the loss of his job, there was little the security officer could do about this problem.

With this being in progress for nearly two years, it had been very damaging to her life. Because of these problems, and the bomb, her fiancée called off their engagement. The man was afraid for both of their lives based on the harassment by Mr. Rose. She took every step that she knew was available to stop the continuous problem.
She had spoken to her own attorney and to the legal staff at the office. Everyone had spoken to Mr. Rose's attorney asking for him to stop the stalking of Dina. None of the conversations were working.

With the constant resistance to his approach, Mr. Rose had started to become more aggressive toward Dina. She started to receive threatening letters, some typed, some written, and some pasted together out of clipping from a magazine. Damage was done to her car with statement of "soon" and "you're next" on the car and her front door. Even her apartment had been broken into without anyone or anything being able to solve that crime. It should be noted that within her apartment was the rough draft of a letter from her attorney to ask Mr. Rose to cease and desist from any further contact with her. After the burglary and before he received the letter, Mr. Rose called the attorney to determine when he would get his copy of the document. That type of action could "rose" one's suspicion about the suspect in the burglary, yet still not probable cause for an arrest.

On one occasion, she even saw a person who looked similar to Mr. Rose in her dark parking lot sneaking around with a bow and arrow in his hands. A man at work told her that he had seen Mr. Rose at work practicing with a bow and arrow in their back lot. Then the final step arose that forced her to call for help. Mr. Rose found a bomb on his car and was blaming her ex-fiancée of planting the device on his car. She was now desperate for help.

My first step was to check with the deputy across the bay investigating the most recent car bomb. To my surprise, that detective did not believe that the victim, Mr. Rose, was being honest with him. They were at a point that they believed the person who put the bomb on the car was the Don Rose himself. On a discussion with the state attorney with jurisdiction on that side of the bay, they lacked sufficient evidence to charge the victim with any crime.

With this being done, the next action was to review this situation with the state attorney on our side of the bay. Now remember we are talking about incidents that started in October of 1982, and we were now at the time of November of 1983 with these occurring crime, occurring nearly daily. At that time, we did not have any state laws against stalking a person. The stalking law would not be enacted until 1997 in our state, over a decade later. The opinion of the State Attorney's Office was that we did not have a crime for which we could arrest the nuisance pest. I still strongly held in my hand that pink phone message from the Sheriff; there would be a resolution to this problem.

# THE EMOTIONS FROM A BADGE

The major put a team of detective to conduct a protective surveillance of the victim. The team of investigators would see Mr. Rose park across from her apartment complex at night; he would follow her to work. He would even use different cars because as a mechanic, he would have to test drive the vehicle he was working on to determine the problem; we know that the test drive was the reason. With all of the special eyes watching the victim, the suspect did not commit a crime; he just watched her constantly. The surveillance was terminated, and the victim moved back home with her parents out of fear for her own safety; now it was still up to me to fix the problem.

Mr. Rose was sure that he was not doing anything wrong, each and every action was legal, and he would continue with his Constitutional rights to live his life to his desire. So since he insisted this was legal, I should investigate the allegations to support his beliefs. In the mornings, I would arise early and drive to the convenience store where he would park to wait for Dina to drive by to work. There sat Mr. Rose so I would park next to him; he insisted that this was proper, so I did the same thing. On exiting my car, I would take photographs with that camera flashing, with or without film in that device. He would act like I was shooting his car full of shotgun rounds as he fled from the parking lot. Other days, the meeting would be as he was driving behind Dina following her to work. As we all know, there are traffic laws that when violated can justify a certified law enforcement officer to stop the driver of the vehicle. When he was stopped, he almost always complained of harassment, no way he was not issued citations for all of the violations just encouragement to abide by the state traffic statutes. This would cause him to stop his stalking, just for a moment before again watching the lady. When he showed up again, Dina called me, and I showed up again to be part of the ongoing party time, peekaboo, I see you too.

The next problem arose when a neighbor, and lifelong friend on Dina, saw a truck parked in an open field of the church located on the next street over from the Garland residence. At that time, an unknown man was walking around the neighborhood, and she called the local police. The subject went back to his truck and was leaving by the time the city police officer arrived at the scene. The good neighbor pointed out the suspect truck and the officer stopped the subject trying to leave; this was without a doubt Don Rose. The officer did a field interview report and released the gentleman who had not committed a crime.

When this news was discovered, I contacted the officer who had been in contact with Mr. Rose. The contact was the same with a man arrogant to the law, insisting he was the victim of harassment and demanding to be released from unlawful custody. That poor officer wanted so much to take some action to fix this forever problem. We agreed that he should contact me if he deals with the subject once again.

With it now being June of 1984, this problem had been ongoing for a year and a half. It was time for me to read the Florida Statutes to find a law that might prohibit this continual harassment; my reading those documents can be dangerous. Within the Florida Statutes, I found the law of loitering or prowling which makes it "unlawful for any person to loiter or prowl in a place at a time or in a manner not usual for law-abiding individuals under circumstances that warrant a justifiable and reasonable alarm or immediate concern for the safety of persons or property in the vicinity." Well, let's look at this, he was loitering in an open field where no one else does; it was at a time and manner not usual for law-abiding individuals because he was doing this to harass someone, and these circumstances warranted a justifiable and reasonable concern for the safety of a person, Dina being that person. Well, that all looked good to me.

A few days later came the phone call that Mr. Rose was again in the open field waiting for Dina to drive by on her way home. The pedal went to the metal with my arrival, just after 5:00 in the afternoon, occurring just before Dina drove by the open lot. Oh, my gosh, it was obvious that Mr. Rose was in a place, at a time that justified the concern for the safety of Dina; Mr. Rose was committing a misdemeanor in the presence of a sworn law enforcement officer. This Deputy Sheriff rushed in to take immediate actions that would "serve and protect" my innocent victim. Mr. Rose was arrested and transported to Central Booking at the county jail. The detention facility was requested in conflict with our normal policy to not release the suspect as he was not a county residence and the fear for the safety of the victim. The detention lieutenant advised me that I did not have to authority for him to fulfill my frivolous request. I made a phone call to update one of my supervisors on the arrest and to the response of the jail lieutenant. A short time later, that lieutenant called me back to inform me that he had just spoken to the Sheriff; my suspect would not be signature released on the charge. Poor lieutenant did not realize my authority on this case.

On the date of July 19, 1984, we were in court standing before Judge Stacy Buckles. This lady is a very good and very realistic judge. Her honesty and integrity have now provided her a position as a federal judge, she is truly an outstand person. With the assistant state attorney having previously been briefed on this multiyear problem and with Mr. Rose defending himself, the prosecutor asked me to tell what had occurred that caused the arrest of the defendant. Fearing that my story would be interrupted before the whole tale could be unfurled, this detective started talking and kept on going. My testimony covered the years of harassment leading up to the offense and the crime itself. Now the crime itself was my concern as the intent of the statute may have been stretched a bit thin for this incident. The good judge saw right through what I was doing and was obviously in total agreement with the need to stop this foolishness. The defendant who claimed his innocence was found guilty sentenced to time served as he awaited bail, required to pay court cost and then placed on six months of probation with a requirement to stay away, absolutely no contact, with the victim. Mr. Rose was ordered to stay a distance beyond the ability to see or to be seen by the victim. It was finally a victory.

The victory was short-lived as with Mr. Rose having contact with Dina, a warrant was issued for his arrest for violation of probation. On August 9, 1984, just twenty-one days after his trial, Mr. Rose was in jail for his disrespect for the order of the court. The court kept him in the county jail until September 7, 1984, that's right, twenty-nine days in the lockup before reinstating the probation, including the requirement to stay clear of Dina. This seemed to stop the stalking, at least for that moment.

The probation lasted until March 6, 1985 which, after the first and only mistake, had been properly resolved by the defendant. On March 7, 1985, Mr. Rose sat on the side of the road and followed Dina to work. This guy must me crazy; hum, let us look at that.

The State of Florida has the Baker Act law that states that a person can be forced to receive involuntary examination, that can be initiated by judges, law enforcement officials, physicians, or mental health professionals, if there is evidence that the person has a mental illness or is a harm to themself, harm to others, or self-neglectful. This can require a confinement for examinations that may last up to seventy-two hours, that's three whole days. A court order or the medical providers can, if so needed, extend the time of the evaluation. The next new law from the state may be one that prevents me from reading the state statutes.

With the assistance of the State Attorney's Office, we obtained a court order for the Baker Act this worthless gentleman. It was now May 24, 1985, almost two and a half years of Dina dealing with this disease of a man, created my next step that required me to track this mentally endangered gentleman down, stuff him behind the cage of a Sheriff's Office marked car, and send him off for a mental evaluation. Is it necessary to explain that Mr. Rose was a tad bit angry over this action? Even the explanation to him defining my persistence and my dangers far exceeded his abilities did not improve his attitude on that trip. It has always been my belief that Don Rose does not want to be my friend.

While the gentleman was in the mental facility, the State Attorney's Office once again reviewed my several inches-thick case file. With their concerns and downright fears, they could find no laws that would help prosecute this continual harassment. They were informed that the subject would be arrested for each and every and any crime that he committed from that day forward; they were informed that this piece of trash was illegally hunting an innocent young lady. Poor Dina had to live with this unbelievable, almost daily terrorism for more than eight hundred and sixty continual days of fear.

We do not know what happened, but after the release from the Baker Act, Mr. Rose no longer stalked Dina; he stopped hunting the poor good women. It may have been the persistent actions of a detective that was meaner and more determined that even that worthless lout. The places that Don kept being placed for short time visits may have been another reason. For whatever the reason or reasons, it seemed to finally come to an end, at long last it was over.

In looking over the following years for Mr. Rose, it appears that his wife divorced him after all of this stupidity. Several years later, he married another lady that obviously had no idea of his personal background concerning women. That time together as husband and wife went through a period where she reported him missing for several days. It make you wonder who he was stalking while he was gone from their home. Eventually, in 2007, the second wife filed some criminal charges against her husband. The charges included domestic battery for hitting his spouse, violation of an injunction that is right ignoring a court order to stay away from the spouse, and of course, one more new crime that was enacted into law in 1997; that is correct, aggravated stalking, the new law that we now have to cover his harassing methods. Later in 2009, he had another trip to jail for once again violating a domestic injunction; Don needs to learn to not disobey a judge's order. In the end, his approach to marriage also ended with the separation from his second wife.

With the passing of thirty years, everyone has moved forward with their lives. Dina is no longer stalked by the worthless scallywag and for years has been off my radar. It would be my hope and prayer that she moved forward and enjoyed a most wonderful life.

Fortunately, the good State of Florida now has a stalking law that can protect a person from the horrible, continual, and disgusting punishment that was endured by my victim. With recalling all of these incidents into a single story, let us all remember to not wait for a resolution to this type of crime. Report the problem early and hope you have a stubborn little detective who can have no problem interpreting the intent of the law and have that detective arrest the culprit for something, something or whatever. We should pray that none of us has to deal with a problem like this, this problem on a daily basis, this ongoing problem for nearly three long years.

# Turn the Power On

Now take a quick break, and we can move on to a story that will have a laughable ending; we need that about now.

The new annual shift bid deployment for my patrol assignment started one year with this sergeant having a brand-new squad on a new shift. On that first day, I met up with the corporal who would be sharing my supervisor responsibilities with me on this new group of deputies. From our many years at the Sheriff's Office, we knew each other but had never actually worked together on any of our multitude of assignments. After the troops were on the road that morning, Corporal LeBron told me he wanted to say something. As I settled in my chair, he notified me that I was the sergeant and that he was the corporal and that to him meant I was in charge, and he was to help me in any way he could. Corporal LeBron continued that he would follow that concept, and that no one, that is correct absolutely positively no one, would cause me any trouble. He would do everything he could to help me with the supervision of this squad. Knowing about this man, I smiled and told him that I knew he would fulfill that promise.

The corporal was a good man who had been with the agency for many years before making the rank of corporal, a person who very much earned his well-deserved promotion. Corporal LeBron's resume with the office included a very wide variety of assignments with many of the jobs providing difficult tasks that he would easily overcome. When anyone would call for help, especially me, being the furthest person from the location, Corporal LeBron was always the first on the scene. He would immediately provide all of the required assistance, and as soon as the problem maker was out of the hospital, he sent them straight to jail. I was very proud to work with this good man.

One normal weekend afternoon, the corporal was doing his everyday good work of helping the squad by taking some of the calls. One of the calls he requested was to a complaint that the owners of a trailer park had turned off the power to the trailer the complainant was renting. This trailer park was one of the locations that not even filmmakers, horror filmmakers, could create such a poor living environment. We often joked that not even the rats inhabiting our local port would want to live in that park. The good corporal was on his way to resolve another problem.

On contacting the owners of the park, Corporal LeBron explained that by state law, they could not turn off the needed utilities, including power or water, to anyone's residence in the park. He also advised them that if this is done, the person who commits this act can be arrested for a misdemeanor crime. They argued with the corporal insisting that he was wrong, and they would absolutely not turn on the power until the renter resolved their late payment. After the disagreement continued, the arrogant landlord insisted that my corporal have his supervisor respond to the scene. Corporal LeBron shook his head and told the landlord that, "Oh no, you do not want to deal with my boss." They were adamant that he have me come to the scene so they could have the sergeant correct his errors. The good corporal sadly agreed but reminded them of his warning.

Corporal LeBron called me to request my presence at the scene as it was very apparent that this group of trailer kings had decided that the corporal was not good enough to solve the problem in their elegant estate. The kind and gentle sergeant was on his way to resolve the problem.

On my arrival, I stood in front of the landlord with Corporal LeBron explaining the situation. When he finished, I asked the corporal why he had not arrested the landlord because he was breaking the law and must go to jail at that very moment. The landlord started to interrupt causing me to stop him and ask why he was denying the victim the need of electricity, why was he violating the state law, and that for doing so, he was going to jail. As the criminal landlord started to speak again, I halted his voice a second time telling the corporal to "read him his rights" before he made any other statement. I continued to rant and rave that Corporal LeBron was too nice, and the landlord was a mean criminal denying the simple needs for existence required for the poor victim. The good corporal continually tried to calm down the furious sergeant.

At that moment, the astonished landlord handed a set of keys to the young man standing next to him. That lad took off running so fast you would have thought both Corporal LeBron and I were shooting all of our weapons at him, and by the way, we were both armed with more than one gun. A few moments passed before the young man returned from his task where he had gone to the power box, removed the lock, and turned on the power. The victim was happy to again have the required by law electricity to their home.

The corporal continued with the extremely difficult task of calming down his irate and uncompassionate sergeant. Explaining that the landlord was such a fine and good citizen who had worked hard to resolve the simple misunderstanding and having corrected the error, Corporal LeBron pleaded with the cantankerous old sergeant not to arrest the landlord. I thought for the moment, beginning to calm down, before telling the corporal that only for him, at his request, and for no other reason would I agree not to arrest the criminal landlord. Corporal LeBron had the situation under control, so I would let him resolve it to his satisfaction. I explained to the landlord that if not for the kindness of the corporal going out of his way to take care of him, he would be in jail where he belonged for his terrible criminal actions.

As this grumpy old sergeant got back into my car to leave, I heard Corporal LeBron tell the landlord, "I told you so." The landlord was very, overly so, happy and appreciative of the corporal for his kindness in helping with the issue. More so, he thanked Corporal LeBron for keeping him out of the hoosegow. Together, the corporal and the sergeant had resolved yet another problem within our community.

After we cleared the call, I had Corporal LeBron meet with me a few blocks from the scene in a local parking lot, so we could converse about his actions at the scene. At that session, we were having trouble discussing the recent incident because we were laughing so hard we could barely speak. Corporal LeBron kept talking about the reactions on the landlord's face as I demanded the corporal arrest the man; that expression was priceless. It was obvious that the landlord should have listened to the corporal's warning about having sergeant grumpy come to the scene. It was also obvious that Corporal LeBron and I do very well working together as a traveling side show act. Heck, we should have both won an award for our acting abilities that day. Overall, we just enjoyed teaching that mean and nasty landlord that he was not the king of the mountain.

Corporal LeBron was a great Deputy Sheriff before finally retiring after many outstanding years of service to the citizens and the Sheriff's Office. To this day, I know that if I called for help, everyone between our two locations had better get out of his way because he would be coming full speed to stand with me. Overall, Corporal LeBron is a wonderful person who gave me one of the greatest gifts of my life, his friendship.

# Victim Refused to Prosecute

Before we can start talking about this story, we have to go back to the very beginning of my days as a deputy while working the streets in a patrol zone. Many a time, maybe a lot more than many, each and every deputy who worked in my area of the county had to respond to a call from the home of Stan and Verna Dillon. Of course, I was one of those deputies with an open invitation to visit this interesting family. Now this couple lived in a home that was beyond human belief that anyone could reside in such a filthy abode. The wooden structure did not have a complete wall on any of the multiple sides as there were gaps throughout the outside walls of the structure. We all remember traveling down an old country road, and there along the side was a poorly built shack that's sole purpose was to sell used tires. That is the best way to describe the home of this loving couple. With the floor being all dirt and the openings in the walls, the goats and cows that were on their property often wandered through the house, I will pass on any other description of that building. With this explanation, it would be oh, so easy to grasp that the home facilities did not include a stash of cleaning materials, none at all. Now Stan and Verna were in their late fifties, but they each looked to be many years older. With their lack of bathing and their unkempt clothing, the overall appearance would embarrass any hillbilly from the highest mountain peak. Before you can even ask the question, the answer would be of course their mental stability was often in question, especially when they drank, and they always appeared to drink.

My first call to the Dillon estate was to the report of a stolen goat; they acted like it was a missing family member. On contacting the couple, Verna began yelling and screaming about the poor little goat being stolen off their private property by a known culprit. It took some time to calm down the lady to a level where she could explain the theft. Apparently, the goat had been tied to the back of a train car that was on the railroad tracks on the north side of their property; and when they went out that morning, the goat was gone. My question was what train car? They informed me the train car was also gone from that location. On looking at the track, there was sufficient evidence that the train car was gone, the goat was gone, and the blood and other animal parts indicated the goat could not be returned to its owner. On explaining this information, Stan and Verna insisted that was what they were trying to tell me the train engineer stole their goat, and they wanted him arrested for the crime. My next stop was down the tracks to the local rail yard.

When the railroad yardmaster heard the story of his engineer stealing the goat, he was speechless. The conversation on how to best resolve this "kid" napping continued with both of us trying our best to be serious, doing so was a very difficult task. We agreed on a solution that sent me back to the crime scene to inform the victims of the resolution of my investigation.

On my return to the residence, Stan and Verna cordially invited me inside to have a seat and discuss the matter. Due to the Sheriff's Office regulations, the one I made up at that moment, they were informed that my investigation needed to be resolved outside of the home in a nonhazardous environment for sure. At that point, they were advised that they were now suspects in the federal offense of interfering with the operation of a train that was needed to supply products to our nation. The railroad was willing to forgive their criminal violation in exchange for their forgiveness with the accident that took their goat. They were both angry and insisted that the prosecution of their goat-napping continue until the engineer was in jail. Sadly, this could not be done until the federal agency conducted the investigation into their federal crime. My next question to Stan and Verna was if they trusted federal investigators? With their agreement to stop all actions on this tragedy, I was back to my regular patrol duties.

Another time, the dispatch to the residence was to assist the emergency medical technicians (EMT) that had been sent to the residence for a man down call. The EMT personnel always requested law enforcement assistance when they were sent the Dillon home. On arriving at the scene, the EMT were already assisting Stan who had fallen off of the toilet. Now that being a bit whimsical, you have to understand the toilet for the home was a five-gallon bucket with a toilet seat attached to the top. Apparently, Stan, in a very intoxicated state, had fallen over on the bucket, or toilet, and was injured to a point of being totally disabled. The EMTs were conducting the proper medical procedures to prevent any further trauma and save the poor injured and paralyzed victim. To assist with this, my first comment to Stan was that he was a worthless drunk and to get up off of the floor immediately. The EMTs were shocked by this statement as they were taking emergency actions to save the victim's life. The EMTs were told to be quiet as Stan was then advised that if he did not get off of the floor, he would be kicked by my large boots until he got off the ground. At that point, Sam jumped to his feet and began yelling and challenging me as he displayed his miraculously and completely healed body. The next information was that if he attacked me, federal investigators would be assigned to conduct the investigation into his criminal actions. With that being said, everything came to an abrupt stop as we all explained to Stan how elated we were for the miracle that caused the immediate healing of all his injuries. Once again, it was time to return to regular patrol duties.

With these previous stories, my hope is that we all can understand that the Stan and Verna were a bit different from the norm of society. Knowing that information, you can be assured that the rest of the story is not even close to being a standard or normal investigation. So unless you need to stop for a refill on your drink, let us move along with yet another interesting tale.

At the time of this crime, Stan and Verna had a gentleman by the name of Louie who was staying at their house with them; anyone living at that hazardous waste site would be a story by itself. Anyway, on the first day of November, Stan and Louie decided to go out and have a night on the town, a men's night out. The two had a taxi cab come to the Villa de Dillon and drive them to a location several miles to the south. This place was a trailer park on the banks of the river that flowed through our community that it's known as the winter home of the carnival. This area is where the traveling carnival workers have their homes and stay when they are not on the road performing. They even bring their lions and tigers and elephants and many other exotic type animals to this winter home.

When the taxi dropped them off, they made arrangements for the taxi to return later to provide a return trip to their home. At this point, Stan, who was fifty-eight years old, and Louie, with the age of sixty, was on a visit to the home of the lovely sixty-five-year-old Missy. During the afternoon as the clock ticked forward, they each had a drink of alcohol or two, maybe a few or more than that small number. Now please understand that this residence was a mobile home that was split in half. Missy rented the southern half of the residence with the other half under the control of another person. The residence had a security wall separating the two living quarters.

It was not long after their arrival of Stan and Louie that a neighbor by the name of Wayne, a twenty-one year old that to this day continues to earn his frequent guest points by staying in the county jail with some even from state prison. The question that will always haunt us will be if Wayne was drunk from alcohol or higher on drugs during his visit to Missy's home that afternoon. For some reason unknown to all, Wayne and Louie started arguing with one another. Eventually, Wayne went over and sat next to Louie on the couch and began a physical struggle with Louie, where the twenty-one year old seemed to have the advantage. Missy was very quick and strong with her actions that stopped the minor altercation. With this, Louie got up from the couch for a trip to the bathroom; this one had a real toilet. As he left the room, Stan and Wayne were starting their verbal disagreement; Stan was always ready to voice his opinion.

## THE EMOTIONS FROM A BADGE

With just the three left in the room, Wayne jumped on Stan and began to beat him as they both went to the floor. Stan was using his cane—yes, the walking cane the fifty-nine year old needed to assist him with walking by holding it across the front of his body and trying to push Wayne off of him. Wayne continued to beat Stan around his chest while knocking his head on the floor and may have even bitten the man on the stomach. Missy was screaming for help while she demanded that Wayne stop the attack. As the fight was ending, four of Wayne's friends came to the trailer and carried him away from the altercation. As Wayne was carted off by his associates, Louie returned to see Stan on the floor and in pain from the attack. Eventually, the taxi cab driver returned and provided them that ride back to their own home.

Without any need for an explanation, it was obvious that Verna was very upset and took the one and only action that she always used to resolve a problem. In response to that telephone call, a Deputy Sheriff responded to the Dillon home. Stan was hurt, upset, and drunk as he reported the horrible attack to the deputy. The main problem was that neither Stan nor Louie knew the name of the young lad who had attacked them. To prevent any further problems with any and all over this matter, Stan demanded to sign a waiver of prosecution, thus ending the investigation of this attack. The waiver is a document that designates the victim does not wish to have the suspect arrested or prosecuted for the crime. With this accomplished, the deputy packed up and went back to his other duties for the evening.

Stan moped and moaned around the house for the next ten days until Verna insisted that he go to the hospital as his condition seemed to be worse every day. The EMT unit arrived in the early afternoon and started their transport to the local Veterans Administration hospital. While on the road to that location, Stan coded out with a cardiac arrest lying there in the back of the ambulance. The transport changed direction and started an emergency run to the local trauma center. With lights and siren, they rushed Stan to the emergency room for the immediate attention of medical doctors. With all of this, it was too late to save Stan; he was pronounced dead at 5:10 on that afternoon in November. The emergency room doctors notified Verna and took the proper step to transfer Stan to the Medical Examiner's Office for an autopsy.

The following day, Dr. Lee of the Medical Examiner's Office conducted the autopsy of Stan Dillon. Dr. Lee, who had been an assistant medical examiner for many years, was knowledgeable and precise, might I emphasize very precise, with the evaluation of an exam. The important facts discovered on this victim were that there were several internal injuries and a few broken ribs that Dr. Lee believed were a direct factor in the death of the victim. To be sure, he reviewed his information over the weekend to justify the final ruling of this incident. On Monday morning, Dr. Lee issued the ruling that the death of Stan Dillon was due to a heart attack resulting from the internal injuries and broken bones inflicted by another person; this was now a homicide.

On that Monday morning, just before noon, Sergeant Randy called Detective John and me into his office to join in on a speakerphone call that he was having with Investigator Nancy from the Medical Examiner's Office. From those many years ago, the three of us had each and all responded to several calls at the home of Stan and Verna. It was a surprise to each of us that Stan had died the week before and worse that Dr. Lee had ruled the death a murder. Investigator Nancy told us that the Police Department had initiated a report at the hospital concerning a natural death, and that the Sheriff's Office had filed a report on the attack. With this information in hand, we set out to locate all of the documents on this new murder case. Sergeant Randy advised the two detectives to go to Verna's home and talk to her about this crime; this was him pulling rank, so he did not have to go to the nasty abode.

Our first stop was at the Sheriff's Office Records Section to obtain a copy of the original report. That is when we discovered that Stan, the deceased murder victim, had signed a waiver of prosecution on the unknown person who killed him. It was back up to the sergeant with the confusion of the document to this crime. This created the first telephone call to the State Attorney's Office where we spoke to the number two man at that agency. The first response of from Chief Assistant State Attorney (C/ASA) Charles was a very amazed,

"What?" The answer was yes, we had a murder where the victim had signed a waiver of prosecution on the killer. The final decision was the waiver was invalid as the state is the one who determines who to prosecute. Sergeant Randy informed C/ASA Charles that his two sleuths were after the facts, and we would call him later in the day. With this, we stopped by the Police Department and obtained their report before we headed south to round up the criminal.

The first stop was to talk to Verna who, of course, invited us into her home to sit down and have a cup of coffee with both detectives reminding her of the Sheriff's Office regulations requiring the investigation be resolved outside of the home; that's right, in a nonhazardous environment. With her interview, it was determined that Louie had moved from the Dillon home and was currently living with Missy at the crime scene; ah, to travel from one resort to another. With little new information concerning the crime, we were again heading south to speak with Louie and Missy.

When we met up with our two witnesses at the trailer, the interviews were very simple. Louie had been in the bathroom conducting personal business, or better defined as hiding from the killer, when the fight took place in the living room. Missy had watched both incidents which made her an eyewitness to the crime. She even talked about Wayne being so intoxicated or stoned that four of his friends carried him from the crime. As there was no evidence to process, the crime scene tech still took some photographs of the scene, and we then started the seek-and-find mission for the killer.

We searched that local community of carnival worker in hopes to quickly find the suspect in this crime. As typical with this close-knit community that word spread faster than we could talk. We chased down leads that he was at his home, another that he was at the grocery store and several other bits of information that took us nowhere. As we decided to stop for dinner, new information arrived that changed those plans and stopped our meal. The suspect was at his girlfriend's house just a few mobile home parks down the road. That is the location where we snagged the young man right out of the protective arms of his cute little girlfriend; from her looks, she was obviously one of the local carnival attractions.

With the waiving of his rights, we had a very short interview with Wayne the killer. He admitted to having a fight with Stan on the evening of his visit at Missy's home. That particular night, he had drank a beer, maybe even two beers, and did not remember everything from the night. Wayne was positive that he did not harm Stan to the point that he would have died from that altercation. Then why did Stan die? That was a question that Wayne could not answer.

Once again, we were on the telephone with C/ASA Charles to obtain his opinion of the criminal charges for this crime. With all of this information, the decision was to charge Wayne with second-degree murder because the intent of the fight was not to kill the victim. With this decided the paperwork was complete, and the prisoner was transferred to Central Booking. The booking time indicated 9:00 p.m. on November 14, which was just ten hours after being notified of the crime. It was also fourteen days after the fight and four days after the death of Stan Dillon.

Now let us move forward eighty more days to determine the final decision of the state attorney on the prosecution of this crime. After a review of the investigation and the opinion of the medical examiner, it was determined that the injuries and the time would not be sufficient to prove the crime of murder, beyond a reasonable doubt. The state attorney initiated a letter of release indicating they would not prosecute Wayne for the murder of Stan. This allowed the release of Wayne from the jail so that he could move forward over the years with many more arrest for various charges.

Verna was quite upset over the lack of prosecution for the murder of her husband. A few months after the decision, Sergeant Randy asked me, well, it was a direct order and a demand, to contact Verna concerning her calls about additional information on this case. When we met at her house, she did not even bother to invite me to come into her home; that was good. Verna advised she had new and additional information concerning this crime. At that time, she would not provide me with the new information that her two detectives had gathered in their search. Verna would not talk to me about her undercover investigation. The little lady would not even identify her investigators; they were surely not federal investigators.

## THE EMOTIONS FROM A BADGE

We never heard any more information about the additional facts uncovered by Verna's special investigation into this crime. The next most amazing fact was that a few years later, Verna was arguing with her daughter who, during the fight, produced a knife and stabbed her mother to death; the girl killed her own mother. It is truly wretched that each Stan and Verna died as the victim of a homicide.

Even with their strange and quirky ways, neither should have been killed by another person, as should no one. The goats and the cows are gone from the little shack where the railroad cars still roll down the rails sending the sound of that train whistle singing past their home. May we forever be remorseful over the way we lost Stan and Verna, as we should for each and every victim of the intolerable crime of murder.

# How Long Has He Been Dead?

No matter why someone dies, a homicide detective is always called to the scene to verify that there is not any foul play in the death. Sometimes, the experienced detective can see things that others do not have the knowledge or expertise for which to look. One day, I was dispatched out to a home where a middle-aged person had been found dead in the home from what appeared to be natural causes. When I arrived at the crime scene, I met up with a Field Training Officer (FTO) and his new rookie Deputy Sheriff for a briefing of the incident. The FTO is responsible for training a new employee through a scheduled process in order to create a qualified Deputy Sheriff. Throughout the training process, there are several levels that the new deputy progresses through to the final goal of being "cut free." This rookie was in the final stage of training where the FTO stands back and evaluates while the recruit does all of the work. The FTO, having worked with me many times over the years, looked at me walk into the room and simply hung his head.

The rookie was extremely professional with his appearance and presentation. He documented my arrival at the scene and began his briefing. The young deputy had done a wonderful job and was obviously near the end of his training. The new deputy knew all of the personal information about the deceased victim, had details on last seen and time found, medical history, and anything and everything else you could ever think of asking, he had it all and more. He com-

## THE EMOTIONS FROM A BADGE

pleted his high-quality presentation, looked up at me, and waited to respond to any question that I could even think of presenting so he could immediately provide the exact answer and of course more detailed information. He was perfect.

The entire scene simply displayed a natural death with no signs of an outside cause or evidence that would support any opinion other than a natural death. To obtain the best view for the evaluation of the scene, I was squatting near the body when I looked up at the rookie, straight into his face and asked, "How long has he been dead?" The deputy looked at his notes, toward his FTO, and back at his notes, shuffling and struggling to find the answer as he was sure he knew all the answers of this investigation. Finally, he replied, "Sir, I do not know." I asked if he had checked for the time of death. Completely frustrated and confused, he indicated that he had no idea of how to determine the time of death. The poor old FTO knowing my history just hid his face in his hands. I asked that highly qualified and professional rookie deputy, "How long does it taste like he has been dead?" The rookie froze, and with his mouth-dropping agape just stared at me in a total state of shock. I shook my head as if I were disgusted over his inability to complete his job duties, then pretended to touch the body, brought my hands to my lips, and then tasted my fingertips. When I announced that it tasted like the subject had been dead between three and four hours, it seemed that all of the blood left the poor rookies face. The FTO in total frustration of me picking on his good new deputy looked to the sky as if he needed help, lots of help, from above.

When the FTO and I explained to our young trainee that I had been joking around about tasting the body, the rookie did not seem to immediately grasp the humorous aspect of my whimsical action. The good young man stated that he needed to walk outside to get some fresh air—yes, a very deep breath. He later, well much later, well maybe a long time after might be the best statement started to laugh about the whole incident.

Over the years, that rookie deputy continued to improve and become a high-quality Deputy Sheriff. On more than one occasion when we crossed paths, he did pick on me claiming it to be more than justified but really more of a required retaliation. My response to his totally unjustified harassment was always to ask him one simple question; do you want ketchup with that?

# Director of Personnel

Refill your drink and get ready to for a strange turn in my career. To add to the confusion of my career, we will of course have to talk about my time in charge of the Personnel Section. That is correct, at one time, this crazy man was the personnel director of the entire Sheriff's Office. Behave yourself and stop laughing at me about this drift from my normal job duties. This assignment added to my various backgrounds to where I could now hire, train, work with, investigate, supervise, fire, and arrest any employee with the agency, not all of that sounds real good.

Shortly after reaching the rank of corporal, it was not long before I was assigned as the administrative assistant to the colonel of the Administration Department. This position provided me with an enormous expansion of my knowledge of the overall operations of the Sheriff's Office. This area dealt with the business side of this law enforcement agency from vehicles and radios, building facilities, and of course personnel. After several years in this assignment, the retirement of the personnel director provided me with a promotion to sergeant and a transfer to that open position. When first advised of this new position, all I could think of was that movie where the old rough and tough police detective who carried that real big pistol tells his current boss, who had previously been in personnel, that "personnel is for a——holes." For one time in all of these stories, the best statement from me about this position would be to say nothing at all and also no need for any comments about me from the gallery.

The lady that had been the personnel director was retiring after nearly thirty years with the Sheriff's Office. During that time, she had always worked in that area as she was moved up the ranks to the position of director. On my taking the position, it was easy to see that the actions and task could be adjusted to improve the overall operations of the office. The easiest way to define this would be to bring the work product into the current century. Now you may have guessed from the previous comments that she and I were not on the best of terms and absolutely not dear friends. Obviously, our personality conflict would be totally and completely my fault, of which I can take great pride.

After a month of watching the operations of the section, it was time to start asking for details on some of the work actions. One of the methods was the completion of a personnel order generated by the personnel clerks. The explanation defined that when an employee had any change in their employment, the personnel order was generated to document the action. Once created, the original was sent to the colonel of Administration for his signature and returned for the next step. From my previous assignment, I knew that the colonel did not sign the form as his secretary rubber stamped his signature on each document, the very large number of these documents. On its return to personnel, they made several copies of the document with the first copy going to the major that was the supervisor of the employee, with the second copy going to the employee, a third copy went to the personnel order file, a forth to the backup personnel order file, a fifth was kept in the personnel sections monthly file, and the original went to the employees permanent personnel file. This created six pages of paper with five of those being generated in the copy machine.

When this was described to me, the next step was to show me how this was accomplished by the clerk. That is when I was shown a room to the side of the office that had an entire wall, from ceiling to floor and wall to wall, a bookshelf that was stacked with loose leaf-ringed notebooks, all of them black in color and the same size. The color and size of these notebooks had to be that same design to not contrast with the other document covers on the shelf. On checking the files, one could see that each folder contained a year of these documents. These dated back for nearly thirty years the previous director had been at the office. Outside of the employees personnel file, the other copies were kept in another backup notebook across the room, but these were transferred to storage after they were three years old. It was apparent that we might be wasting money on some of the extra copies of copies which also required the extra and extra copy and storage cost.

The next question was to explain how the document was created by the clerk. That was easy; it was created in a computer file, and the original was maintained in the computer. You might want to read that sentence again to see that the document was also stored in the computer. With all of the trees cut down to create the paper to generate the multiple copies of a personnel order, it can easily explain the creation of the Sahara desert.

With the approval of the colonel, the ancient yellow faded Orders that covered the wall were all shredded to clear space in the facility. The multiple numbers of copies were reduced to one that was stored in the employee's original employment folder. The major of the employee received an e-mail copy of the computer-generated document. The final was to eliminate the backup copy that was stored on the other side of the room and to destroy the old copies that had been sent to storage so that the storage cost could also be eliminated from the budget.

On explaining this new concept to the personnel clerks, there was an immediate need to call in the SWAT team, or in this Sheriff's Office the Emergency Response Team, as the employees went berserk. One of the supervisors of the clerk told me that we could not change the method of this perfect and long standing operation. My only question to that was, "Why?" The response to that question simultaneously came from several of the employees, "Because we have always done it that way." They were stunned by the order from this grumpy and crazy new sergeant who lacked any experience with the personnel, remember "personnel is for a——holes." With the order in place, the new methods were implemented on that day.

Within a week, a group of the clerks requested to meet with me over the change in the operation. These people were elated over the reduction in workload by eliminating some of the frivolous work requirements with the personnel orders. That is when they pulled out a list of other suggestions to improve on the work product within that section. Heck, we even eliminated the written payroll card that was required to be turned in with the computer-generated payroll document. Still, some of their ideas were not able to be eliminated, and we also could not allow the extra paid day off for a trip to the beach. They were very happy with the idea of moving the work methods to match the current world.

After two years as the director of personnel, my ability to continue in the assignment was not high on my list of things to do. With this being the case, my request for transfer was completed and forwarded to the colonel. This generated several meetings with the colonel and others in the command staff. At that time, we were in the process of implementing a new computer program within the Sheriff's Office that would work on the business aspects of the agency. This operation was being supervised by a gentleman in the Fiscal Section and included the director of payroll, the sergeant of recruitment, and of course, the director of personnel. With this being in progress, the bosses decided that I would remain in personnel until the activation of this program was complete. What did that detective say about personnel in that movie?

The project that was keeping me in personnel had been in progress for several months. Now the manager of the project Mark Flasher, a gentleman from fiscal, had his eyes set on this being established for fiscal and not for any of the other areas included with the program. This was not progressing very well, and it was a frustration of its own. The computer company that was creating the program had a part-time person working on the payroll, recruitment, and personnel areas of the project. When she had her nervous breakdown and left the project, she was replaced by one of the people who had been working on the fiscal side of the job. That person was then part time to our side of the program. Menial and laborious task were given to us to train our people on this program or to simply keep us busy.

## THE EMOTIONS FROM A BADGE

That gentleman from fiscal had little to no knowledge on computer programs or the best method to implement the system.

With all this in place, my desire was to move forward and complete this slowly dragging process. At a meeting with the manager from the computer program company I wrestled the conversation away from Mr. Flasher, the fiscal gentleman, and asked when the non-fiscal side would receive some help on the project. That request was quashed by the computer manager and the fiscal gentleman as they both advised we had sufficient help to complete our task. That response was to request that we had mastered our foolish tasks, and the remainder of those actions should be downloaded from the current files rather than hand entering the thousands of pieces of data and speeding up the process. That was also shot down, and the meeting ended with the two gentlemen not being happy with my challenge to their work and their authority. I forgot to remind them that I was from personnel.

After the meeting, the fiscal gentleman summoned me to his private office—yes, this command leader was the only one on this project with a private office. As I sat on the opposite side of Mr. Flasher's desk, the wimpy little accountant jumped from his chair and screamed and yelled at me as he pounded his fist on the desk and chastising me for challenging his authority and status. As much as he is an accountant, he did not calculate that I would not allow anyone, not a single person on earth, to treat me in that fashion. Flasher seemed a bit shocked when I stood up from my chair with his entire attitude changing as I grabbed his large wooden desk and shoved it completely to the side. Without anything between us, his ashen face melted into an appearance of shock and fear as he backed into a bookcase behind him. As he banged into the bookcase, some of the books fell to the floor as his shaking body also slithered to the ground. As he bundled up into a fetal position with his arms covering his head, it was apparent that any physical confrontation would be a total mistake, my mistake. I did not bother to determine if he wet his pants before I left the room to return to my office in personnel.

Back at the office, I made the proper notifications to my supervisors concerning the difference of opinions at the project site that day. The following morning, the office received a request from the computer company manager, the one who is the friend of the Mr. Flasher or the wimp, indicating they could no longer work with me requiring my transfer from the project. My very unhappy supervisors removed me from the project and transferred me to night shift in patrol. The punishment for this error was more like winning a huge prize. Yahoo! this old cowboy was back on the wide open range.

A little side note to this would be that the program was completed to the requirements of the fiscal gentleman. Therefore, the program was a complete failure; and after ten years, the office is still trying to correct the problems with the worthless system. The disastrous problems created out of this project were those defined in several of my arguments in the meeting that created my removal from that project. The good part about this waste of manpower and money was a major step to correct the problem. You are correct, based on his unforgivable blunder, the fiscal wimp decided to resign at the request of the staff officers who are also still irritated with my actions over this ridiculous project. So is there anybody here who would like to take a bet that the fiscal wimp is in total agreement with the statement of the detective in that old police movie?

# One Boring Day with a Detective

Throughout my life, great fortune has rained on me with the ability to meet so many people who so often have become one of my many good friends, often creating friends with them and their entire family. From my days in high school, one of my friendships was with a great family that had some younger members who also became some more good friends. With this association, many trips took me to one of the great universities in our state to watch one of these friends playing on the university baseball team. It was always a good trip to watch the good team and visit with my buddies. During these many trips, one of the baseball players, another hometown resident, approached me about an internship at the Sheriff's Office to assist him with obtaining his degree in criminal justice. With this simple request, there was no doubt that the internship would be accomplished for the award-winning athlete.

When the time arrived, Rick was immediately accepted into the program at our Sheriff's Office. Now normally, an intern will ride with a patrol deputy and maybe have the opportunity to go with a detective; these special assignments rarely provide a trip with a homicide detective. Of course, we now have to remember that Rick was one of my friends, so it was time for me to visit with the boss. After a short conversation, arraignments were made for him to include a time in his internship riding with this detective. Now when he looks back on this, the good man rarely talks of his time riding with me.

On the first day that Rick rode with me, he had been in a patrol car for several weeks. It was important that he understand that the detective position was more mundane, more boring, than the activity of a patrol deputy. The detective goes to the office in the morning and obtains the new assignments with the actually crime or action way in the past, and the investigation begins the tedious steps to solve that problem. These actions are all simply after the fact. Rick seemed to understand that riding with a detective can be a boring day.

A couple of days into the ride along, we had resolved another case where a gentleman, now that he was sober, did not want to continue the investigation into him being hospitalized after the bar fight. As is normal with these cases, the gentleman signed a waiver of prosecution, and the investigation was complete. With documents in hand, we were driving through the town on our way back to the office to complete all of the paperwork. At the main intersection, we were waiting for the red light to change as we were both singing along to a Michael Jackson song bouncing from the radio. In the middle of that song, an alert tone sounded from the other radio.

With that sound, the reflex is to turn up the radio and listed to the dispatch, a very interesting one for that day. The dispatcher announced a bank robbery in progress where the robbers, armed with rifles, had kidnapped a citizen and was forcing them to rob the bank. The robbers were outside the bank, sitting in a car in the parking lot. The most interesting part of the dispatch was the location of the bank; it was two blocks south of my current location. It was time for action.

Without waiting for the light to change and to the anger of many other drivers, my left hand turned sent me toward the bank. The turn also made Rick stop his sing along with Mr. Jackson. The main instructions for my intern were to stay down and stay in the car. The instructions were quick as we were already pulling into the parking lot of the bank. Moments later, the marked units were coming down the street. The described car being used by the robbers was easily located in the parking lot. They were in the far corner of the lot and backed into the parking space to assist with a quick escape. The marked units were advised to delay a second or two so that I could place the unmarked car in front of the robbers. This would stop them from driving away and help prevent a pursuit. As soon as I stopped, the four marked units were to pull in from all directions. We all drew our sabers, and the charge was on.

As I touched our front bumpers, the robbers had a look of shock on their face. That look quickly worsened as the marked cars completed the encirclement of the bad boys. With my pistol drawn and many more weapons pointing from the other deputies, the suspects were easily apprehended in the middle of the crime. As I turned and looked back, there was Rick on the floorboard of my car with just his forehead and eyes above the dashboard. He looked so much like that Kilroy cartoon of the eyes and nose looking over the fence. When I got back to the car to check on his well-being, the only comment from Rick was that it was not true that a detective's job is always boring. My response was that things can happen, happen at any time in this work. That must have been a major factor that changed his mind about detective work.

Well, old Rick graduated from college and became a Deputy Sheriff at our wonderful Sheriff's Office. During his career, he had many assignments with, of course, one of those being a homicide detective. His cases where always solved and resolved in the best of fashion. Even some of those were major investigations that received national news coverage. Eventually, he worked his way up to master sergeant and achieved his own retirement. That goes to show you what riding with me a few days can teach a new troop how to become another great deputy. Okay, that may sound good; but the real story is that Rick was a good detective and is a good person. I am very lucky to be able to include him in my list of friends.

# Shooting in the Park

Let us take a stretch and get ready for another interesting story, a wild ride.

As a patrol sergeant, I was driving down the road on a beautiful day in December observing all of the holiday decorations and enjoying the cool Florida weather when the radio squealed with an alert tone. A shooting had just occurred in the playground of an elementary school located within my area of patrol. My deputies were en route to this heinous report of such a horrible crime which also requires a supervisor to respond to the scene. The engine roared as I stepped up the pace racing to the scene of a very serious criminal act. This type of call always sounds like it would be a serious emergency. On that particular day, it was the last two days before the beginning of the school's Christmas break. The schools were on a half day schedule, so nobody was at the elementary school. Some students from the local high school had finished their end-of-semester exams for that half day with the second portion of exams scheduled for the following day. So having the beautiful afternoon off some of the high school boys were playing around in the park next to the school. Then it happened.

As the boys were running in the park, a pickup truck drove out onto the field. In the vehicle were the driver and a passenger hidden in the bed of the truck. As they drove by the group in the field, the armed person in the back of the truck stood up and emptied the rifle at the crowd. Many of the people were hit as the shooter was quite the marksman. Now step back and calm down, it was a paintball

## THE EMOTIONS FROM A BADGE

gun. Most of the guys running and the guys in the truck were friends who were continually playing tricks on each other. They were out just having a good old boy time.

One of the boys running in the field was not part of that group of pranksters who exchanged those tricks back and forth. One of the paintballs struck him in the chest with another in the throat. The throat shot missed an area of the body by less than an inch that could have caused a very serious injury; I have seen lesser injuries result in death. Still, this was all meant to be in fun, yet on that day, not everyone saw the humor in the event.

The victim, a young man named Lee, walked to his home just a few blocks from the school. His parents were very irate and called for the Sheriff's Office demanding justice for this criminal activity. This was a situation that could have been but fortunately was not a tragedy. The outcome did not calm the parents from their fears of what could have been. They insisted on filing criminal charges!

As we were initiating the investigation, the pickup truck from the attack drove by the house. When my good deputy, Michelle, stopped the truck with only the driver from the crime spree, who she identified as Zack, was still driving the vehicle. The investigation of this ambush shooting was all coming together. While Deputy Michelle was interviewing, the driver of the truck, the shooter, who we determined to be Steven, came strolling up from the crime scene and joined up with all of us. Steven, who was very concerned, stated he heard that Lee had been hurt and wanted to make sure he was going to be okay and also wanted to apologize for the incident. Everyone needed for the investigation was now together and the case of this vicious crime spree would now all come together.

The victim's family was adamant about pressing charges repeating their concerns of the serious injuries that could have occurred to their victimized son. They were convinced that Lee was very lucky to survive the shooting and still be alive. It was easy to understand their point of view as a parent and concern for their child and his well-being. Still, there was a very important fact to be considered; the injury was just a red spot on his throat. Trying to convince them that the best solution would be to handle this between the families was just never going to work. They knew this was an attempted murder, and the sadistic killer should be sent to death row. The heathen must be arrested, at this very moment, immediately and now!

Steven and Zack were both very good young men who had been joking around with their friends. Without any desire for it to become such a bad event, the joke had still gone way too far. The "by-the-book" investigation would require that any suspect in this type of criminal act be arrested and transported to a detention facility. The very intelligent and compassionate Deputy Michelle did not want to arrest anyone for this incident that was a game that turned into a bad mistake. Without regard to her opinion, the job required her to be diligent with her duties.

The deputy and I got together and tried to reduce the serious level of the incident to make the system deal with this situation in a method more suitable and based on the actions and reasons for this error. First, we consoled Lee and his family showing our concern for their moment of terror and our joy of his survival with minor injuries. The driver of the truck, Zack, was a very big and very humble high school football player who we transformed into a witness of the crime. Even though he was driving the assault vehicle as a witness, he would not be charged as being a criminal involved with the shooting spree. In the end, only Steven had to be arrested for the shooting of only Lee, the one victim out of the many that was reporting being shot by this terrorist sniper. On a review of the various state statutes that would cover this type of incident, we determined the least Steven could be charged with was throwing a deadly missile, which is still a felony requiring detention.

As Michelle wrote up the arrest papers, I went over to the patrol car and spoke to Steven who was sitting in the backseat of the caged car. As he sat in that car which is designed to transport the hardened criminals, we looked at each other face to face. I felt like the worst person on this entire earth. Steven was a seventeen-year-old junior in high school. The polite, well-mannered, and good-spirited boy had never been in trouble in his life. He was the picture of that perfect young man that we all know. This was all supposed to be a joke; instead, it was tragedy that had turned into a situation that should not have happened to this young man. Deputy Michelle and I believed the crime we selected, being a lower level felony and his clean record would justify his quick release from the juvenile detention facility. So with all the paperwork signed, Deputy Michelle hauled the hardened assassin off to the juvenile prison.

Another part of this story was that Steven came from a very good family. They lived in the area for many years and knew many other people in the community. They were just darn good folks. When Steven's family discovered that he had been arrested, they contacted most of those many other people in the community. The shooter's mother was not at all happy with the outcome of the investigation. Nor would my mother have been, both mothers love their boys.

Thursday afternoon was the day of this bit of craziness, and with our work schedule, we did not return to work until Monday. When we got back to work on Monday morning, Deputy Michelle updated me on the outcome of this Wild West shootout. The charged crime calculated to enough points that the shooter had to be kept overnight to appear before a judge the following morning. That next day, a very disgruntled judge ordered Steven to be detained until his trial date. Apparently, there had been several throwing deadly missile crimes recently covered in the media with one involving rocks thrown from an overpass bridge that caused a fatal traffic crash. The media frenzy helped keep our fine young man, who made a mistake joking around with his friends, locked up in the juvenile detention center. This continuation of jail time had also caused Steven to miss the second day of his end-of-semester exams. You are correct; his mother was more than very, very mad being angrier with the Sheriff's Office than with her own son. Michelle also told me that Steven's detention status hearing was set for that morning. This was all so wrong, so again, my patrol car engine roared to life.

When I got to the courthouse, there were probably fifty people packed in the lobby. The shooter had fellow students, friends, neighbors, teachers, and family wanting to speak up and defend him. By court rules, none of them could enter the juvenile courtroom which created a screeching halt to their crusade to save the young lad. As a uniformed Sheriff's Office sergeant, I went directly into the courtroom. There sat the young terrorist sniper in a jumpsuit, ugly plastic flip-flop shoes, and of course, handcuffs and leg irons. Again, our eyes met for a moment, and then Steven looked down to the ground; it was a very pitiful sight of such a fine human. Steven did not deserve that type of treatment, especially for almost five long days. It was now time for the hearing to begin.

The prosecutor and I had spoken about the lack of any need to continue detention of the defendant. He believed that the judge, due to recent events and his honors regular tough attitude, would not be agreeable to a release of this good person. The prosecutor stated that he could not promise but would try to allow me to speak to the judge. The shooter, his attorney, his mother, and his father stood before the judge while on the other side of the bench stood the prosecutor and the grumpy old uniformed sergeant. There was a quick presentation from the two attorneys concerning the incident and a disagreement over the need to continue detention. The judge then looked at me and smiled, which I returned, and he ordered me to identify myself to the court.

Without anyone else knowing what was happening in the courtroom at that moment, it was all a bit comical to the judge and me. During my career, I was involved in numerous investigations concerning corruption and several other criminal offenses within the courthouse. During this time several judges resigned, a few lawyers went to prison and a couple of law enforcement officers went to jail. This judge was accused of using his position on the bench to commit one of these criminal acts. My investigation into the allegations determined that the judge was innocent of any and all allegations of the lies raised against him. His innocence, proven by my very professional investigation, caused him to warmly greet me from that time forward.

I advised the judge that the shooter was not a threat to the community or for flight from justice. If there was a fear of either or both, I was willing to take that fine man to my own family home rather than leave Steven in the confinement of juvenile jail. After I spoke, to the surprise of both attorneys, the judge without question or hesitation immediately released the young man from detention to house

## THE EMOTIONS FROM A BADGE

arrest. This action would allow him to go home and stay with his wonderful family. The judge after preaching to the young man about the danger of the crime ordered that Steven would not be allowed to leave the home to go anywhere that was not required by school, medical or judicial needs. Fortunately, I was able to help convince the judge, maybe with a wink and a smile, or some other information from that past investigation into the honorable judge; that this good man should not stay in the confinement of the degrading detention facility. The shooters mother was not quite as mad as she had been.

The frustration over this incident is that a Deputy Sheriff puts a longtime juvenile criminal, once again and again, in detention for another burglary or a theft. Some of these hooligans should be locked up until they are more than past the age to be eligible for Medicare. With the methods of the juvenile justice system, the bad boys may be released before the arresting deputy finishes writing the offense report. Now in this case, the system requires this good person with absolutely no history of criminal activity to sit in detention for five very long days for playing games that went too far. Now as we sit here believing that his release from jail can put an end to this crazy mess, we have to change our opinion and open chapter two.

A few days after Steven was released from detention, I received a telephone call from the victim's mother. She told me that during the night, Lee, who barely survived the first attempted murder, was driving his truck home when someone threw eggs at his truck. This attack created a reaction where he nearly wrecked his vehicle in response to items striking the windshield. Once again, Lee had a horrible moment, but for the grace of God, this did not become his final tragedy and end his life. His mother was convinced, more so she knew that the shooter had tracked down her innocent son and committed this crime to finally succeed in his strong desire to murder her boy. She demanded that we take all efforts to stop this grand conspiracy of retaliation as she did not consider this current crime a yolk. (I am sorry, a joke.)

Once again, the car engine roared to life as I went to work on trying to resolve this new offense before it could get further out of control. From the previous investigation, I knew which individual would tell me the truth about this new attack. I tracked down my source so I could get the real story, yes the correct information about this current crime. At the beginning of our conversation, he stated he did not want to be involved in this new situation. As this bit of tomfoolery needed to be brought to a stop, he was told that I would loosen my grip on his throat, return his feet to the ground, and keep his name out of the case if he would tell me the truth right now. With a quick reconsider of his original comment, he agreed to assist with this investigation and told me the entire tale. After getting that story off his chest, he took a breath and his feet back on the ground, we both moved on down the road.

The story was that since Steven had been released from detention, he totally obeyed the order from the court and stayed home. His friends would come over to the house where they played games and watched videos. The night of the egg throwing, Steven got a cell phone call from three of their friends. They informed Steven that they had gone out to egg another friend's car. During the evening search for this other friend, they were not able to find him or his vehicle. They finally gave up on their plans and decided to drive on over to Steven's house to play cards when on the way, they saw Lee driving down the road. They immediately went on the attack to get this poor boy and threw the eggs at his car. When they told Steven of this great accomplishment, he did not laugh. Steven told the trio that what they did was more than stupid. He informed them that they could not come to his house that night; he insisted that if they did show up, he would not let them inside his home because of their thoughtless act, and then he hung up on them. Steven, the good young man, the very angry young man, had learned the bad circumstances that can be created by one's mistakes. My source also gave me the names of the people in this criminal gang, better known as Los Muchachos Huevos (The Egg Boys).

At this point, I had most of what I needed to solve the new investigation. With my source not wanting to testify and complaining about his sore throat, there was not enough legal information to justify an arrest. The next step was to contact the victim and his family for an update on this criminal investigation. Lee and his family were told that I had most of the answers without having any evidence that could be used in court to justify any arrest. I advised them that if they would sign a waiver of prosecution on the subjects, I would promise to get them all of the answers on this situation. Even with this preventing any criminal proceedings, this would be the best method to give them peace of mind in knowing that there was not some ongoing plot of treachery planning to kill their son. This would also be very helpful with my plans to convince everyone to immediately stop any and all of this foolishness. They all agreed that this was the best way to resolve this problem and signed the waiver with the hope that I could get all of the answers and create a future safe environment.

My game plan was in progress with the next stop being at the shooter's house. I had not seen Steven since that day I spoke up for the gentleman's release in the courtroom. When I arrived at his home, Steven was in the front yard doing some gardening work. As we approached each other, Steven dropped everything that he was holding, ran up to me with a huge smile on his face, and gave me a strong hug. Steven told me that he could not express how much he truly appreciated what I had done for him in the court hearing. I told him his thanks were more than enough because the system did not work well with his situation, and it created problems that he should never have endured. That day, we both had very large smiles on our faces. As we talked, I told Steven that I knew the very first thing he did when he got home from the detention facility. He told me that was easy to figure out because he went to bed for a long time as he had not slept anytime while in the facility. I told Steven that was not correct, the very first thing he did was take a shower, a very long shower. Steven started laughing, indicating that I was very knowledgeable, and agreed that was the correct answer. Still the hour or longer shower seemed like it could not wash that horrible feeling of the jail off of his body. From there, we went inside the home so that we could talk with his parents about the current problems.

Both his mother and father joined us for the meeting concerning the topic about the latest crime, which I knew Steven was not involved, and how to prevent the problems from continuing. When

I told them the story that I was looking for the egg gang for this new crime, Steven looked at the floor. It was obvious that he did not want to tell me about the crime or who the egg launchers were; you could see that Steven did not want to lie to the man who helped free him from jail. Watching him shrink from the story, I did not ask Steven if he knew anything about this current event; it seems that each of us had developed a special respect for the other. I made up my mind that he needed to be left out of this part of the story, and that I would do everything in my powers to accomplish his separation from this action. The family agreed to talk to everyone about leaving the victim alone and to put a stop to all other shenanigans. They were sure that everyone would want to go along with this decision. As I left the house of my new friend, I felt so much better than I did that day in courthouse. The family, and especially Steven, was very appreciative for my help in this incident. Even his mom was happy.

Later in the afternoon, I found two of the egg gang as they returned from their morning fishing trip. As I stepped out of the car, they looked at the uniformed sergeant; they looked at each other and turned back to me. Without saying a word, they were both showing faces that were screaming they were guilty of the crime. One of the boys was a strong and solid defensive back on the local high school football team, and both of them were very nervous. I assured them that if they told me the "truth and nothing but the truth," I would resolve this problem in a fashion that would prevent their arrest. After having heard Steven's story about his time in detention, they were both willing to do anything rather than spend time in the jailhouse. Their story was the same one that I heard earlier about them driving around looking for a friend to throw eggs at him, his car or both. When they could not find the desired target, they gave up the quest and started toward Steven's house. On the way to the card games, they happened upon the victim. They decided to go after Lee, as a joke, and throw the eggs at him thinking it would be funny after all the trouble he had created for their friend. They often played this game with their band of friends not thinking that this action could be a dangerous crime. After they launched the attack, they called Steven who became irate with them for what they had done. It was unbelievable that Steven would be that mad, so very mad, he was furious at them over this incident. They never wanted to hurt Lee and were very sorry for what had occurred promising that they would not do anything like that again. They also agreed to tell everybody to stop all of this foolishness of playing jokes on each other. This was originally meant to be fun, but as it progressed, it kept getting worse and had developed into a very bad problem. Preventing either of these young men from being arrested was the best way to resolve this bit of stupidity and allowed the football player to keep his sports scholarship to college which could have been cancelled with his arrest.

Finally, I was able to contact the third egg delivery boy at his home later in the afternoon. In the original conversation with him and his mother, he spoke a bit short and nasty with me. His defiant and rude attitude required me to explain that I had a piece of paper in my hand that was a waiver of prosecution which would prevent his arrest for this crime. I again interrupted his sassy mouth and followed with an explanation that it was obvious he was an intelligent person with a keen understanding that a piece of paper, like a waiver of prosecution, could be torn into little tiny pieces while he and I travelled to the detention facility. As if a magic spell was cast into the room, his total attitude changed, and he became a very polite and totally cooperative person. His story was the same old tale that I had heard several times that day. The same agreement was reached for him to stop any and all actions and to encourage all others to prevent any further aggression directed at the victim or anyone else. This might require them all to grow up just a little bit.

By the end of this story or stories, the victim and his family were completely satisfied by the outcome of the investigations and the judicial process. The egg gang had been "broken and scrambled" with no future threats or problems. The group of friends decided they would grow up and move away from the pranks and other jokes being played against each other. This also stopped other innocent people from being caught in the middle of their "playtime." Steven received his punishment through the court and fulfilled the requirement of his sentence. At long last, finally, the saga was over and done.

After several months, Deputy Michelle received the evidence disposition request on the paintball gun. When a piece of evidence is no longer needed, the impounding deputy receives a disposition request form and has to determine what to do with the evidence. She brought this document to me requesting what should be done with the dangerous sniper weapon. On calling the shooter's house, his mother was the person who answered the telephone. We asked her what she wanted us to do with the paintball gun as we were preparing to release the item. Laughing with me or maybe at me, she told me exactly what to do with that device including exactly and precisely where I could put the weapon. Michelle, with a big smile and a good laugh, completed the evidence form indicating destruction of the paintball gun. As Deputy Michelle walked out of my office, she stopped and asked if she needed to indicate on the document exactly and precisely where the evidence personnel had been requested to put the item. With my laugh and smile, I gave her a direct order not to include that information on the document.

Steven got back to school, resolved all the issues with his missed exams, and graduated the following year. He even sent me an invitation to attend his graduation party the family had at his home. As time has moved forward, the good man has obtained a job in sales for a national company that has transferred him to several different locations around the country. I will forever believe that it was the right thing for this grumpy old sergeant to stand up in the courtroom and defend such a fine person who made a simple mistake that sadly was defined as a crime. Over time, we have become one of those friends who rarely see each other; but every so often, sometimes on a holiday or one of our birthdays, we will talk on the telephone and have a good laugh. We both agree that neither time nor distance can separate true friends. When we do happen to see each other, we both get a big smile back on our face. By the way, Steven's mother now thinks that I am a pretty good person.

# Closing a Business

It was a very beautiful day just a short time after the start of the spring season. The nice Florida sun was shining so bright with just a few clouds floating across the pretty blue sky. Sergeant Randy, Detective Lee, and I were on the way back from a nice quiet lunch; with our busy schedule, rarely did we have the time to dine together. For the past few weeks, the homicide activity had been sort of dead, maybe I should change that to quiet or not so busy. As the experienced and well-nourished group of investigators was driving back to the office, the sergeant's phone began to ring. The caller was advised that the good sergeant had the information, and he would respond with two of his detectives, that is right, the two in his car.

The call from the dispatcher informed the sergeant that a man had just been shot to death in the driveway of his home. The location was just a few minutes from our location that we would have passed on return trip to the office. The time span between when the call was received by the dispatchers to our arrival at the scene was thirty-two minutes. That short time was probably a record for the homicide detectives arriving on the scene of a murder. The rest of the beautiful spring day would continue to be a short time span for a murder investigation.

The home where the crime occurred was a block or two off of a large major highway that would take you from one large community to another in our large county. The street of the murder was in a nice area containing better homes with that road extending down to a dead end into the large river that flows through the county.

This home was the second house on road in this quaint quiet little neighborhood. At the scene, the patrol deputies had secured the location and were prepared to brief the investigators of this current crime. Everything was moving along so very well just like it would be defined in a homicide training class.

The quick story was that the victim, Dean Darrell, had just had a lunch meeting at his home with Bill Simpson, his business partner and friend. As they were leaving the home after the meal, Dean had gone to his car parked in the driveway and Bill to his parked in the street. While Dean was getting into his car, another vehicle pulled in behind him; the driver exited the automobile, walked up to Dean, and shot him to death. The killer then walked back to his car and strolled away without the appearance of any concern. This entire incident happened while Bill stood and watched the callous murder of his business associate and friend. Mr. Simpson was without a doubt very upset over the tragedy that had just unfolded before his very eyes. When asked if he knew the killer, it was a very simple answer for him; the killer was Andy De Leon the third partner in their business. Most business lunches have a much better resolution.

With Detective Lee and I being assigned the investigation, we started with the interview of the eyewitness to the murder. Mr. Simpson told us that Mr. Darrel, Mr. De Leon, and himself had created a business concerning investments and financial advice. Recently, Dean and he believed that Andy De Leon had been cheating them and filed a criminal allegation of stealing from the business. Since that time, the bad blood between the two sides had continued to boil. Even though the friendship had ended and the business was in disarray, he did not believe that Mr. De Leon would go to the extent of killing anyone over this simple business disagreement. As Dean and he left the house after the lunch meeting, they each went to their own vehicle, Dean's in the driveway, and he's parked at the front curb of the yard. At that moment, Andy De Leon drove into the driveway stopping behind Dean's car, walked up and continually shot Andy until the gun was empty. Andy then turn and walk to his car driving away like nothing had happened, just a nice departure from a lunch meeting. This all seemed like a pleasant meeting of business associates except that one of them was now dead.

We finished the interview with Mr. Simpson and helped him get back to his home where a marked patrol car was placed outside to protect him from any other business transactions. After his noon meeting, it was obvious that Bill Simpson's next meeting would be with a very large and very strong drink of hard liquor. It was now time to move on with our investigation.

The first step was to place alerts for the suspect in our homicide. The alerts for Mr. De Leon were broadcasted to all of the law enforcement agencies in the county. Other detectives were sent to the De Leon residence, business office, and other locations to find the fleeing murder suspect. The suspect would be easy to identify as so many of us in this community knew the vicious assassin.

This person being a murder suspect was a shock to so many of us in the agency and the community. Mr. De Leon was a longtime resident of our town and had an outstanding reputation for helping in the various areas of our county. At the time of the murder, he was still a leader in the district offices of Little League baseball. Over the years, he had even been the baseball coach of some young lads who were now some of the detectives that were on the trial of the murder suspect. In my own past, I met Andy and his family on many occasions in my days as a patrol deputy. The family had a son who was an excellent athlete who played football, baseball, and wrestled on the local high school teams excelling in all of these sports. Outside of school, he was also an accomplished expert in the sport of judo. With all of the great abilities of this young man, he had a small problem, drugs. His drug use would cause him to go berserk where he would use his fighting skills to attack others and most often his father. Several times, I had to arrest the young man for his attacks on the family members. Most of the arrests were accomplished at a ten-yard distance with him facing the barrel of my rifle. The young man and I had a mutual respect for each other. The problem was finally resolved with these terrible drugs taking the young man's life. Now the kind and well-mannered father had taken another man's life and destroyed his own.

The simple crime scene was very easy to process for this very serious crime. The victim was lying on the ground just outside of the open driver's door of his vehicle. There he lay on his right side with his arm stretched out above his head. One of the bullets had missed the victim and hit the windshield of the car. Pieces of the bullet were scattered along the car's dashboard. There were other bullet entry wounds around the body with one being in the victim's back. The shot to the back would indicate that he was shot after he went to the ground. At the distance between the victim and the suspect, it would be difficult to miss the target. The fact that only four bullets were discharged by the suspect was a bit confusing as the witness stated the suspect shot until the gun was empty. The number four does not match the number of bullets that would be in a small revolver described by the witness. Yet, at the end of the driveway were four empty shell casings. At that location appears that the killer empty the spent bullets and reloaded the handgun. This makes one realize how fortunate for Mr. Simpson that he was to still alive. We would have to answer that question of only four bullets later in the day. The photographs were taken, the measurements completed, and the scene was searched for any other evidence. The medical examiner completed his actions at the scene and removed the body for an autopsy. The final bit of evidence was recovered from the victim's briefcase that was lying on the seat of the car.

Within the briefcase was a photocopy of a newspaper article. This article had a very large photograph on the front page showing two Sheriff's Office detectives recently escorting a local politician out of the courthouse. The headlines spoke of the corrupt person being arrested for his crimes. This particular copy had an alteration to the large photograph. Placed over the face of the arrested politician was a cropped photograph of Andy De Leon's face. This was a cute little joke where it made one believe Mr. De Leon had been arrested for corruption. It was obvious that Dean and Andy were no longer retaining their friendship from the past. With Mr. De Leon never knowing about this bit of comedy, one would have to ask if Mr. Darrell and Mr. Simpson continued to see the humor on this piece of paper. Unfortunately, Mr. Darrell would not be able to answer the question.

With the crime scene completed, the interviews conducted; and sadly, the next of kin notified we packed up and went back to the office. Sitting down at the typewriter, I began to create an arrest affidavit and a warrant for the arrest of the elusive Mr. De Leon. It was almost time to end our work day and just two and a half hours after the murder when we were notified that two detectives had the killer in custody. Mr. De Leon had met up with his lawyers to notify them of his afternoon outing. These gentlemen decided that poor little Andy needed the professional help of a psychiatrist. To interrupt his arrest, they rushed him to the local mental facility to place him away from the hands of law enforcement. While going through the admissions process, Detective Rock and Detective Leon were notified by a confidential informant of the whereabouts of the wanted man. Knowing Detective Rock and his reputation with the ladies, we never knew if the informant was a nurse at the facility or maybe the wife one of the attorneys, regardless of that he found the suspect.

At the mental facility, the attorneys informed the detectives that they could not take their client from his need for professional help. The good detectives informed the attorneys that they could arrest the killer and anyone else who interfered with their duties, including the attorneys. Needless to say, the legal eagles did not continue to disagree with the highly skilled investigators. While a patrol deputy impounded the subject's vehicle from the parking lot, the two detectives transported the suspect to our office. It was a hard trip for these detectives as they were two of the Sheriff's Office employees who had been on Mr. De Leon's baseball team. A Deputy Sheriff doing the right thing is not always the most enjoyable of task. Still, these two good men did their job, as always with these two gentlemen an outstanding job.

At the office, we sat down with Mr. De Leon to conduct an interview concerning the day's events. Of course after the reading of his Miranda Rights, Mr. De Leon told us that on the advice of his attorney, he would not make a statement about the crime; it was a rather quick interview. While completing the paperwork and finalizing the arrest actions, I stopped by the holding cell and asked Mr. De Leon if he needed anything before we transported him to jail. Andy looked at me and said, "That's okay, thank you. I won't ever be going anywhere again. "From his decisions and actions earlier that day, it was easy to determine that he was absolutely correct.

We later served a search warrant on the car of Mr. De Leon and recovered the murder weapon. This firearm was one of the small revolvers that you always see the detective in the movies and on television shooting the criminal fleeing from the scene. Those detectives always take one shot and wound the criminal at more than a mile away, which cannot really happen. This small revolver is a gun that can be loaded with five bullets and has a two-inch barrel which is accurate at very short distances, a short distance of standing outside of an automobile while shooting the man standing next to the car. Many people believe in that old cowboy way of not loading a bullet in the chamber that is under the hammer of the gun. In the old days, this was a safe way to carry the gun with this no longer being necessary with the improvement of the firearms over the years. Even with the changes, many people, like Mr. De Leon, do not like to carry a revolver with a bullet in that active chamber. With the gun in custody, it was easy to see that Mr. De Leon did empty the gun into Mr. Darrell. With the five-shot pistol loaded with only four bullets, all of the projectiles struck the victim and the car. Mr. De Leon was so frustrated over the business problems that he kept shooting till the bullets stopped firing; it was good the gun didn't have more bullets.

We should add here that Mr. Darrell also had two pistols in his own automobile. The quick attack by Mr. De Leon prevented him from arming himself and preventing a big shootout. The two guns did nothing to prevent him from dying on that nice afternoon.

When we went home that day, we had spent just over seven hours on the investigation. This very short murder investigation was completed with everything needed for the prosecution packed together in that short time span. This was a very quick investigation with the time to commit, investigate, and complete the overall actions of a murder, being like a drive-thru restaurant purchase rather than a sit-down dinner.

## THE EMOTIONS FROM A BADGE

The murder trial was also very short and an easy case to resolve in that very short time. The conviction for the murder required the life sentence to be imposed for this foolish action by a usually good man. So at the age of forty-nine, Mr. De Leon killed a thirty-seven-year-old man over a disagreement concerning their business. Now at the age of seventy-six, twenty-seven of those in prison, we wonder if Mr. De Leon regrets his terrible decision on that beautiful spring afternoon. The actions of Mr. De Leon have kept him in prison for one-third of his life, and in the long run, the final outcome will be close to half of his life, all over a disagreement over the business. With such a terrible action occurring on that beautiful spring day, maybe everyone should learn a great lesson that there are many other ways and better ways that a person can close a business.

# Endangered Quarterback

If you are ready for another strange story, sit back for to this one. Do you need a refill before we start this saga? So let's get going.

Let me tell you that my time as a supervisor of the district detectives was more than a wonderful ride. The squad of investigators was a group of good workers and overall outstanding people. Each was able to fulfill their own job duties while at any time being ready and willing to drop their assignments and help their teammates. This bunch of wild ones made it easy for me to take great pride in the outcome of their superior work product. More than that, I can tell everybody that each one of these heroes became my friend. I am truly a lucky man.

One morning, one of my detectives wandered into my office and simply fell into a chair. With a perplexed look, Detective Will told me he was concerned about one of his recent investigations. He did not know if he really had a problem with the case or if his past knowledge of the victim and his family was creating more of his anxiety. The family, both the mothers and fathers side, had lived in our little town for several generations with this current part of the family having two teenage sons. One of the two boys, Jordan, a junior, and the quarterback at the local high school had recently been the victim of a crime. His car had been parked in the school parking lot, and someone broke into the vehicle and stole several items. One of the two suspects went around the community bragging about his theft from the quarterback while he proudly boasted about his crime to everyone and even giving people some of the items he had stolen from the truck. This thief was just overly elated that he had stolen from this particular victim. With all of the street talk about the suspect, it was very easy for Detective Will to complete his investigation with the arrest of both of the criminals.

Over the past years, Will had known Jordan and his family as the boy was growing up and along with his brother both played football and baseball in the community. The detective's son also played baseball in the same leagues as the victim's family. Currently, Jordan's younger brother Brian and Will's son were teammates on the high school baseball team. Even though he knew the victim and his family when they were away from the sporting events, they had not been real friends but very good acquaintances. The best description of the relationship would be they were "bleacher parents."

The original crime seemed to bewilder the detective because the suspect acted as if he had some vendetta against the quarterback. It was just that investigator's extraordinary gut feeling that there was some other reason for the story far beyond just stealing the items. Part of the concern was that after their arrest, the two criminals continually approached and threaten the victim at various locations in the community. Jordan's parents contacted Will to discuss the criminals harassing of the young man, their little boy. This added to Will's concerns and feelings of this incident seeming to be more than just the simple crime of the burglary of a vehicle.

At the time of the crime, both of the suspects had physically entered the car to commit the felony. One suspect was the driver of the getaway car and the other seemed to be the leader of the two. The driver was much more timid and reserved compared to his much more aggressive partner. So to help me tell this story, we will give these criminals the names of Sam the driver and Leon the thief.

Since the arrest of the criminals, there had been several contacts between them and Jordan. One time, our victim was shopping at the local mall with Brian and some friends. While in a sporting goods store, of course where else would these young men go, they were approached by the two criminals. The subjects confronted Jordan and his group and started to be aggressive and challenge them. Leon kept encouraging Jordan to go to the parking lot so they could have a fight. Jordan simply made fun of the worthless thief and then took his group and moved on down the mall. Later, while they were still at the shopping mall, they were approached a second time with Leon again talking about how he was going to defeat the quarterback in a fight. Again, Jordan knowing that he would easily stomp the little thief to pieces laughed at Leon and moved on with his friends.

On another day, Jordan's mother, while standing in the front yard of their home, was approached by several cars full of boys and girls from the high school. They stopped in front of their house, and she asked if she could help them. One of the subjects asked if Jordan was home with her responding that she would go inside and get him. She went into the residence to tell her son and her husband about the strange group of visitors. As they all three returned to the front yard, the group jumped into their vehicles and sped away from the home. Jordan recognized both of the criminals as being within that group of young people. Mom decided to stay in the front yard to see if the gaggle of kids would return so that she alone could stand up and protect her poor little boy from any and all harm. You can bet that young Jordan, the high school quarterback, is a very tough and strong young man. Still, I believe I would rather fight with Jordan than with his mother, who is a very nice lady, especially when she would decide to stand up and protect her precious little children. If that situation were to arise, I am positive that Jordan and I, along with Brian, a defensive back on the football team and no doubt the father also a past football player, would all be running at full speed away from that confrontation with that kind and gentle lady. Alright, let me return from my tangent rambling and proceed with the story. Occasionally, one of the several cars would drive by without stopping. They did not ever return as a group only one of the cars at a time randomly passing by over the evening. Her neighbor later told her that a bunch of kids came by on another day, and they were also asking for Jordan. The neighbor said that he told that other throng of kids that the family no longer lived in that house having moved to a new and unknown location.

Then there was the third contact occurring on a weekend evening. Jordan with some friends and also with younger brother Brian went to an evening movie at the local theatre. After the movie, they went to a nearby fast food restaurant for some food and friendship where the parking lot is the location for the high school students to meet and socialize with one another. Sam, the driver from the crime, was also in the parking lot that evening and walked up to Jordan stating that Leon was looking for the victim. Jordan told Sam to go away as he did not desire to associate with criminals like him. Sam simply walked away without saying another word. A short time later, Leon, with two other people in the car, arrived at the gathering spot ready and willing to confront Jordan. When they started to approach Jordan's group, it appeared that one of Leon's cohorts was holding a pistol in his hand. Leon told Jordan that tonight, right then and there, he was going to fight him and if need be in the end would kill him. With Leon and his partners approaching, one of which was possibly armed with a gun, Jordan and his friends, in direct conflict with all high school teenager rational, made a very intelligent decision and hit the road. Leon was left standing in the parking lot in a cloud of dust and looking like a fool.

Obviously, the victim's parents were concerned about this ongoing harassment. The strange part was Leon having this impelling and great desire to fight the victim. Leon had also made several threats that before it was over, he was going to kill Jordan. Earlier, I told you that Jordan was the quarterback for the high school football team which had won the state championship on several occasions. Even though not a huge person, this young man was a good looking, very strong athlete who was built like a sculpture. The strongest part of his body, however, is his heart. Though still full of the mischief that is required of a high school student, Jordan is a very good person and a very strong athlete.

On the other side of the battle, Leon was a small built person with a horrible background of criminal activity that was very descriptive of his worthless personality. Leon lived with his grandparents most of the time until he would create a problem and move to his mother's home. That length of stay was dependent on the next error where he would be back living with grandpa and grandma. With his arrogant attitude and lack of direction, Leon was not a person who was interested in school. Just prior to his crime of stealing from Jordan, our little Leon had made his mature and intelligent decision to quit high school. That action alone can help anyone understand that Leon was not just a fool but a total and complete idiot; Leon is a very bad person and a very weak loser.

It would be an easy guess of where to bet one's money on a fight between the athlete and the wimp. The problem would be that the odds would not pay much money on the quarterback's obvious victory. The detective was still bewildered over these continual occurrences with this situation; why was Leon so persistent with his attack on Jordan?

All of the people involved in this investigation attended a local high school. This educational institute is well-known for its high-quality athletics. The school also had a rough reputation for the histories and personalities of its scholars and athletes. From the demographics of family backgrounds and individual personalities, these students cover the gambit of the best to the worst in the community. The football team players and several other sports earn multiple college scholarships every year. Many of those scholarships have been lost after the player was arrested by one of my outstanding detectives for committing felonious crimes. It had reached a point that the football coach and I exchanged cell phone numbers so he could immediately be informed of my detectives creating a need for changes to his daily lineup.

Combining the environment of the school with the criminal act then adding this continued harassment, Will was uncomfortable about the whole story. While Will and I debated this situation, we developed an opinion that one of two scenarios were in motion. The first was that Jordan and Leon knew each other prior to the incident, and that beyond our knowledge, there was a closer relationship. Had the two been involved in some activity where the victim offended the thief, did one owe the other money, an argument over a girlfriend, drugs or alcohol? Will and I both had a long history in law enforcement which creates a very inquisitive and suspicious personality. During my career, I have more than once investigated and even arrested the best of people who were so perfect they could of course do no wrong. The question had arisen; did our quarterback have a secret?

The other possibility we developed was that the thief was a crazy maniac. We wondered if Leon had developed a jealousy over the achievements and status of Jordan. In other words, he was not after Jordan himself rather he was after that person who was the star quarterback of the award-winning school football team. Did Leon believe that defeating the local quarterback hero would place him in the status of being much more than even a super hero? This was a task which we all knew Leon would not be able to achieve as the fight would absolutely be his loss, a complete and total loss. This being the case to achieve his ultimate and demented goal would require Leon to fulfill his threats by forcing him to kill Jordan.

Will and I were now both wrestling with this concern for the safety and well-being of the young athlete. What could we do to obtain the right answers so we could create the best solution? In law enforcement, one should always try to stop a crime before it can happen, especially murder. We created a plan of action believing the best start was to talk with our victim. Will said he wanted me to help with the interview because I was an expert on making people uncomfortable. My detective of course was completely wrong about my persona; still, we were going to get to the bottom of this; we would obtain the compete truth. Do you understand me? The truth!

We went over to Jordan's home to meet up with him and his parents. After a short conversation, we all agreed to take the victim to our office so we could talk to him about this situation. No one had any problem with just the quarterback going with us, and of course, Jordan had no concern because Jordan is a tough man.

At the office, we all went into the interrogation room. This is a small—yes, a very small—room with no windows and plain white walls containing a small desk that splits the room in half and a chair on each side of the desk. Will took the chair on one side of the desk with Jordan on the other side requiring me to bring in a third chair where I squeezed in and sat next to the victim. Jordan and I were physically very close to each other in this small confined area. I then activated my interview methods learned from my training in the interview techniques class, my past and various law enforcement experiences and maybe a little from those overly exaggerated allegations of me having a brusque personality, it was now time to invade his space. As we talked about the situation, we continually pressed Jordan on how he knew Leon. He stated that he knew him from school but never had any real contact with him. I inched my chair closer to Jordan. We continued to question him about any contact with the thief in or out of school. He insisted there are many students at his school, and he doesn't socialize with everybody. The chair moved closer as I became stronger, very much stronger, with my questioning. Jordan denied having any involvement with drug activity or any criminal actions with Leon. Yes, closer and closer, stronger and stronger. He insisted that he had no contact with the thief at school or in any other way, none at all. By this time, I had moved so close to Jordan that he was squeezed into the corner of the small room. One of the legs of his chair had lifted off the floor. He was in a position against the wall where he needed to have both of his feet on the ground and his shoulder to the wall to keep himself in his seat. There had been so much pressure put on him that he was sweating and stammering. It became obvious to us that Jordan was telling us the truth, the whole truth. Jordan showed us that he is a tough man, well to a point.

With Jordan having no previous association with Leon, we faced our second option as the answer to this perplexing situation. This thief was such a crazy lunatic that Jordan's life could be in danger. We ended the interview, packed up, and took the young man home to speak with his family. Jordan was very—yes, very—happy, maybe ecstatic, to leave that interview and be home. Our discussion with the family was for them to be cautious and notify us of any contact with the thief. We had enough information to currently arrest the heathen Leon for the crime of tampering with a witness. At this point, we did not explain our fear of the level of danger to Jordan.

With our attempt to locate Leon not being successful, the word of our search still spread over the streets, and through the sewer to him. A short time later, Leon, with his attorney, having heard we were looking for him, surrendered to us at our office. At the time of his arrest for threatening a victim, the attorney advised his client not to answer any questions concerning the crime. Leon was informed he had the right to remain silent, forever. Before he was transported to jail, Leon claimed that during this contact with the investigators, someone threatened to harm him if he did not stop harassing Jordan. You know that one cannot trust what a criminal might say or even make up to interfere with his prosecution.

Now let me add a little information that came out of the clear blue sky and increased our concern for the safety of our quarterback. During the time of this investigation, Will and I were concerned about other odd things happening in our community. We heard that this one place in our town was buying stolen property, yet our bosses told us not to investigate these stories. Eventually, we discovered that the Sheriff's Office was conducting a top secret undercover operation. No one outside of the investigation was allowed to have any knowledge of this exploit. All personnel were ordered to keep this totally secret, or they would be dismissed for violating that direct order. I had a very bad habit; some called it a sickness of knowing more about the people and actions of the office than I or anyone was ever supposed to know. This illness forced me to become aware of this secret investigation, and that the Sheriff's Office had opened an undercover pawnshop. They convinced the local criminals that they would buy any and all stolen property, especially firearms. One of the investigators on that project advised me that this undercover operation was of course not in progress because if it were true, he was sure that Leon would be stealing guns and selling them to the operation. The final count of stolen firearms sold by Leon to the sting operation could be more than a dozen deadly weapons. With Leon having all of these stolen guns in his possession, our concern increased for the safety and the life of Jordan. No need to worry I do not remember the name of that investigator who gave me this confidential information, and with what I know about the secrets in his life and career, he still owes me many more favors.

After the thief was released from the detention facility, things continued to happen including one night when the window was smashed out of Jordan's vehicle while it was parked in his front yard. We again investigated to attempt additional charges with the dangers and concerns for Jordan's safety being in the forefront but still not being able to establish probable cause to justify a new arrest. The juvenile court, a strange and complex system, was our only hope to create a solution to this dilemma. From the previous multiple charges, some were dropped, others adjusted, and finally, the courts settled on a sentence of probation for some of these crimes. Detective Will and I made sure that the probation included a caveat which required Leon to have no contact whatsoever with Jordan. This step seemed to bring our investigation to an end. Again, Leon made claims that a member of the Sheriff's Office had once again threatened to kill him if he continued to stalk or did any harm to Jordan. So again, I had a conversation with Leon about his fabrication of these ludicrous statements allowing me to convince him that he should retract the nasty allegation and stop his attacks on Jordan. Many of my detectives strongly believe in my abilities to fully communicate with an uncooperative person. Also, we all know that one cannot believe a thief!

With the probation for this crime and his later arrest for the gun thefts, Leon became so busy with the courts and crimes that he could no longer seek to harm Jordan. I am not sure if Jordan and his family ever discovered the level of danger to his life created by the ranting and raving of the armed thief. We do not know if our continuous investigation was part of the reason that helped keep Leon from taking any further actions with his threats against Jordan. Some may believe those false allegations about the thief being threatened by some obviously unknown individual at the Sheriff's Office may have helped convince Leon to move on down the road. No, I of course cannot believe that could ever happen. Still, for some reason, Leon moved along and ended his threats against Jordan bringing an end to all this foolishness.

That next year, Jordan continued to play football with a strong team that once again moved forward to the state championship. The only team they lost to that year was the team that became the state champions. With all of his athletic skills and other qualities, the young man earned a football scholarship to a well-known national military institute. On several occasions, I had the opportunity to travel and watch some of his games. One time with my family, we went up north to see one of Jordan's home games; he always smiled up at us on those days we were sitting in the stands. My young early grade school daughter thinks that Jordan and Brian are so cute, and that they are of course "her" friends. His family has been to my house on several occasions to feast on a terrific meal cooked by my wonderful wife. The quarterback has now graduated from college and working in a job where he has already achieved a promotion. Jordan often tells the story of that first rough interview by a very intimidating and mean aggressive sergeant. To me, it sounds like a bit of an exaggerated tale. Still, we have all become good friends both as individuals and as families. On one occasion, Jordan and I went to watch a college baseball game where Will's son was playing. We sat there in the stands, Jordan, healthy and alive, in the middle with Will on one side and me on the other; that was a very wonderful day.

Leon continued to have his own problems with the legal system. His crimes with the burglary of Jordan's truck, the multiple charges with the theft of guns that he sold to the undercover pawnshop along with several additional felony crimes that were committed after those convictions resulted in him to be currently serving a multiple year's sentence in state prison. The lack of a high school education apparently helped him with his stupid decisions to continue to commit one after another and another felony crime. It is sad that anyone can chose to have a life like his. It is even sadder that once chosen, that type of worthless person does not spend the rest of their criminal life in prison, as should Leon.

The detective—well, as I said earlier—Will is one of my heroes.

# The Never Again Will I Ride in Your Car

Now before we go further down the road, I need to add a little story about my good detective. Please do not laugh too much at this downright true story.

As a detective sergeant, I always went to work earlier than the rest of our squad. This early arrival allowed me to review the overnight incidents, assign cases, and prepare for the morning briefing with the boss. One morning, with the sun just rising and a cool morning breeze blowing, I was met in the parking lot by one of my detectives. Detective Will had just finished an all-night stake out that was completely and totally an unsuccessful waste of time. We stood there so he could give me a quick update before he went home to get his much needed sleep. More than anything else, his face alone explained that he was exhausted beyond description. As we spoke, he held his radio in his hand with the volume turned down so low that most people could not hear the transmissions, Deputy Sheriffs are not most people.

Some sound or noise, maybe the stress in the voice or the radio code alerts a deputy to the radio transmission. This particular transmission was a School Resource Deputy (SRD) assigned to the local high school. The siren in the background did not stop us from fully understanding that the deputy was calling for help. A suspect vehicle with two occupants had fired gunshots at a school bus full of students, and the SRD was in pursuit of that vehicle which was traveling toward our location. When a deputy asks for help, everything else stops.

Detective Will told me good-bye and started for his car to respond to the in progress action. I hastily stopped him stating that he was too tired to drive in a car chase with armed suspects, and since we were together, he would ride with me in my car. The look on Will's face displayed total disappointment. He knew that as a supervisor, I would lag behind the chase, piddling around to prevent being involved in the direct pursuit and take command by radio to control the incident. We both ran to the car, but before we sat down in the car, I stopped, opened my car truck, and obtained one of my special pieces of equipment; my AR-15 military assault rifle.

My detective had forgotten that my career included being a member of the SWAT team and also a time in the Selective Enforcement Unit, I was not like most sergeants. Remember from earlier tales, this was the old deputy from the SEU squad that would receive the special assignments from the command staff, a task that was almost always on the pink phone message slip of paper with a note to "fix" the problem and with no requirements to explain the resolution of the concern. The pink phone message was always quickly returned to the boss with the inscription "Done." Now this could be another story, maybe many other stories, but they would have to stay in that old coffee can and be told at a later time. For now, let us continue with this story.

Driving down the road, lights glaring and siren blaring, we caught up with the pursuit and began passing the other deputies involved in the chase. The road was blocked and full with morning traffic making it difficult for many to keep up with the fleeing suspect vehicle. My past experiences had shown me that one does not need a road to drive a car; heck, what are the reason for sidewalks and medians? With this knowledge, we continually passed the citizens and patrol cars eventually becoming the first car behind the suspects. These active criminals took various actions while attempting to lose the pursuing car; alas, they could not lose the highly experienced driver, the old gray-haired man that was pursuing them.

My poor detective was buckled in with both hands in a very strong rigid grip clinging to the seat of the car. I did not know if Will was a religious man, but at that time, he was praying, or should I say begging, for God's help. He also assisted with the chase with screams of "Look out!" and "Oh no!" and many other very loud and short four-letter-word phrases. Based on his extremely loud screams, he appeared to be a bit concerned.

With the helicopter flying above and the grumpy old sergeant in the unmarked car behind, the suspect's time had arrived where the criminals decided that the car would not generate their escape. With this decision, they stopped in the middle of the road, jumped from the vehicle, and started to run on foot. I exited my car with my rifle in hand which caused the suspects to increase their foot speed to the level of a track and field championship meet. Even the neighbors on seeing my rifle started to scream and swiftly returned back inside their homes while shouting praises to the good lord. All of the other units seemed to be stopping with absolutely no clue of their next action. The helicopter called on the radio and yelled that a detective was chasing one of the criminals to the west. Of course, that was the very tired Detective Will, just one of my many exceptional troops. Someone replied over the radio asking the helicopter chasing from where? The pilot replied that the chase was from where the guy with the rifle is standing. I was not standing long.

Along with others, we chased after the other bad boy all the way to a fence where he was snagged and arrested as he screamed and begged for me not to shoot him. He should not have been that nervous; I was only armed with a military assault rifle. My detective, on the other hand—yes, the one who was so tired from the all-night job—single-handedly caught the other criminal after running him down and putting him into, or should I simply say onto the ground. Finally, other deputies arrived at that location, and they helped Will cuff and stuff bad boy #2. Yep, partners, both of those criminals were in custody of the posse.

The suspects were placed behind the cage of marked patrol cars and transported to the office while Will and I got back into my supervisors vehicle to also return to the office. On the way back, my detective told me that he could not believe that I could drive like that. He corrected himself with that anyone could or would drive like that. He then took an oath. Will swore and avowed that he would never again, for the rest of his life, for any reason whatsoever, ride in a car that I was driving. Will just wanted to get to the office and out of my car. I responded that we did accomplish the job as we caught the suspects. His rather loud response, with a very strong glare, was only by the grace of God was he alive. Will acted like he was serious.

Within the year, Detective Will, on another investigation, had developed information to obtain a search warrant for a location containing stolen property. It was late in the day, and we needed to contact the judge at his home to sign the warrant. The detective and a college intern riding with him were not sure how to locate the home of the judge. From my past corruption investigations, I knew the exact location of that judge's home. I told both of them to hop in my car, and I would drive. Will started screaming at me ranting and raving that he would not get into my car; he would not allow me to drive, not now, not ever! As we went down the road in the detective's car, the intern asked why the detective got so upset. Will told the college student that I was beyond dangerous and past crazy. That college student was the same high school quarterback that Will and I assisted by arresting the maniac who was trying to kill him. Jordan, remembering his own interview from that case where the good sergeant nudged him into the wall, laughed and with a very huge smile on his face was in total agreement with Detective Will. I do believe that they were both serious.

# *Disrespect One's Oath*

With your new cup of coffee, this story may require a little whiskey be added to the cup. This one truly upsets anyone who wears a badge.

At one time in the recent history of law enforcement, someone with an office located in the state capital came up with the great idea of identifying the best college students to push toward law enforcement careers after they obtained their college diploma. These volunteers would be evaluated, selected, and assigned to the law enforcement agency within our state prior to their senior year. On graduation, they would attend a special state-sponsored training academy to earn their certification in law enforcement. Special financial benefits would be provided to this new super cop and extra money also to the agency that hired the excellent new professional. Several people jumped on board for this new job and for the financial bonus not being aware that concepts often seem to look better on paper than in reality. My opinion has always been that being a law enforcement officer is like eating liver; you love it or hate it with nobody having a wavering opinion, and if you love it, then you are stuck forever. For those who do not like the job, it would be the worst experience possible, an unbearable task.

At the onset of this new program, my agency hired three of these college graduates to become the new mega deputies of the future. Of this group, two of them did not make it to the end of the time period required for the extra bonus money promised by the state. The third subject was that perfect gentleman that was eager, anxious, and ready to become the best deputy in the entire office. This gentleman was so enthusiastic and so dignified that everyone knew that if he ever made a mistake, he would most likely contemplate suicide. Deputy Roy came from an Oriental family background with that culture that establishes a very dedicated and professional personality. His zealous approach to his work was always at full speed to accomplish the perfect solution. On one occasion while talking with Deputy Roy, I told him that I would give him the best advice he would ever receive as I took out one of my business cards and wrote one word on the back, "Relax." We both smiled and proceeded forward with our own assignments for that time. Several years later, we were once again in the same work area where I asked him how things were going with his job. Deputy Roy smiled and took my same old business card from his pocket replying that because of excellent advice from his coworkers, all was going very well. It was surprising and a bit of an honor that he kept that note of advice for such a long period of time.

One evening in early April, another deputy working in the area with Deputy Roy believed that he had located the suspect in a crime that he was investigating. To help establish enough evidence to generate an arrest, the other deputy needed the witness of the crime to come to his location to verify that the person in custody was the one who had committed the felony. The dilemma that evening was the witness was not able to get to the deputy's location which was a short distance from the crime scene. Without any hesitation and as always, Deputy Roy was willing to assist his zone partner in this ongoing investigation. Deputy Roy went to the crime scene, met up with the witness, and took her to meet up with the other deputy. The good lady was not really anxious about being involved in the situation but in the long run did agree to assist the deputies. On seeing the person who was talking to the other deputy, the witness, with a slight reluctance, notified the deputies that they had located the criminal who committed the crime. The suspect was off to jail, and the witness was taken back to her home.

A short time after Deputy Roy returned the good citizen to her home, his sergeant was notified that the lady wanted to talk to the supervisor. With the sergeant not being far from the home of the victim, she drove to the house to meet with the lady who had helped take another felon from our streets. At the residence, Sergeant Moe met up with a very upset woman who was crying and in an extremely disturbed status. As the sergeant was trying to calm the lady from this unknown predicament, the woman through all of her tears, fears and shock told the sergeant that she had been raped by Deputy Roy in his patrol car. Sergeant Moe was then herself in a state of shock.

We often have complaints against our deputies with many of them being unfounded allegations or misunderstandings some that may even be a justified misunderstanding. When a violation is determined to be true, the discipline can be of various stages including up to termination of employment. This was more than a simple violation, this was a report of a major and terrible felony crime. The hardest part of this story was the alleged suspect being Deputy Roy which created the suspicion that there had to be some other reason to report this as a crime because this accusation against the perfect deputy could not be true. An allegation of this nature requires an investigation both on the criminal and the internal affairs' side to assure the proper outcome for all parties. The sergeant had a different deputy respond to the scene and initiate a sexual battery report which requires the victim to be examined to establish the offense occurred and to recover evidence. This was just the beginning of a long process that was now in progress.

The victim claimed that she was picked up at her home by Deputy Roy, placed in the back of his caged marked patrol car, and transported to the other deputy where she identified the criminal. She said she was not happy about being involved in the other incident but was assured by the deputies that she was required to assist them. On the way back to her residence, Deputy Roy pulled down a dark road, entered the rear of the car, and forced himself upon her. He told her that she had to have sex with him, and that she could not tell anyone for if she did, he would make sure she went to jail. With him being a deputy and wearing a gun, she was afraid to resist or struggle with the man. The deputy forced himself upon her and committed the sexual act. After the incident, Deputy Roy returned her to her home where she felt obligated to report his crime. The entire incident only added a few minutes to her trip home from the meeting with the other deputy. The assigned deputy and the Internal Affairs investigators were in full motion to conduct a proper and professional investigation.

The next step in the investigation was to take the victim to have an examination at the rape crisis center. At that location, a trained medical professional will exam the victim and determine if any evidence can be recovered during the examination. This portion of the investigation indicated that the lady had recently been involved in a sexual act, and they were able to recover semen from the vaginal area. The center provided the information for counseling and assisted the deputy in returning the troubled woman to her home.

With this side of the case actions completed, it was time to interview the suspect of this terrible crime, so Deputy Roy was brought into the office for questioning. On hearing the allegation, Deputy Roy appeared stunned that the lady would make up a story like this about him stating that it was not true, a complete untruthful story. This good man could not understand why this woman would fabricate this story and unjustly accuse him while demanding to tell his side of the story. He told the investigators that he took the lady from her home to meet the other deputy and then returned her to the residence. It was a short trip to and from her home, and that there was no time to complete the alleged action. Even if the woman had offered him the opportunity, he would have had to decline because he was on duty and would not take part in that improper act. Deputy Roy said that he does not know why she would make up this lie, insisting that nothing happened between the two of them. On completing the interview, the detectives took a sample of the good deputy's saliva in order to conduct a DNA comparison test with the evidence recovered from the victim. These actions would surely prove this wonderful deputy innocent of these allegations.

As the evidence was packaged and sent to the crime lab for examination, all that could be done was to wait for an answer. The rules that cover this type of investigation require the ongoing case to be held in strictest confidence. Now we all know how inquisitive or better stated nosy Deputy Sheriffs can be, so keeping this a secret would be like trying to convince a University of Alabama fan that their school does not have a perfect football team, I beg that all of the Alabama State Troopers will forgive me for that comment—Roll Tide. With the story of the allegations rumoring throughout the office, nobody could believe the lady would create this outlandish story about such a good deputy. There was no way that Deputy Roy would commit this false allegation because he was such a perfect and dedicated employee. It was believed that if one would throw Deputy Roy in a mud puddle, he would walk out and be squeaky clean. Everybody believed that the lady was a complete nutcase because this deputy was just so perfect he could not commit this or any crime.

Eventually, Deputy Roy was requested to return for an additional interview with the Internal Affairs investigators. The change in this interview was that the lab test had been returned with the comparison of the evidence on the victim and the test saliva from Deputy Roy indicating a positive match, the DNA showed that Deputy Roy raped the victim. This time, the interview was very different with the ex-deputy breaking down and confessing to his horrible crime. Just twelve days after the offense now, Mr. Roy, stripped of his badge, was transported to the county jail for the charges of sexual battery and kidnapping.

With the announcement of the arrest, everyone was shocked at the final outcome. It was very hard to believe that a person who was so dedicated to his job would commit the illegal act that he had sworn to prevent. That perfect deputy had become a no good criminal who had lacked all respect for his oath, the badge, his obligations, and duty. Our anger over his worthless action was the hurt by how he damaged our badge, that beautiful star. In reality, there is only one badge, and we all wear that magnificent symbol; with his stupid act, the badge was tarnished.

With the delays of the justice system and a little attempt to avoid justice, it took over two and a half years before the rapist returned to the courtroom with a plea of guilty. The judge sentenced the criminal to five years in state prison on each of the two offenses and to ten years of probation after his prison time. He was now headed to the terrible location that he had previously sent other criminal violators to his well-deserved new home at state prison.

Every law enforcement officer believes that they can look at a person and define that person, yet in this case, we were each and everyone wrong. This in itself is a horrible crime because it is also such a horrible invasion of a person, the personality, safety, and their life. There is no cure for this injury that will stay with the victim the rest of their life. To make this even worse was that a uniformed Deputy Sheriff sworn to "Serve and Protect" had hurt this poor little lady. We were all as shocked as we were angry over the perfect deputy doing this crime. That great deputy who I was so proud to know in the long run simply spit in my face, what a disgusting animal.

# Cuff and Stuff

With modern law enforcement, there is a new concept originating from college research doctorates of how to reduce crime in the jurisdiction that is covered by one's law enforcement agency. This starts with determining the types of crimes and the locations of these criminal offenses while using the modus operandi, that is the MO or methods used to commit the crime, calculating the times and days of the week when the crime is committed and any other information that would be associated with the type of offense. Based on that information, the data is combined with the known criminals who live or are known to frequent the area of a defined crime spree. This information is calculated by the crime analyst who provides the document to the proactive squad leader to develop a plan to stop the defined crime explained in a usually very large document. For those of you without a PhD, the basic concept is to take the active criminal off the street with the concern being to determine who the active criminal is for that ongoing crime spree.

With all of the thoughts and plots and plans that were stirring for my Sheriff's Office to move to this type of enforcement, I decided that rather than wait for the committees and subcommittees to meet to decide the next date to meet for another meeting to form a new subcommittee under the subcommittee why not just try something new. As the sergeant in charge of the district detective squad, I decided to try a new approach based on the idea of attacking the active criminal. With documents and charts in hand, the corporal and I went to meet with Major Paul to present him with a great idea

## THE EMOTIONS FROM A BADGE

knowing that if it were to work, he would gladly take full credit for the outstanding concept. The presentation showed that the detective squad was understaffed for the amount of crime that was occurring within our district. With that information, we then told Major Paul to be quiet and listen to the entire presentation before he said anything else, please be quiet and listen, even Captain Steve knew that stopping Major Paul from talking is just as easy as stopping the water flowing over Niagara Falls.

As we moved forward with our exhibition, information was provided on how the detective receives their new assignments each morning, investigates the crime, and in some cases attempts to locate the criminal. With the search for the bad guy, the street talk flows to the subject making them aware that the detective is on their trail. This usually causes the criminal to run and hide to prevent the ride to jail. The next morning, many more assignments are provided to the detective. The time used in the search for the criminal is a detriment to the productivity of the detective with their continual new investigation assignments. With the time constraints, the work load and the criminal in hiding the detective issues a warrant for the felon and moves on to the other cases. This leaves the active criminal on the street to commit more crimes.

The request was for Major Paul to assign two uniformed patrol deputies to my squad. These two would be assigned to track down each and every criminal whom the detectives were searching for and take them off the street before they could commit the additional crimes. This would attack the criminal thereby preventing the scoundrel from committing additional crimes; this would reduce the total number of crimes in our district.

Major Paul responded with the statement that he knew that the detective squad was short of manpower but so were each of the patrol squads; this shortage would not allow him to take the two deputies from the ten busy squads. Ah, but major if we use the two deputies to arrest the many active criminals then the crime reduction would create fewer report calls allowing the marked cars additional time to serve and protect rather than sit and write more reports. At that moment, a little light illuminated above Major Paul's head allowing him to believe that this would be a great method to stop the active criminal; he also knew that if it did not work, the debacle would be totally my fault. Major Paul also remembered when he was a detective and my wild idea of the matching shoeprints solved the stabbing and stomping murder that he personally solved with an arrest and received an award, he knew it was often best to try my wild ideas. With his approval to start the following Monday, this all being accomplished without even a single committee meeting; we were ready to move forward with this very different approach to reducing our crime. Major Paul told us that he had the two perfect deputies in mind to assign to this new approach to law enforcement, which of course started our next battle, and in this corner...

The two deputies that Major Paul selected were some of the nicest people in the entire district; they were both excellent at fund raising and public relations events. My adamant disagreement to his selection of personnel was quite a surprise to the good boss. The argument was that the two deputies in this assignment should not be so warm and cuddly, as his two gentlemen were mostly worthless in their enforcement duties, rather they should be aggressive law enforcement deputies. In response to his question of who I would select, poor Major Paul nearly fell out of his chair over my selection of Deputy Jack and Deputy Brian to be the two attack dogs. The major indicated that each of these two had recent problems with their independent actions and required very close supervision on all of their work with my response of that is exactly what I am seeking, aggressive deputies. With his face displaying a questioned look, he was reminded that I have disciplined, fired, and even arrested Deputy Sheriffs and of my very strong reputation from those actions. These two deputies would be under my control, and he knew what "my control" would mean to these two or any deputies. The ultimate results of this job would need the aggressive deputies, and the decision of Major Paul was to assign Deputy Jack and Deputy Brian to this project. As the corporal and I were leaving the meeting, Major Paul told me that he would pray for the two deputies who would have to work for me; he also added a statement of good luck.

## THE EMOTIONS FROM A BADGE

Notifications were made to the supervisors and to Deputy Jack and Deputy Brian who reported to duty at the detective office on Monday morning, with no one having any idea what was in progress. Before the morning meeting, the two deputies, the corporal, and I met in my office to discuss the plan with my new troops. The simple plan was to have them work with the detectives, obtain information on wanted suspects, and bring the criminals to the detective; their only job was to bring in the criminal. To achieve this assignment, they would have to work for me and absolutely not cause me any problems. If they did create a problem, then I would resolve their error, and that they needed to totally and completely understand that they did not want that to happen, now or ever. The looks on their faces were enough of a statement to indicate they fully understood my presentation. The final question was for them to let me know if they wanted this assignment with both responding before I could complete the question with a strong and excited approval for this new job. With their hunting license being issued, it was time to start our new approach to street cleaning.

During roll call that morning, the new methods were provided to the detectives who were confused with the need for this action. They were assured that this would not take any of their actions or numbers from their precious statistics. They still seemed a bit concerned or confused about this different method of their work assignment; a new method is always difficult to accept. At this point, the sergeant explained that whoever was in their position, the current detective or their replacement would totally and absolutely help with this new action, for which I received a response of complete agreement from each and every eager investigator wanting to help with this new plan. The names of some wanted subjects were provided to our new apprehension team who headed out to complete their assignment.

Over the next few months, a dramatic change occurred with our work product. A criminal was identified, my two deputies were notified, and the criminal was scooped up for the detective; the investigators loved this new method. On some days, these two would bring in one bad guy; and while that detective was conducting an interview, they would go out and get another suspect. We often did not have enough interview rooms for the detectives to complete their job tasks. In the long run, the active criminal was taken off the street and unable to commit those additional crimes. The arrest numbers went up, and the crime numbers went down. These numbers were very confusing in the big staff meetings forcing Major Paul to brag about his own personal great new concept of reducing the crime and creating the command staff's concern if this was an appropriate action as it had not been approved by a committee, not even discussed in a subcommittee. Major Paul was not concerned and continued to brag about *his* productive program.

With this working so well, it turned into a process of a detective telling Deputy Jack and Deputy Brian who they wanted; and on arriving at work the next morning, the suspect was in the holding cell waiting for the interview. The word even got out on the street that nobody could hide from these detectives because they would send out the pit bull deputies to drag the criminal into the jail. Anytime the detective needed a cage car, we had one available without bothering the patrol zones freeing the zone cars for their own work, which included fewer crimes and fewer report calls. The idea was working so well.

While sitting at my desk one morning, the phone rang, indicated the desk deputy needed me to come to the front of the office. Standing there in the lobby was a person who told me that Deputy Jack and Deputy Brian were looking for him, and he knew that it was a waste of time to try and hide from those two wild animals, so he came here to surrender to them or the detective. The man also asked that I help him avoid having contact with their sergeant because he had heard the sergeant was a dangerous man. On asking how he heard about that mean sergeant, the suspect stated that the two deputies always warn people to surrender to them, so their crazy and savage sergeant does not come looking for the criminal. That soon-to-be-arrested subject was turned over to the detective, and the deputies were called to my office.

While sitting in the office across from my desk, the two deputies were notified of the story that had just been provided to their sergeant. As the story unfolded, their faces dropped more and more toward the floor. At the end of the story, I told them not to look at their feet but to look at me to look right in my eyes so I could congratulate them on doing such a great job. These two had created a reputation that when the word on the street was out that they were looking for a person, that criminal knew they had to give up. They were also reminded that the only people who really needed to fear me were the two of them which resulted in their immediate response of total agreement, a complete confirmation. They were also informed that if using me as the bad guy was working, then keep spreading those terrible rumors. The question of how mean this sergeant could be was never defined as that was just a rumor with positively no supporting facts; of course, it was a total rumor, just a frivolous rumor, and don't you dare believe them, do you hear me! Well, let's just move on.

One of the other good catches was when we were looking for a very violent criminal that had recently committed another crime, leaving the victim in the hospital. This suspect, who was once again recently released from state prison, was a very large and aggressive person who had a reputation of fighting and resisting in every one of his previous arrest; this time, he was also armed with a pistol and a rifle. The detective had been unable to locate this current customer so that morning our "seek and find" team was notified of the suspect. That afternoon, we stood in the office deciding on an arrest plan for the hideout where they discovered he was secreted from society. During the planning, it was announced that I was going to be involved in this arrest which caused the whole squad to demand they attend this event; they felt it was like going to a Broadway show without having to buy a ticket. From our designated placements, the whistle was blown, and the home was attacked by multiple unmarked Sheriff Office vehicles and of course two marked cars. A large group in the front yard was taken to the ground, and the suspect was pulled from the house. The bad man was facedown in the yard when he turned his head to look up at me, straight into my face that he could barely see as the barrel of my AR-15 assault rifle was pointed directly at his face. As the suspect looked into the hole of that rifle barrel, he decided that he was not going to resist arrest this time. Another criminal was removed from our streets.

With all of this good work, our activity numbers began to drop on the monthly reports. With the reduction in the number of offenses, we were investigating fewer cases, and the criminals in jail created arrest numbers that were very low. With that, it was determined that this project was no longer effective, and the use of uniformed deputies in only our district was not a proper deployment of manpower. It seems that no one wanted to understand or admit that the low numbers were based on us removing the active criminal from the street, and with these habitual felons in jail, they could not commit more crimes; it had reduced the crime rate, therefore, the numbers. With the decision made, the effective project was completed and the deputies removed from the detective squad. The other patrol majors were happy to see this change as this action had outdone their own work product.

Based on the work and all the help that those two men had provided to the office, the district, and most of all to me, it was time to stand up and help them with a reward for a job well done. In Major Paul's office, I presented the need, requirement, and obligation to provide these two with special assignments rather than a return to a patrol zone. In the long run, each of them was placed in assignments that would be a better and more enjoyable job. Both earned their positions, and both of their new sergeants were happy to have such good troops.

Before they left the squad, we did have a going-away lunch party at my home, better known as Café Patty. My great wife put together another wonderful meal, and we, all, each and every member of the squad not wanting to miss my wife's outstanding cooking, celebrated their work and their friendship. They both told me how much they appreciated being selected for the job and how they respected me for how well they were treated by this sergeant. Their worst remorse over this move was losing the ability to have any more meals cooked by my good lady. On many occasions since then, we have often spoken of the accomplishments and the just plain fun of that special assignment. It is always enjoyable to overcome difficult tasks by working with such good people.

In the long run, you must realize the foolishness of how frivolous this concept was of attacking the active criminal. Several years later, a new method of reducing crime was created by the command staff based on recommendations from several committees and subcommittees. Currently, each district has an entire squad supervised by a sergeant who is dedicated to identifying the active criminals and taking all steps to remove that offender from our streets. By taking the criminal off the street while and even before they commit the crimes, the overall crime numbers can be reduced within our communities. Tell me that is not a great idea, I just wish that Major Paul or even I could have thought of that newfangled concept for crime reduction.

By the way, Deputy Jack and Deputy Brian, good job with all your cuff and stuff actions. Thanks!

# Not Invincible

With my many years as a Deputy Sheriff, there was no doubt that I was invincible, just perfect and could, of course, do no wrong. That statement was about me, not about you as we all most assuredly believed reading the comment defining a perfect person would be about ourselves. Though we all believe that we can accomplish any job and climb every mountain, there will be at least one moment in our life that will make us each come to a screeching halt and be forced to reconsider our own world. With all of my accomplishments, I had one of those moments, maybe not a moment, it was more a smack in the face with a huge cast iron skillet, hot cast iron skillet. So let me talk about my little bump in the road and hope we can all learn to face some of our many moments in life and relax and have a great day.

It was just a few days after my forty-second birthday as I drove down the road on a beautiful fall evening thinking of my wonderful life and feeling totally invincible. The trip that evening was to meet up with some of my comrades who were gathering in a large upscale neighborhood to celebrate the upcoming wedding of my good friend who would eventually become one of my great cousins. This entire community is surrounded with a security wall that encloses the very large area of land that requires homeowner's permission to go past the security guard at the entry gate. With my name on the guest list, the guard saluted me through the entrance allowing me to proceed down the roadway. This main thoroughfare is a long road that ambles along through the beautiful golf course within this large community. Driving down the road, heading to the party and singing along with the radio, I approached the T-bone intersection which would require a full stop and a turn to the right. At that moment, everything in my life was about to change. Without any warning, I passed out at the wheel of the car, still moving down the road without the ability to slow down or apply the brakes due to being totally unconscious caused the vehicle to crash into a fire hydrant and then a tree that were both on the far side of the intersection. The vehicle damaged beyond recognition, rolled over, and eventually stopped on the crushed top and part of the side trapping this lifeless body in the wreckage. The neighbors who heard the very loud crash immediately called the Sheriff's Office for this emergency and responded to assist with the incident. When these citizens arrived at the scene, they found that nonresponsive body ensnared inside the mangled vehicle creating the belief that this was a traffic fatality.

Emergency vehicles from County Fire Rescue and the Sheriff's Office quickly arrived at the scene to begin their amazing actions. The paramedics determined that the unconscious driver was alive and would need to be extracted from the twisted steel that wrapped around his body. The Sheriff's Office deputies looked at the wad of metal that had been a car and were not able to recognize that it was an unmarked Sheriff's Office vehicle. The Jaws of Life, power saws, and other various tools were put into action by the fire rescue personnel allowing them to cut the metal pieces away from the trapped body. As they were in the process of removing this victim from the remains of the mangled car, a paramedic made an unusual discovery; on the driver's ankle was a concealed pistol. The Deputy Sheriffs were notified of this discovery, and they moved closer to see the still motionless body. One of the deputies, who had worked with me on several assignments throughout our careers, immediately identified me to the entire group. The radio transmissions came alive advising that a Deputy Sheriff was down creating a change in everything at the scene.

With me still not responding, the first approach decided on by the scene supervisors was to airlift me to the nearest trauma center. This decision was changed when I became conscious though still incoherent and combined with the fact that Sheriff's Office staff officers had arrived at the scene, and also with all of the many people now in charge, the decision was to immediately transport me by the Fire Rescue ambulance to the closer hospital. This movement was accomplished with an escort of Sheriff's Office marked patrol cars. It is incredible to know that an injured deputy causes, and justifiable so, the actions of all others to stop and deal with that emergency.

At the hospital, I started to become more aware of my surroundings but was still in a confused state. Tests were conducted, exams were performed, and many people stopped to check on my condition. The amazing part of this incident was there were no injuries caused by the traffic crash, not a broken bone or even a cut. As all of the many procedures continued, the on call doctor arrived at the hospital. Dr. Donald was a high-quality neurosurgeon who was not out to have a friendly conversation; he was there to heal the injured party. His evaluation of the tests created the opinion that the X-ray to my head showed something behind my left eye. To better determine the definition of this item would require a magnetic resource imaging (MRI) examination. At that moment, the MRI at that hospital was not operational. Dr. Donald ordered that I be kept overnight in the intensive care unit (ICU) to assure that the problem did not recur over the evening. If my condition improved, I would be released the next morning and an MRI would be conducted at another location to determine the reason for this strange event. So on that evening, I would spend the first night of my entire life in a hospital bed.

One of the requirements with this type of event is to notify the next of kin of the victim. At this time in my life, I was still the single man living all alone, so the notification would have to be to my parents who were listed in my Sheriff's Office files as my emergency contacts. This would be a little difficult at that time because my parents were out of town visiting some of their friends in the mountains over a thousand miles away and several states from our home. This forced the notification to jump to the next one on the list, my older brother who, on being notified, responded to the hospital. The easier way to notify someone would have been to simply go to the emergency room waiting area as that place was stuffed with my many friends and future family. There was no need to worry about me as many of these good people were ready to become my caretaker. You can be assured that more than one prayer originated from that loving group on that October evening.

I should add that on meeting up with me at the hospital, my brother insisted that the medical staff was totally wrong because everyone always knew that I had nothing in my head, absolutely nothing at all. On hearing from my brother that their little baby boy was in the hospital with a boo-boo injury, Mom and Dad loaded up their car and were southbound and down. I do believe that if they were clocked by police speed radar that the officer, driving a Formula One race car, would not have been able to catch up with them to make the traffic stop. After poking fun at me as we always do to each other, my brother went home also concerned for his baby brother.

With the rise of the morning sun, I awoke in an ICU bed with the feeling that nothing had happened and with a sense of perfect health. All of the vital signs and test indicated that I was fit as a fiddle and ready to be released from the medical facility. On my release, my brother returned to the hospital to help me get back to my home. The release included several requirements listed by Dr. Donald that included I could not drive a car, do heavy work, and must have an MRI conducted as soon as possible and to get some rest. The papers were signed and stuffed in the pants pocket of this antsy gentleman who was ready to get out of the hospital. It was not very long after my brother got me to my house that my parents arrived to check on my well-being. The medical advice to rest should have been given to their poor automobile that sat in the yard with smoke coming from several areas. My parents were concerned for the health of their little baby boy.

Now this all seemed so ridiculous because I knew this incident was a single happening and that no one should be concerned about my health. Throughout my life, I had the normal illnesses of chicken pox, the mumps, and other childhood illnesses with never having a broken bone, a stitch, or even any medical procedure to the point that at that time in my life, I still had my tonsils. That night of the accident was the first time in my life that I ever went to an emergency room and the first ever to stay in a hospital. Having never ever been sick, I knew that I was invincible.

Without being able to drive my father became my personal chauffeur while I traveled to my various appointments. The first was to my MRI examination and my new experience in this medical field. The technicians had me strip down to assure that I had nothing that was metal on my body then dressed me in a hospital gown that was obviously too small for me before marching me into the MRI room as I tried to hold closed the back of that open gown . This large room is maintained at a very cold temperature to keep the MRI from overheating. So dressed in my very little bit of clothing, I was helped onto the very cold table where I laid down, so they could strap me to the board and finally cover me with a very welcomed warm blanket. That nice and polite technician then told me to lie very still and not move so that the test could be completed without an interruption. As she fled from the frigid room, she once again shouted, "Remember, don't move!"

As the test began, the machine rolled me into the interior of the device which is like a very small tunnel. The area was so small that if I moved, I would bang into the sides of the small little pipe where I was stored at the moment. The test began with the sound of *click, click, click* followed by the sound of *buzz, buzz, buzz*, and repeated one time after another as the table moved between every round of buzzing. Finally, the technician returned and removed me from that tiny little tunnel of confinement, finally freedom. She then notified me that the physician requested the test also be conducted with contrast. Of course, that was followed with my question of, with what? Yes, they injected some ink directly into my blood, wrapped be back up, and returned me to the tunnel of claustrophobia. It was now time to begin again with *click, click, click, buzz, buzz, buzz*, adjust the table and over and over and over again. The short test was taking forever with me believing that it would never stop, on and on, it just kept going; I wanted this horrible bit of torture to stop right then and there, now! Finally, at long last, it came to an end allowing me to escape from the icy and uncomfortable conditions inflicted on me by the test. You can only imagine how hard this test was on me as it took almost thirty whole minutes even though it seemed like it took hours.

The next afternoon, my father picked me up at my home and drove me to my appointment with Dr. Donald. This would be the meeting to get everything cleared up with my clean bill of health allowing me, the invincible one, to move on back to work. After a short wait, Dr. Donald met with us in his office rather than an examination room strengthening my belief that it would soon be over. The good doctor looked directly at me as he explained that the diagnosis determined the cause of my blackout was a tumor in my brain. This tumor was approximately the size of a tennis ball located just behind my left eye. They could not determine the type of or if this was cancer without removing the object from my skull. My response was what if I just left this alone, could we not wait to see what would happen over time? Dr. Donald informed me that without surgery, this condition would be fatal, probably within six months. My following question received more terrifying news as the surgery could cause me to lose my sight, my ability to speak, my ability to hear, use of my legs, and use of my arms, any of these, or all could be temporary or each and all could be permanent, if and only if I actually survived the dangerous surgery. Sitting in the chair, I was having trouble breathing with my next statement given to the doctor being that I had to leave the office immediately. The good man totally understood and helped me set a new appointment later in the week as I quickly as possible left the building. At that moment, I no longer felt invincible.

As we drove home in the car, the tough old retired railroad man and the unconquerable Deputy Sheriff could barely say a word. My father, believing he had lived a long and good life, was upset asking why it could not have been him instead his young little boy. I apologized for creating such a problem and asked him to take me home. At that time, I needed to be alone to make some decisions for my future course of action. During that ride, I was so scared that I could not even cry.

Once home, I started with my new concept of life, one that is so familiar to any cancer patient. At one moment, I would want to be totally alone with no one that is right absolutely positively nobody around; then moments later, I had to be with people, anybody and everybody. There was no way to determine which mood I would have at any time or any moment as it would constantly change without any method or warning to predict the attitude. On that day, it was important to be totally alone not even a telephone call, except for my mother. When I spoke to Mom, it was hard to understand the conversation between all those tears.

Sitting alone in my chair in total silence, my tumor-infected brain was trying to determine the best answer to this dilemma. The doctor told me that without the surgery, my life would end within the next six months. I was not anxious to die at my young age. With the surgery, it could cause me to be unable to use my arms, to walk, to talk, to hear, or even be able to see, if and only if I lived through the procedure. The image of me confined to a wheel chair being totally crippled and simply a burden to others would not be worth continuing my life; death would be better than being that crippled burden to others. What is the best decision when the outcomes all seem to be that you lose the game? Throughout my life as a Deputy Sheriff, I have faced many difficult tasks with my personal safety. One time, a gentleman paid another street urchin to kill me, with another time, a subject who was under investigation for murder was determined to be researching me to become one of his next victims. During my days at work, I have wrestled many weapons including knives and guns away from criminals while also fighting these armed villains down to the ground and into their handcuffs. Many of those ragamuffins went to the hospital before they ever made it to Central Booking. Now finally for the very first time in my life, I was the one that had to go to the hospital. I did not want to die and am certainly not at all a strong enough person to live life as a wheelchair-bound cripple.

I don't know how long I sat in that chair before I realized that the sun had gone down and without a light on in the entire house, I was sitting in a very dark room. When I turned on the light, it illuminated that very dark room and maybe a light within me. I began to realize that one cannot win the game if one does not play the game. There was another outcome for that medical procedure one that could remove the tumor without any crippling of my body and leave me completely healthy. Like any of my criminal investigations that were resolved with the felons going to jail, this healing could not be achieved by sitting around mopping and doing nothing. I had to strap on that old six-shooter and charge into the surgery room to stand up and defeat another bad guy who wanted to attack me. That worthless tumor had to go, and the surgery was the only answer. Now realizing that I was not invincible, what was the right answer?

The next meeting with Dr. Donald went much easier than the previous one. We discussed the fact that I had great confidence in his abilities and his opinion but still thought it would be best to obtain a second opinion considering the gravity of this situation. The good doctor agreed with my concern suggesting that I should check with not one but two other doctors and suggesting one who was considered a local expert and with the second being my choice. The surgery planning would have to wait until after the other physician's opinions. So the next step was for dad and me to get out of his office and schedule the other appointments.

The first review was with Dr. David, the expert who had been suggested by Dr. Donald to review my condition. This man worked at the local main hospital as a neurosurgeon and as a teacher for the college of medicine at the local university. He was considered one of the two best local physicians in this particular field; Dr. Donald was the other of the top two. On his review of the MRI, he provided his diagnosis of my medical condition which sounded like he had pushed the play button on the recording of Dr. Donald explaining the issue. Dr. David's main interest was that he was anxious to be the physician who would conduct the surgery because this would be such a challenging procedure. Dr. David was much more anxious for the surgery than me. With all that mimicked information, there was still a requirement for the next opinion.

Two hours north from my town is the home of that best university here in the United States of America. You are correct, that is the school that I attended after graduating from high school and the school I failed out of creating my need for employment as a Deputy Sheriff. At the university, their college of medicine has a teaching hospital that has international recognition for its outstanding achievements in medicine. My primary care doctor is also a good friend of mine who I grew up with in our good old town. On hearing the need for the third opinion, he made arrangements at that fine hospital for me to visit a doctor who is another national expert in this field. It is always a difficult moment when your own doctor holds back tears while you converse about one's illness though this also helps one realize that you have such a fine friend.

The next step was for Dad and me to head up north to the hospital at the university. On packing the car we ended up with three additional passengers, my mother and two of my aunts. Since my cousin, the daughter of one of these aunts, lived near the hospital, they decided to take the trip and visit these relatives. This was a quick road trip to meet up with the third well-renowned doctor allowing us to obtain another opinion about my condition. It is not hard to guess that I once again we heard a replay of that original recording of Dr. Donald defining the tumor. These opinions seemed in some ways to be a worthless expense of time though they did help strengthen my belief that they had each defined the same problem, and they all independently agreed on the resolution which created an understanding without any doubt that it was the correct diagnosis and the proper solution. Still, it was hard to get that old six-shooter strapped on for the shootout with that darn tumor.

At this point, it was time to pick up the good ladies at the cousin's house, stuff the three of them in the backseat, and for dad to drive us all home. As we traveled home down the middle lane of the interstate highway, a semitruck driving in front of us suddenly came to a screeching stop in the middle of the road. The right-hand outer lane was full of traffic, and the inside left lane had a car that was also stopping in the roadway. The old railroad man tapped the brakes and swerved into the grassy median of the highway resulting in the car spinning in circles and coming to a halt as the left rear tire was ripped from the rim. It took a few moments before the first words were

# THE EMOTIONS FROM A BADGE

finally spoken when I inquired about everyone's well-being obtaining the response that everyone in the vehicle was doing very well and even able to once again start breathing. I stepped out of the car, saw the damaged tire, and looked up to the good Lord to tell him that he did not have to keep dropping these hints to show me he was taking care of me that a simple note or e-mail would suffice rather than continually scaring me to death. We both knew that I had already decided on the next step. With the tire fixed, we loaded up the car and once again headed south with that last segment of our travels on that day being a very rare historical moment, none of the petrified ladies in the backseat said another word. Those ladies not talking is something the entire rest of my extended family, one and all, to this day, believes is a flat-out lie a totally unbelievable story that I completely made up; those ladies always have something to say.

My research for the best doctor to conduct this dangerous procedure resulted in friends and contacts in the community telling me that the two best neurosurgeons in our town were of course Dr. Donald and Dr. David both who had evaluated my condition. The folks also told me that Dr. Donald was a gruff person who does not have a warm and cuddly personality. My friends included that Dr. David has the same personal touch, but he is a tad bit warmer than Dr. Donald. On asking who was the best doctor, the final answer would have to be decided by the flip of a coin. With the situation at hand, I believed that the coin tossed in the air would fall to the ground resulting in the edge sticking in the dirt preventing a heads or tails answer as either of these good physicians could do this task. At this time in my life, I was not out to become best friends with a doctor; I was looking for the best man who could fix my problem. So what should I do to resolve the dilemma, wait and die, become a cripple, or stand up and fight the battle to recovery? All of my decisions were made, and it was time to move forward with the best resolution.

When I got back home, we again met up with Dr. Donald and set a date for the surgery. Prior to the action, he would like to have a new MRI to determine if there had been any changes. It was scheduled, and of course in that cold room where the freezing nearly naked young man went through the old *click, click, click, buzz, buzz, buzz*, adjust the table and over and over and over again. Then to my chagrin, the doctor had once again asked for the contrast so I was shot full of ink and then back to the *click, click, click, buzz, buzz, buzz*, adjust the table and over and over and over again one more time. They did determine that the tumor was still there without any change.

The time finally arrived with the requirement to meet with the doctor at his office the day before I entered the hospital for my scheduled surgery. On the day of that appointment, there was no need for a licensed medical doctor to determine that I was suffering from a horrible cold. Through the sniffling and sneezing, Dr. Donald said that he could not conduct the surgery on a sick person creating a postponement for the procedure. I now had to sit and wait even longer.

With time moving forward, my cold ran its course and left the sick little boy free of the nose problems. It was obvious that I was not concerned about that cold because I had "other things on my mind," stop that moaning at this moment, we needed a little laugh because back then, it was often hard, nearly impossible to find a laugh or even a simple smile.

It was once again time for me to have another scheduled meeting with Dr. Donald at his office. My father gave me a call on the telephone to let me know that he was on his way over to shuttle the patient to the appointment. That morning, the tumor had again taken over my body causing me to be lying in bed and in a totally confused state. When I answered the phone, my father was getting strange and very weird responses from my dazed condition. My parents called Fire Rescue and rushed to my home; that poor car was having yet another moment of its own. On their arrival, the paramedics and my parents found me to be awake but totally disoriented with their attempts to communicate with me requiring them to contact the doctor whose decision was to transport me to the hospital for treatment. The paramedics assisted me in getting out of bed so they could walk me down the stairs to the exit. With my mother standing there, I had to stop everybody in their tracks as I was about to leave the house which was against my mother's rules from childhood because I had not yet brushed my teeth. As I stood in the bathroom brushing my pearly whites, everyone else stood there staring at me and waiting for me to complete the task so we could leave. Remember you always do what Mommy says, so you don't get a "pow-pow." It was obvious that I was not on planet earth at that moment.

The doctor, being a highly trained professional, ordered another MRI to review the current condition. The cold conditions and the *click, click, click, buzz, buzz, buzz,* adjust the table and over and over and over again were not quite as bad this particular time as I must have been sleeping during my return to my home planet. By the next morning awaking in the hospital bed, everything was again just fine without having any aches or pains from the previous day's downfall.

With Dr. Donald's examination, he determined that we could not wait any longer, and that the surgery should be conducted as soon as possible. As I sat there in the hospital bed, I was in total agreement with that medical decision; it had been two months since the accident, so let's get this thing over with. During that meeting, Dr. Donald introduced me to another good doctor who was going to perform a new procedure on me prior to the surgery. Dr. Evan was going to enter into the arteries in my thigh and work an instrument up through my body into the tumor behind the left eye. Once the probe was within the tumor, he was going to pump a liquid into the object to harden the soft glob. The coagulation would help stiffen the tumor making it easier to remove from the area of the brain. The medical procedure would take less than an hour.

That afternoon was a very difficult time with me trying to cope with everything in progress while all I could do was to simply wait, waiting for the others to do the work. It was not like me to have others do the work to take the step to complete the action; I was independent and would do everything single handed for myself not allowing anyone else to do anything for me, I never needed help. Now I had to sit there and do nothing but let others do everything for me as I could do nothing, nothing at all. Lying there in the hospital bed waiting for the next procedure, I did not feel as worthless as I felt scared, scared to death. There was no doubt that I had lived a wonderful life growing up in a great family and having so many experiences that so many people can only have in their dreams. I was a man who has many very good friends that cover large areas within age groups, personalities, races, and genders who each give me great pride knowing these relations are so strong. The two months between the accident and the surgery allowed for plenty of time to debate and to cry, now it was time to act. Still, as I waited in the bed feeling so totally helpless and worthless, all that I could do that day was cry.

That evening, Dr. Evan took me into a surgical area, gave me some drugs to relax me, and conducted the experimental procedure. Most of the time, the drugs kept me asleep, but I would come in and out during the process. I later discovered that the one-hour procedure took over six hours to complete because Dr. Evan wanted to do the very best with this action. These extra hours took him late into the evening causing him to miss dinner with his wife that night. I should have sent the lady an apology and a thank-you note for allowing him to stay with me to complete his superior medical action.

Once again, I awoke to the morning sunrise in a hospital bed, but this time with the worst headache in my life. That soft tumor squashed in my head was now a very solid and hard object that was creating a strong and serious pain. The orderly whisked me down to the surgery area with the pain, and my complaints increasing, this grumpy man was hurting. While I was being prepped for surgery, Dr. Donald stopped in to check on me and let me know that he was going to be assisted by Dr. David on this surgery indicating that my luck was improving as my surgeons were those two best in the area for this serious procedure. Now it was time for the anesthesiologist to prepare me for the surgery. That poor man was trying to conduct his business of explaining the procedure while my head pain was continually increasing in strength and severity. A lady in labor with twins is probably easier to communicate with than I was at that moment of agony. The doctor told me to calm down and wait just a minute as he did something to the IV plugged into my arm, and it did not take a minute before I was out. That was the last moment I remember from that day.

## THE EMOTIONS FROM A BADGE

Apparently during the ten-hour surgery, many of my friends and family filled the surgery waiting room. At lunchtime, my forever best friend went out and bought sandwiches to feed the large group of people. Had my good friend been the one in surgery that day, he would have had the doctors stop the procedure so he could have joined in with the others for lunch, especially if they were serving chocolate chip cookies or dear lord even more so cinnamon rolls. At the end of the day, the doctors had achieved more than they even believed could be accomplished with the surgery on that day. The biggest question was how the procedure affected my abilities with movement, vision, hearing, and speaking would have to wait for the following day when I would eventually awaken from the anesthesiologist actions. With the task accomplished, everyone packed up and went home to rest and to provide some additional prayers, this was all after having receiving the best news of that day; I had survived the surgery.

The morning sunrise was one more day for me to wake up in a hospital bed with me making a wonderful discovery; I could see that beautiful sunrise as the surgery did not blind me. As I laid there in the bed, it was time to test myself discovering that the right arm worked, then the left arm, both of my legs moved allowing me to walk, all of the movement could be heard; and finally, it was time to talk. Trying to talk I could create the words in my mind, I knew what to say, but the words would not come out of my mouth. It was a tough roadblock to my recovery, but I had to be positive as everything else worked, and I would have to fight this battle and would again win allowing me to eventually be able to speak.

By the time that Dr. Donald arrived to check on me, my brother had already arrived at my hospital room. The doctor was checking on me asking how everything was going, and I could not answer him with my inability to talk. Dr. Donald looked at me and said to wait just a minute as he reached over and removed the trachea tube from my throat. Once again, he asked how I felt with me replying that I felt fine. It was the tube in the throat that had prevented me from being able to speak a single word. With the object pulled from the throat, I could talk again creating a recovery from everything once again I was whole—yes, I was whole. At that moment, my brother asked the doctor if it would not be best for all others to put the trachea tube back in so I could not talk. Even Dr. Donald got a laugh out of that statement.

The explanation from the surgery was that the tumor was a meningioma. This is a mass that is similar to a wad of cold spaghetti that has all the strings wrapped into a ball with these strings extending out from the mass. The doctors had been able to peel back my scalp, saw open my skull, and move my brain in order to get to the large clump and remove it from my head. The procedure conducted by Dr. Evan solidified the tumor making it easier to pull this large lump from the brain cavity. The bad news was that they had to leave some small pieces in my head from the end of the extended strings as they could not get to them without creating damage to the brain. This meant that there were several particles of the tumor still in my head with the bits and pieces requiring the future treatment by a doctor of radiation oncology to resolve that condition. Dr. Donald then said the good news was this tumor was benign. I told Dr. Donald that the good news was that I was alive, and he did an unbelievable job in keeping me in that condition. The man that many claimed to be a gruff person showed that like me, he was happy, lets up that to ecstatic with the outcome.

Later in the day, a physical therapist came to my room to evaluate my need for his services. We once again tested my legs and arms and other body movements with a final decision that I was in tip-top condition. With my sincere thanks for his evaluation, I apologized for the fact of my happiness as I would not need his services where he returned the smile responding that he fully understood and agreed with my happiness.

For several days, I stayed in the hospital to recover from my amazing surgery. The interesting point is that there was little to no pain from the surgery. Apparently, this is an area of the body that does not create the severe pain from a surgical procedure. This allowed my recovery from the procedure to be an easy task as the days passed by in the hospital. The biggest problem was that I had little to no energy sleeping through most of the days. Eventually, I was able to take a look at myself in a mirror realizing Holy Cow, I looked atrocious.

My normal daily appearance and my personal attitude often give a bit of a strong approach to others. At this time, my head was half shaved with hair hanging out of the side that was not bald with that open side having the huge gash stapled together to create the appearance of a character in a horror movie. It would have been great to be home looking like that while having some unwanted person ringing the doorbell so I could answer the door and just stare at them. Without me saying a word, they would certainly take off screaming as they ran away from the horrible monster man. Without being able to do that, I simply put the mirror down and took another of my many naps.

My stay in the hospital was during the Christmas holiday season with many a friend and family coming by on more than one occasion to keep me company and lift my spirits. The couple who were the guests of honor for the party that I was travelling to on the night of the accident had their wedding during my stay in the hospital. On one evening, a beautiful lady whom I had dated on several different occasions and left her on each of those several occasions even came by to check on my well-being; it was more than nice to see her. The hard part for me was to see these big tough friends of mine come to my hospital bed and simply cry over my difficult trek and terrible appearance. On one evening, a mother and her daughter stopped by to bring me some gifts of food and check on my condition. They are one of my many families who are good friends as the group and each one as an individual. That poor lady sadly told me that one of her boys would not be able to come see me at the hospital because he was such a close friend and could not bear to see me in this condition. She added that she knew the boy did not want me to see him cry as he has been doing over his concern for me. That poor little young man the ex-college athlete who is married with three children in his own way showed me his true and strong friendship being unable to deal with viewing the injuries of his great friend. That evening, I explained to her not to worry about that as it was not a problem and then demanded to know what was in the food basket because her daughter bakes such delicious cookies. Man, those cookies were so good that evening.

To celebrate New Year's Day, the doctor gave me the most wonderful gift, a set of discharge papers from the hospital. The papers included that I was not able to stay alone which required me to move in at Mom and Dad's home so they could take care of me; Mom still had some of my old cowboy pajamas. The surgery had sapped all of the energy from my body creating a chubby little boy taking steroid medicine and eating everything while sitting around all day watching television. Doctor Donald had advised that I needed to start doing some simple movement to help me get back into society. His suggestion was to take a walk around the block when I felt up to this major exercise. He also gave me a new prescription ordering me, maybe demanding me, to get my haircut, so I would stop scaring the residents of the local cemetery.

Finally, my energy was returning so I made an announcement of my plan to walk around the block all by myself that is correct alone. It is a waste of time to argue with one's mother who, of course, is the doctor in charge of her poor sick little baby when she states you are not going alone, and she was going with me, said and done. So we got together and started out for that trip around the block by starting off across the front yard. By the time I reached the street that was within ten yards of the front door, it was time to return from the exhausting physical exercise. Every day, my energy improved to where I, and of course Mom, eventually made it around the block and then several blocks. The outcome of these journeys continued to improve every day.

During this time, I continued to have follow-up visits with Dr. Donald to assure the surgery was healing. Most of the time, this required me to have yet another MRI with the *click, click, click, buzz, buzz, buzz*, adjust the table and over and over and over again tedious procedure. These tests indicated that the recovery was going well, and the leftover particles were not growing. Dr. Donald also referred me to two other doctors, a neurologist to review the surgical effects to my brain and an ophthalmologist as we had discovered my left eye had a problem moving the full length of the eye socket. Dr. Donald also made a wonderful decision that would allow me to move back home and once again live alone, allowing me to leave those cowboy pajamas once again with Mom. The most important part of the news was this meant that I was getting better.

With Dad still having to drive me around town, he would pick me up for the next visit for whichever location was scheduled on that date. My neurologist Dr. Edward was astounded over the recovery from such a difficult surgery. This poor man seemed to be frustrated that he did not have to do anything to help with my medical condition. Every visit, he tested all of my movable body parts to determine that my body was healing properly. Things were moving along so very well.

The next step was to meet up with Dr. Mitchell who was a well-trained ophthalmologist in our area. This time, I provided him a copy of the most recent MRI with him being very appreciative responding that was going to be his first request, hallelujah missed another one of those clicking test. On viewing the exam, you can see that the optic muscle from the back of the left eye is touched by the open hole filled with body fluids that was left by the removal of the tumor mass. The pressure on the optic muscle restricted the left eye from looking down to the ground forcing this one eye to stop at three quarters down its path to the bottom of the eye socket and creating double vision in the lower area of my vision. A questioned looked developed on the face of Dr. Mitchell as he requested to hold my eyeglasses. It was then my face that changed to a questioned look as I handed him my spectacles where he took possession of the glasses and pulled a strip of frosted plastic tape from the dispenser then affixed the tape to the bottom of the left lens. The glasses were returned to my face ready to perform another test that showed the tape blockage corrected the double vision in my lower area of view. This would eventually be corrected by making the left lens a bifocal allowing this to be a total fix which meant that out of all of the fears of the damage that would be caused by the surgery, I had to change my eyeglasses prescription to correct my vision; you know that's not at all bad. With Dr. Donald stapling my skull bone back into place and Dr. Mitchell using Scotch tape to fix my eyes, I was beginning to wonder if the proper business for medical assistance would not be the drug store but an office supply depot.

About six months after the surgery, Dr. Donald, who had already taken a pair of construction pliers and yanked most of the staples out of the top of my skull, determined it was time to have a doctor of radiation oncology determine if the remaining particles stuck in the area of the brain could be treated. Following his recommendation, I met up with Dr. William who immediately requested, that's correct, another MRI. Off once more of the *click, click, click, buzz, buzz, buzz*, adjust the table and over and over and over again, don't forget a second test with contrast. With the new results, Dr. William met with me again at the MRI machine to define the method that would be used to destroy the particles in my head with a radiation treatment. This required a large plastic mesh screen to be heated and the melted plastic placed over my face to form a mask that was then attached to strong plastic brace at the back of the head. This would allow me to lay on the table for the MRI and have the mask bolted down onto the table. Markings were drawn onto the areas of the mask so Dr. William could aim the rays from the radiation machine to the points on the mask allowing the alignment and destruction of the particles that remained in my head. These treatments or should I say these many treatments would each and all occur inside of the MRI machine with the new *click, click, click* and now *zap, zap, zap*, adjust the table and over and over and over again. I could write a thesis on living inside of a soda can.

During these treatments, Dr. Edward had approved for me to return to work on a light-duty status. At that time, my assignment as a corporal was the assistant to the colonel of Administration allowed me to work some in my duty assignment and part of the day in communications. With me receiving radiation treatment, everyone in the executive offices was concerned that my hair, the little bit that had grown back from the surgery, would begin to fall out causing me to become totally bald. It was my duty to relieve those fears and comfort my fellow workers so I put on a multicolored clowns wig and ran into the office of Sheriff Cal yelling the treatment was changing my hair. After a laugh and a smile, his next step was to do what he believed that no one had ever done before and threw me out of his office. The boss didn't realize he was not at all the first or for sure not the last person to achieve that moment of office tossing. It was good to see the smiles on the faces of my fellow workers.

In a relatively short time based on brain surgery recovery, the treatments and follow ups were all completed with a final stamp issuing a clean bill of health. The head was healed, the leftover particles destroyed, the eyeglasses changed, and all of the medications stopped allowing me to reinstate my driving license and return to full duty. Even though I was in good health, we agreed to have the MRI conducted on a continual basis until we could be assured the particles would not start to enlarge. Finally, I was in good health—yes, finally. Hoorah!

This medical condition and all of the events surrounding my recovery affected many parts of my life, one being the required revocation of my aviation medical certificate causing my airplane pilot license to be suspended and grounded me from flying. To prove to myself that I could keep going with my life required me to discover and overcome a new challenge by reaching another wild accomplishment. Looking around and checking my life list of wants, I made the decision and took the next step to obtain my bareback sailboat captain's license allowing me to sail a large sailboat. On reaching that level, the accomplishment only caused me to desire the reinstatement of my airplane pilot's license. It was time to once again strap on the six shooter, mount up, and charge into another of life's battles. With the results of the medical tests, additional flight examinations, and other administrative actions, this fight was also won with the approval by the Federal Aviation Administration certification to once again fly. So from the ship's deck at sea to a pilot's seat in the air, I could once again announce, "Ahoy, mates at sea, I'm departing on Runaway 18. I had played the game and won.

Through all the fears and tears, this challenge in my life had been conquered, allowing me to move forward with the reinstatement of my driving and flying licenses and many more. With all of these actions, there were changes to my overall outlook on life in general and in me. First, I do realize that I am not invincible, and that one needs to fight to survive and not surrender without fighting to achieve one's desire. Another realization was that I had dedicated myself to my job not being aware that there was life outside of my duty assignment. I also realized that there were more people that I could ever believe that continually honor me with their friendship and their love. There were so many reasons to show me how lucky and happy how fortunate I was to have survived this difficult life challenge by facing the demons head on with a very positive attitude, and yes, I survived!

This change in my life created a belief that I had to live life and enjoy life so much more. There was not a need to be alone in the world, and that it is not a sin to allow others to help you with the trials and tribulations of life. During that time, I remembered the beautiful lady that came to visit me at the hospital during my recovery. We had dated several times in our lives with each time coming to a screeching halt by this selfish fool walking away. She was the only lady that I had ever truly loved in my entire life, and I did not let her slip away like as an idiot, I had chased her off three different times. Now remember that this fiasco taught me many lessons which included not giving up and fighting to achieve what one truly desires in life. It was three years after the accident when I dropped to my knee and begged that perfect lady to be my wife. Six months later, the wonderful and beautiful lady gave me something that was more valuable than any of the doctors or medical procedures provided to me by simply saying, "I do" as we gave each other a ring. Not only was I alive, but now today with my wife and daughter, my life is truly perfect.

With all of my test and tribulations, I was able to strap on the old six shooter and once again charge into battle. It is the best step for anyone, even the ones who are not invincible, to face the challenge, so the final solution can be the best solution. So when you cannot figure out what to do, just remember, before you ask yourself why, ask yourself why not and just do it, only if it is legal.

# Last Day

Okay, let's finish this up so we can get off the porch and put away these coffee cups. We might need to get inside before it rains.

So it is June 30, 2009, and I am standing in the roll call room of the district office. As I look around, there are many people, of many ranks, that have been with me throughout my career. The news media and some other people from a variety of places are also in the crowded room. The most important folks are my family, my wife and my daughter. As the most senior deputy of the Sheriff's Office, the day will be my last day as a Deputy Sheriff. It took thirty-five years before I was once again a civilian.

As the Sheriff spoke of my many accomplishments, our friendship and my great career, it was a great honor. Then it was my turn to speak. As I looked across the room and all those faces, many old stories came to mind. Those many faces looked very nervous about the story that would be told about any one of them. The crowd was on edge.

My speech began with thanking everyone for being there for me. The next sentence was my pride over my wonderful time at the office. Sentence three was informing all that I had been reminded that if I had nothing good to say, then I should say nothing at all. So sentence four was a good-bye and good luck. Many, oh so many and most, were happy about me not reminiscing with a story about them.

The thanks and conversations were completed with a piece of cake. Then it was time to move on. With this being my last day, I drove the unmarked car to the garage and turned in the vehicle. The next and last stop would be return the radio to the shop.

As I stood at the counter, the memory arose of the beginning of my career in the radio room. I just had to take one last action. The radio was turned on, and here it was:

I called "2810 to Hillsborough."

When the dispatched responding "2810"

Then it was time to log off with a final "2810 place me 10-102 forever and thanks!"

There was a moment before the dispatcher responded "2810 10-102"

It was final, the original unit 619 was now ending the job as 2810 and signing off the radio.

With all of my equipment returned and all of the hands shaken, this grumpy old master sergeant climbed into the car and his family drove him home. It was truly a great and wonderful occupation and life.

# Epilogue

Throughout this book, we have talked about some horrible stories that have occurred in our society. When these tragedies arise, we must each determine to stand tall and face the horrible moments in our own life and the lives of others as we defend those loved ones who have been left behind by the tragedy and demand that those who committed these ghastly criminal acts be held responsible by lady justice, both with her scale and with her sword. We must also move forward with our own lives, our own moments of fear, and our own difficulties while we help so many others with their own trip through their difficult treks in our world. Within my trek or career as a Deputy Sheriff, I had the honor of working for a most outstanding agency, the very best of Sheriff's and overall wonderful people and partners of which I take great pride in serving for the benefit of our county. Occasionally, we also each and every one of us need to stop, look around, and as we smell the beautiful day around us to realize how many great friends and wonderful family members surround us as we move through our own magnificent life.

As I mentioned in the beginning of this book that within these stories, we will each have our own moments where we are angry, other times we may want to cry, some moments we will take great pride with our personal actions, and frequently, I hope you and everyone will give a little laugh or more so a huge and joyous roar of laughter during every day of your life. Throughout my career, I have learned that death will come to each of us someday; it does not mean we cannot fight to live as we enjoy each and every day of our wonderful life. So at this very moment and so many—yes, so many—moments more in the future, we should all stand up right here and now to raise a glass and share a toast with all of the so very many just plain good folks of this wonderful world, so raise your glass high while we recite:

"May the beauty of each sunset be a preamble to another glorious sunrise. Enjoy life!"

## The End

Oops! After all the stories of death, maybe I should say "The Finish" as "The End" could have a more morbid meaning with all of these homicide investigations, how about…

## Case Closed

# About the Author

For his entire life Stephen Cribb has been a resident of Hillsborough County Florida, creating a rare third generation of Florida Crackers. At a young age, he became the first teenager to be a Deputy Sheriff with the Hillsborough County Sheriff's Office in Tampa, Florida. During his thirty-five of years of service as a Deputy, he worked in a wide variety of various and interesting job duties. With these many challenging tasks, his career took him from Law Enforcement Deputy up to the rank of Master Sergeant at his time of retirement. These jobs covered law enforcement, investigations, administration, training and supervision at one of the largest Sheriffs Offices in the United States. This lifetime has provided him with great knowledge and appreciation of the community and citizens.

During his career he achieved an education that includes a degree in Engineering Technology and one in Business Management. Master Sergeant Cribb is married and has one young daughter, with many other numerous family members and friends. With all of this variety in his life he has archived a large amount of information that is included in these entertaining and interesting tales for a career of a Deputy Sheriff.

CPSIA information can be obtained at www.ICGtesting.com
Printed in the USA
BVOW08s0334260216

438022BV00001B/1/P